POSTCOLONIAL PRACTICES OF CARE

Postcolonial Practices of Care

A PROJECT OF TOGETHERNESS DURING COVID-19 & RACIAL VIOLENCE

Edited by Hellena Moon & Emmanuel Y. Lartey
With a Foreword by Gary Y. Okihiro
and an Epilogue by Pamela Cooper-White

PICKWICK *Publications* · Eugene, Oregon

POSTCOLONIAL PRACTICES OF CARE
A Project of Togetherness during Covid-19 and Racial Violence

Pickwick Publications
An Imprint of Wipf and Stock Publishers
199 W. 8th Ave., Suite 3
Eugene, OR 97401

www.wipfandstock.com

PAPERBACK ISBN: 978-1-6667-3204-7
HARDCOVER ISBN: 978-1-6667-2529-2
EBOOK ISBN: 978-1-6667-2530-8

Cataloguing-in-Publication data:

Names: Moon, Hellena, editor. | Lartey, Emmanuel Yartekwei, editor. | Okihiro, Gary Y., 1945–, foreword. | Cooper-White, Pamela, 1955–, epilogue.

Title: Postcolonial practices of care : a project of togetherness during covid-19 and racial violence / edited by Hellena Moon and Emmanuel Y. Lartey ; foreword by Gary Y. Okihiro ; epilogue by Pamela Cooper-White.

Description: Eugene, OR : Pickwick Publications, 2022 | Includes bibliographical references.

Identifiers: ISBN 978-1-6667-3204-7 (paperback) | ISBN 978-1-6667-2529-2 (hardcover) | ISBN 978-1-6667-2530-8 (ebook)

Subjects: LCSH: Postcolonial theology. | Theology, Practical. | Pastoral care. | Postmodernism—Religious aspects—Christianity. | COVID-19 Pandemic, 2020-. | Racism.

Classification: BV4011.3 .P695 2022 (print) | BV4011.3 .P695 (ebook)

DEDICATION
This volume is dedicated to
Mother (*ohmma*) Theresa Eun Sook Moon
Elbert, My Love
to
"STOP AAPI HATE"
And all other organizations fighting for a more just
and equitable society
And to
BREONNA TAYLOR (1994–2020)
And all other victims of colonial power killed while they slept

we are not better *than* one another
we are better *with* one another
—Brother Ishmael Tetteh

TABLE OF CONTENTS

Contributors

Namju Cho is a writer based in Seoul with a passion for food and social justice issues. Her work has appeared in the *Wall Street Journal, Los Angeles Times, KCRW*'s Good Food, *KoreAm Journal,* and the *Korea Times,* where she wrote a Korean-language column about Korean-American issues.

Pamela Cooper-White, PhD, is Dean/Vice President for Academic Affairs and Christiane Brooks Johnson Professor of Psychology and Religion at Union Theological Seminary. An Episcopal priest and licensed psychotherapist, she has published nine books. She serves as President of the International Association for Spiritual Care. She also serves on the Steering Committee of Psychology, Culture and Religion unit of the American Academy of Religion.

Miranda Dillard has been teaching music at The Paideia School since 1996. She believes that music instruction can be a mirror that helps with self-awareness and mindfulness and be a window that allows students to explore, develop compassion, and learn about the world.

Jillian Eugene is an educator, gardener, herbalist, and world traveler. She earned her degree in anthropology and Spanish from Eckerd College, during which time she studied in Spain and did ethnographic research in Mexico. Since graduating she has taught English in Thailand, served at FoodCorps, and taught environmental science in Atlanta.

Anne Gardner spent twenty-five years working at two of Boston's premier educational institutions, Harvard University and Phillips Andover. She currently leads the chaplaincy program at Harvard-Westlake, a private school in Los Angeles. Her debut book, *And So I Walked,* recounts her journey across the 500-mile *Camino de Santiago*, an exploration of faith, family, and friendship.

Phebian Gray is an incoming freshman at Yale University who enjoys crocheting and making music. As part of her work with @blackatpaideia and beyond, she aspires to create environments where everyone's truths and perspectives are heard and valued.

Jen Ham is a second-year doctoral student in the History of Consciousness Department at the University of California Santa Cruz (UCSC). Jen's research centers on reimagining accessibility for disabled folk. She is interested in exploring how the socially built environment of cohousing communities (originating in Denmark) can help us reimagine access as relational, co-creative, and reciprocal.

Won-Jae Hur, PhD, is Assistant Professor of Comparative Theology at Xavier University in Cincinnati, Ohio. His areas of research include the fields of comparative theology, Buddhist-Christian studies, Edith Stein and phenomenology, and contemplative studies.

Sophia Huynh is an incoming freshman at Columbia University. She is the founding member of Paideia's high school student Asian American Alliance and the Diversity Equity and Inclusion (DEI) Committee. She loves to write poetry, listen to music, and engage in discussions on DEI topics from across the spectrum.

Lori Klein is a Board-Certified Chaplain and Director of the Spiritual Care Service for Stanford Health Care. She worked as an oncology chaplain at Stanford for seven years. She has taught health care providers, attorneys, and spiritual leaders, both in the United States and in Central Europe.

Sarah Lapenta-H, an Episcopal priest with experience in hospice and hospital chaplaincy as well as congregational leadership, served as Decedent Care Chaplain for Stanford Health Care from December 2019–November 2020, and continues in a relief capacity. She earned a Master of Divinity degree with foci in Pastoral (Spiritual) Counseling and Global (Multicultural) Leadership.

Emmanuel Y. Lartey, PhD, is Charles Howard Candler Professor of Pastoral Theology and Spiritual Care at the Candler School of Theology and the Graduate Division of Religion at Emory University. He has taught at Trinity Theological Seminary, Legon, Ghana; The University of Birmingham, UK; and at Columbia Theological Seminary, Decatur, GA. He is the author of six books including *In Living Color: An Intercultural Approach to Pastoral Care and Counseling.*

Lahronda Welch Little is a doctoral candidate at Emory University. Her studies are centered in what she calls "holistic soteriology" and how practical notions of salvation affect the whole person, community, environment, and world systems. Central to her academic research are spirituality, Africana studies, womanist and feminist discourse, Wesleyan theology, and intercultural encounters.

Hellena Moon, PhD, is part-time Assistant Professor at Kennesaw State University in the Interdisciplinary Studies Department. She is co-editor of *Postcolonial Images of Spiritual Care: Challenges of Care in a Neoliberal Age* (Pickwick, 2020). She is also author of the forthcoming book, *Mask of Clement Violence Amidst Pastoral Intimacies: Charting a Liberative Genealogy of Spiritual Care* (Pickwick, forthcoming).

Benjamin Moon-Chun is a rising sixth grade student at The Paideia School in Atlanta, GA. He likes to play baseball, bird, take photos of birds, read, and build legos. He loves school, watching movies, and playing outside with family and friends.

Madeleine Moon-Chun is a rising eighth grade student at The Paideia School in Atlanta, GA. She likes reading, cross-country running, swimming, poetry, photographing nature, science experiments, and dancing. She also loves family dinners, nightly family games, and hanging out with her friends. She loves school—even when it is virtual.

Kafunyi Mwamba is a Board-Certified Chaplain, an Anglican Bishop, and Palliative Medicine Chaplain and Volunteer Coordinator at Stanford Health Care. Previously, he worked as a Palliative Care Chaplain at Redding Mercy Medical Center. He earned a Doctor of Veterinary Medicine degree in Congo and a Doctor of Ministry degree in Ohio.

Anna Nikitina, staff chaplain, came to Stanford Health Care with years of experience working with diverse populations of patients. She was born in Russia where she majored in Civil Law (Legal Studies). She obtained a

Master of Divinity degree at Torch Trinity Graduate School of Theology in South Korea.

Samuel O. Nkansah is a Board Certified and Interfaith ICU Chaplain, as well as a Catholic Priest at Stanford Health Care. Previously, he served at several hospitals in the East Bay. He earned a Master of Theology and a Master of Philosophy from seminaries in Pennsylvania and California.

Gary Y. Okihiro, PhD, is professor emeritus of international and public affairs at Columbia University, and a visiting professor of American studies and Ethnicity, Race & Migration at Yale University. He is author of twelve books, including *Third World Studies: Theorizing Liberation* (2016) and *The Boundless Sea: Self and History* (2019). He received the Lifetime Achievement Award from the American Studies Association and the Association for Asian American Studies. He also received an honorary doctorate from the University of the Ryūkyūs, Okinawa.

Tom Painting was born (April 1, 1951) in Rochester, NY and currently lives in Atlanta, GA with his wife Laura Brachman. They have three children, Edith, Sarah, and Phillip. Tom teaches junior high humanities at the Paideia School. He enjoys birdwatching and reading. He is making slow but steady progress on the acoustic guitar.

Taylor Powell is a seventeen-year-old black female who has been fighting for justice since she could speak. From defending her best friend in an unfair playground game of tag, to creating a committee that would better her school community, Taylor's beliefs have never faltered. Her passions for justice are reflected in her work for this volume.

Loretta J. Ross is an Associate Professor at Smith College. Her career began as an activist in the 1970s. Her recent co-written books are *Reproductive Justice: An Introduction* and *Radical Reproductive Justice*, both published in 2017. Her next book is *Calling In the Calling Out Culture*, forthcoming (2022).

Leenah Safi, MDiv carries her Syrian heritage and US upbringing with her into the field of pastoral theology. She has served as a university chaplain and is currently a PhD student at the Chicago Theological Seminary with special interests in theological education, reflection methods, and moral injury.

Jetta Strayhorn was born and raised in Atlanta, Georgia. She has been dedicated to the liberation of Black and brown peoples for years now. She is a student at Harvard University where she is studying theatre arts and creative writing with the goal of improving media representation in the film industry for marginalized communities.

Yukiko Takeuchi is a most-of-the-time homemaker and part-time attorney in Atlanta, Georgia. Prior to moving to Atlanta to focus on family, she lived in New York City for thirteen years where she attended law school and practiced law.

Jackie Weltman is a former professional baker, passionate home cook, and historian of religions. She cooks, bakes, and gardens year-round in the San Francisco Bay Area. She was recipe editor and co-writer of the vegan, punk rock cookbook, *Soy Not Oi 2*. She holds an MTS from Harvard Divinity School.

Foreword

Reassessing Third World Liberation: A Conversation

THIRD WORLD STUDIES IS a conversation about liberation. To converse, we need to speak the same language and hold ideas in common. By language, I refer to the English language in which this Foreword is written but also to the language of fields of study called disciplines (disciplines are bodies of knowledge with their methods and theories, subject matters, and practices, and organized broadly as the sciences and humanities in the European tradition). A system of ideas comprises ideology. Together, language and ideology constitute discourse or, in my rendering, a conversation.

This discourse on liberation is in dialogue with you, the reader. As a transaction, what I intend to convey might not be the meaning you grasp; despite speaking the same language and sharing ideologies, the speech and its hearing are related but not necessarily corresponding. In addition to that uncertainty, consider this conversation as contingent and never closed or complete; it is in process, open, and accommodates contestation and change.

Our conversation's subject matter, liberation, entails discourses of abolition and emancipation. It is thus dialogical. Third World studies conceives of liberation as sustained struggles, on shifting grounds against oppression and exploitation. Oppression is the curtailment of agency, wherein agency is ability or influence. Exploitation is the expropriation of surplus product. Under capitalism, the surplus product is the profit taken by those who own the means of production. Liberation from oppression and exploitation, accordingly, involves the discourses and material relations of power, which is the ability to move.

So again, Third World studies is a conversation about liberation from the powers that oppress and exploit.

Power resides everywhere. In the physical world, power is expressed as energy. In the social world, power is agency, ability. We, humans, all possess power albeit in differing degrees. Concentrations of power facilitate the ability to name, describe, and rank. Through assignments and enforcements those taxonomies, or classifications produce subjects as individuals and groups.

In concrete terms, the empowered elite specified races, genders, sexualities, and abilities, assigned natures or attributes to those categories, and placed them on hierarchies of merit and worth. Those social constructions created, where none existed before, the four principal races—European, Asian, African, and American (Indian); the two genders—man and woman; the two sexualities—heterosexual and homosexual; and able-bodied and disabled persons. Those were not ordered by divine law or natural law, but were inventions by those with the power, the authority to name, describe, and rank. They are social and not scientific truths. They are fictions of the mind.

Although imagined, their creators produce (interpellate) those categories in the lives, the lived experiences of their subjects. Coercion and consent are involved in that production of bodies. Laws and the policing of those laws are examples of coercive actions. For example, racial segregation, when required by law, defined races as well as imposed borders between those so designated. Schools for whites and schools for nonwhites illustrate that classification and divide based upon alleged differences and abilities. Violations might prompt courts and the police to impose fines, corporeal punishments, and imprisonment. But coercion is one method of oppression; consent offers another.

Consent occurs when subjects agree with those powers to name and enforce. We understand that as hegemony. Subjects might choose acquiescence to avoid penalties. Others might comply because they learned, perhaps through the example of role models and schooling, that those categories are real and true; they are self-evident, discernible and visible, and based on reliable evidence and science. Still others might conform without having given it much thought. In those ways, consent can be active and passive.

Resistance against those forces of oppression and exploitation constitutes the struggle for liberation. Coercion and consent fail to exhaust
the possibilities of agency. As in the reading of this text, readers can agree
but also disagree. Resistance, therefore, is an exercise of agency. We can
refuse to accept the named and imposed categories that divide us and
pit us against one another. The strategy of divide and rule is not the sole
option. And in turn, that resistance can modify the forms and strategies
of oppression and exploitation, leading to other, mobile fields of contestation and struggle. That is how liberation is an ongoing, unfolding, and
indeterminate process.

*Power, then, is the ability to influence. Despite its distribution among
all, power is not possessed or exercised equally; there are accumulations
and more significant exertions of power by the few over the many. Thereby
empowered, the elites can oppress and exploit the masses. But the oppressed
and exploited, having agency, can resist power, and thereby mobilize and
enjoin the struggle for liberation.*

Third World Studies was introduced to US higher education in 1968
at San Francisco State College, where students of the Third World Liberation Front (TWLF) identified and affiliated with the oppressed, the
exploited peoples of the Third World. The field emerged from an affiliation with and a commitment to "the people," not "we, the people" of the
US Constitution. "The people, united, will never be defeated!" and, as
the Black Panthers declared, "All power to the people!" were more than
empty slogans for the TWLF. "Serve the people" was their guide, and "for
my people" they labored.

In their statement of purpose, the TWLF declared, "As Third World
students, as Third World people, as so-called minorities, we are being
exploited to the fullest extent in this racist white America and we are
therefore preparing ourselves and our people for a prolonged struggle for
freedom from this yoke of oppression." Our people, the oppressed, the
TWLF understood, extended beyond the borders of the United States.
"We adhere to the struggles in Asia, Africa, and Latin America, ideologi-
cally, spiritually, and culturally.... We have decided to fuse ourselves with
the masses of Third World people, which are a majority of the world's
peoples, to create, through struggles, a new humanity, a new humanism,
a New World Consciousness, and within the text [sic] collectively control
our own destinies."[1]

---

1. "A Non-White Struggle toward New Humanism, Consciousness," *Daily Gater*
[San Francisco State College], May 22, 1969.

The TWLF thus demanded of the college the institutionalization of a "Third World curriculum," which they believed would educate them, indeed all students, to the realities of their communities in the United States and their connections with the oppressed and exploited peoples of the Third World. This was not a course of study intended to lead to an appreciation of the nation's diversity as multiculturalism is designed to achieve, nor was it about fostering hatreds and divisions within the US nation-state as caricatured by critics of ethnic studies. Third World studies is not ethnic studies, which is primarily about the racial formation in the United States. From our conversation about liberation thus far we understand the subjects of Third World studies to be the human condition broadly, the locations and workings of power to oppress and exploit, resistances, and the approaches to liberation.

The Third World contexts of that TWLF strike supply some of the influences at work in that struggle for liberation in US education. Of great significance during the 1950s and 1960s were the Cuban revolution, the related movements for national independence from French colonialism in Algeria and Vietnam, and the liberation movements directed at Portuguese colonialism in Guinea-Bissau, Angola, and Mozambique and against Belgian colonialism in the Congo. Those anticolonial revolutions were allied to freedom struggles in settler nation-states in Palestine, South Africa, and Bolivia. From those years emerged notable revolutionary figures like Ernesto "Che" Guevara, Patrice Lumumba, Ho Chi Minh, and Nelson Mandela; as well as intellectuals like Frantz Fanon, Amílcar Cabral, and Eduardo Mondlane.

The year 1968—when students organized the TWLF—was remarkable. In January the Vietnamese launched the Têt offensive that led to the war's end, and some 47,000 Japanese antiwar protesters converged on the US navy base at Sasebo, Japan. In March over 10,000 Chicanx high school students in Los Angeles staged a walkout against racism, and for a relevant, quality education while at San Francisco State, the TWLF formed. In April, an assassin silenced the incomparable voice of Martin Luther King Jr., and protests engulfed over forty US cities. In China tens of thousands marched, condemning racism against African Americans, and in New York City a student strike at Columbia University protested that institution's expansion into Harlem and its complicity with the imperial war in Southeast Asia. In May, students and workers erected barricades in Paris, and that summer activists formed the American Indian Movement. In September, the National Organization of Women protested the

Miss America beauty pageant in Atlantic City, and students, peasants, and workers demanded an end to government repression in Mexico City. In November, Richard Nixon captured the White House.

Those Third World revolutionary movements against colonialism and settler colonialism—as well as student and worker mass protests against imperialism, wars, racism, sexism, and state violence in Japan, China, France, and Mexico—informed and inspired like resistances in the United States. Students of the TWLF linked their movement for educational transformation with those multiple and interrelated global struggles for liberation.

But 1968 was not the start of Third World studies. Its origins reach back to 1900 when the African American intellectual and activist W. E. B. Du Bois famously declared: "The problem of the twentieth century is the problem of the color line." He delivered that prophetic announcement, appropriately, in London, the seat of the British Empire, on which the sun never set. Imperialism closed the nineteenth century and its counter, the decolonization struggles of Africa and Asia, ushered in the twentieth century. Self-determination and antiracism—the dismantling of the material relations and ideologies that justified and supported colonialism—were the central aspects of those liberation movements, which promised a new dispensation for humanity and, after two global wars and the Cold War's onset, world peace.

The color line, to Du Bois, was the divide between the colonizers and the colonized, what became known during the Cold War as the First (capitalist countries led by the United States), Second (socialist countries led by the Soviet Union), and Third World (the rest). The Third World for Du Bois was the world of color; it was racialized because the colonizers justified their imperial rule based on racism, the inferiority of the colonized. An ideology of oppression thus accompanied and advanced the material relations of exploitation. The solutions to those problems created and installed by Europeans was, therefore, anticolonialism and antiracism. Those causes were central to the field that began as Third World studies.

The problem of the twentieth century was transformative in world history. For over 400 years, Europeans—through imperialism and colonialism—had dominated the world. They created a world-system of oppression and exploitation in which flowed capital and labor. That structured relationship enriched the core (Europe and the United States) by impoverishing the periphery (the Third World). The core thereby amassed wealth at the expense of the periphery, installing dependencies. It was precisely because the Third World was enormously rich in resources and labor that the core conquered, colonized, and drained it of its capital using its labor. The revolutions against those forces of oppression and exploitation, the problem of the twentieth century, changed 400 years of world history. Third World studies was a part of that global revolution and advance.

But since 1968 and after the end to formal colonialism, Third World studies in this iteration concerns itself with liberation, broadly conceived, from all forms of oppression and exploitation. At the same time, I believe keeping the name "Third World" studies is an important reminder of its history, origins, and purposes. I realize many of us today recognize the term "Third World" with its associations of bankrupt nation-states, dictatorships, extreme poverty, civil wars, and violence against women, queers, and social outcasts. An answer to those conditions comes from a consideration of imperialism and colonialism and their afterlives, what some have called neocolonialism.

Third World studies emerged from "the problem of the twentieth century." The problem was European imperialism and colonialism that was justified by racism to oppress and exploit the Third World. Since the formal end of colonialism, Third World studies examines all forms of oppression and exploitation for the liberation of all.

The objective of oppression and exploitation is to rule, that is, to exert controls over and benefit from unruly (resistant) subjects. Modernity justifies its worth on that basis, the imposition of order in an imagined disorderly world. That mission is achieved through science, reason, and evidence, called the "Renaissance" or rebirth, life anew, eclipsing the superstition, faith, and experience of the former, called the "Dark" Ages. That duality of death and birth mirrors the mind and body distinction, rationality versus empiricism, man as opposed to woman. Therein we see values, virtues attached to discourses, history, and bodies and their assigned names, natures, and abilities.

Under modernity, those exertions of power to oppress and exploit work upon the individual (subject) and the social (society). A key instrument in that contest is the discourse and practice of sovereignty. The Treaty or Peace of Westphalia (1648) defined the contours of that relationship between ruler and subject. Westphalia provided for the nation-state comprised of property or bordered space within which sovereigns (the state) ruled over subjects (the nation). Sovereignty, thus, involved private property, the rights (divine or natural) of the state and its subjects (citizens), and self-determination or the ability of nation-states to direct their own destinies without outside intervention.

From Westphalia and its subsequent modifications descend the sovereign nation-state and sovereign subject. Those divisions of the individual and society, premised upon divine and later natural rights, are, of course, the manifestations of power. Rights whether granted by god or nature are appeals to human-assigned authorities, the sureties (positivism) of science notwithstanding, and as such are neither absolute nor eternal. Clearly borders and property include as well as exclude, and private property is a cornerstone of capitalism. Boundedness and ownership can betray the promises of liberation. Individualism can reduce collective identifications and solidarities. Finally, and as we will see, there are compelling reasons to reject the idea of a solitary self and society.

Humanism arises from the Cartesian (named after the 17th-century French mathematician René Descartes) formulation, "I think, therefore, I am," which is wonderfully optimistic but also woefully negligent. The statement reaffirms the human ability to think, which distinguishes that species from other life forms, and it posits the notion of self-determination. The self, through thought ("I think"), calls forth existence ("I am"). That rebirth arose amidst doctrines of predestination and divine will that determined and directed human, indeed all, life. Humanism, by contrast, expressed a confidence in human abilities to make history.

But as we now know, speciesism or the belief in the primacy of humans is debatable. How is superiority measured, and is human existence separate from and unrelated to other life forms and the environment? Moreover, is cognition a unique human trait or can other species or robots (artificial intelligence) think, plan, and act? The dividing line, if one exists, is certainly thin and porous. Anthropocentrism is a supremacy claimed by its creators and is patently false in that humans relate to, depend upon, and sometimes are subject to their environments, including plants and animals but also the lands, waters, and skies of their planet earth.

In addition, Marx (1818–83) and Freud (1856–1939) cast doubt on the complete autonomy of the human subject. Marx argued that one's class position or location within the relations of production shaped consciousness, while Freud found the unconscious dimension of the self that was inaccessible to thought. Marx pointed to the social context as central to the constitution of the self, while Freud identified the inner workings of the subliminal within the human mind. More basic than thought, the Swiss linguist Ferdinand de Saussure (1857–1913) explained, is language, which is the way humans conceive of themselves and articulate with their worlds. Without language the Cartesian formulation "I think" is impossible; nothing can exist outside of language. In that way, language structures consciousness and the subject.

The French psychoanalyst Jacques Lacan (1901–81), like Saussure, saw language acquisition not as a solitary but as a relational act, a submission of the self to the power and rules of language and its source, the other. For Lacan, language produces the subject in a process he called subjectification or the creation of the subject-self. Besides language, the Italian Marxist Antonio Gramsci (1891–1937) and French philosopher Louis Althusser (1918–90) described how intellectuals produce ideology, which the state uses to interpellate consciousness and subjects. Together, the French philosopher Michel Foucault (1926–84) held that language and ideology (comprising discourse) are what make subjects. In that sense, subjects are variants of discourse, and as such they are social constructs.

In sum, then, power names, describes, and ranks subjects to rule and exploit. That imposition of order, called modernity, began with the idea and practice of sovereignty and its rights of authority, property, and self-determination. Humanism upheld that sovereign self, which was undermined by subsequent ideas of class-consciousness, the unconscious, and language and ideology (discourse). Even as language acquisition is relational, the subject-self is produced in conversation with society.

Civil societies are organized within and ordered by nation-states. They comprise its members or citizens with rights and responsibilities. The nation is a narrative in the making because the official version of a chosen people with a common purpose is at odds with the varying realities of porous borders and diverse peoples. Still race is a foundational feature of the nation-state as we see in the term "nation," which comes from "by birth" or "to be born," indicating kinship of blood, which is a race. That fiction of nation starts with one people, one race, united by blood, sharing a single language and culture, history and destiny. As John Jay, a founding father of the United States and the first chief justice of the Supreme Court, declared: Americans were "one united people—a people descended from the same ancestors, speaking the same language, professing the same religion, attached to the same principles of government, very similar in their manners and customs."

That nation-state, in addition to race, is implicated in the production and management of gender, sexuality, and ability. As shown in the United States, the state has an interest in distinguishing and therewith instituting prohibitions and rights to men and women, heterosexuals and homosexuals, the abled and disabled. Patriarchal order installed men in the public sphere because of their ability to self-determine and govern and women in the private sphere because of their "inabilities" and hence "dependency." Men held ownership rights to property, including slaves, women, and children, while women had diminished rights to possess because of their incapacities. Those conjured abilities and therewith rights entitled men to occupy the state and rule while women only achieved the vote in 1920, nearly 150 years after the nation's founding.

Compulsory heterosexuality, including sexual behaviors and marriage, is a state prerogative as the guardian of public "morals" while its self-interest requires the reproduction of racialized citizens. The US Naturalization Act (1790) restricted naturalized citizenship to "free white persons." Therewith, freedom, white, and citizen formed correspondences, as opposed to bondage, nonwhite, and alien. Race, freedom, and sexuality also figured in those relations of power. In 1664, colonial Maryland in a single act banned interracial marriage and made slavery a lifetime condition. Also in US law, homosexual and interracial prohibitions often formed equivalences. As "immoral" and "unnatural" acts against god and nature, homosexuality and interracial sex and marriage were denied and punished.

The state—as a locus of power—rules through a strategy of naming, describing, and conferring rights and privileges on the bases of race, gender, sexuality, ability, and nation. Through the apparatuses of language and ideology (discourse), the state produces those subjects as dualities of one set against the other: white v. nonwhite, man v. woman, heterosexual v. homosexual, abled v. disabled, and citizen v. alien. By segregating and pitting one over the other, the state imposes order and rule or hegemony through coercion and consent. Its constitution and laws bestow and deprive powers, and transgressions of those polarities are deviations and threats to the national security. Since the US nation's founding, for example, migrants of color were "aliens" and as such imperiled the homeland.

Even before the US nation-state in settler colonial Virginia we see that term "aliens" used to identify people of color as nonmembers and thus deprived of rights. Anthony Johnson, an enslaved African, arrived in the Colony in 1621, two years after the first Africans landed. He worked on a settler tobacco plantation along the James River, and over twenty years married, Mary, an enslaved African, and together had four children. After gaining their freedom in the 1640s, the Johnson family farmed some 250 acres on the Colony's eastern shore. They kept cattle and had two African servants. In 1669 a settler jury of white men ruled that Anthony Johnson was "a Negroe" and by consequence "an alien" or noncitizen. As such he could not transfer his land to his son, and instead awarded the property to a white settler. Therein we see race, citizenship, and rights of possession conjoined; white, citizen, and owner stood in opposition to black, alien, and dispossessed.

The social, in addition to race, gender, sexuality, ability, and nation, includes the provisioning function to sustain life, societies, and the nation-state. Human labor exerted upon the land (environment) produces goods or value. Food, clothing, and shelter provide for those basic needs. The economy is that process of creating value. Capitalism is but one of several economic systems. We should remember that because in our time capitalism is the dominant world order, and we can easily see its triumph as vindication of its verity and powers. In fact, capitalism emerged in a place and time, and its spread and growth can be attributed in large part to its role in imperialism and colonialism.

Simply, capitalism is an economic system based upon private property, the ownership of the means of production, and upon surpluses or profits derived from the labor of workers. Those constitute classes, those who own and those who work for returns. Whether enslaved, indentured, or free, laborers produce wealth for the owners in exchange for sustenance (food, clothing, shelter) or wages. In that way, accumulations accrue to the owners through the impoverishment of those who create value. The expropriation of surplus product is what we know as exploitation. Super exploitation occurs when profit margins widen from labor systems divided by race (nonwhite), gender (women), or nation (alien) to lower the costs of labor, and from environments such as colonies where resources are more abundant, and labor is plentiful and cheap.

Sovereignty, as ideology and practice, abetted the rise of capitalism. As we saw, property and rights were features of the sovereign state and sovereign subject. Those possessions formed a basis for the ownership of the means of production (resources, factories, and so forth), and ownership of one's own labor. Humanism and individualism, however, were not universally or equally possessed because of assigned abilities and inabilities that merited and denied claims and powers. Accordingly, nonwhites and women were dependent upon white men because of their lack, mainly their mental inabilities to comprehend complexities. Similarly, workers were poor because of their deficiencies, whether of drive and initiative, intelligence, culture, or bad choices. Discourses thus installed and explained social locations and hierarchies.

Imperialism or extraterritorial powers extended sovereignty's reach by advancing the ideas of possessions and rights to places outside the nation-state. Imperialism is both discourse and material relations. Colonialism is an aspect of imperialism as discourse and sites of those extraterritorial powers. Colonies involved military and provisioning bases to defend and facilitate the expansion, and extractive and settler colonies to produce wealth for the imperial power. Gold, silver, tobacco, and sugar flowed from America to Europe while spices, silks, cotton, and porcelain moved from Asia to the core. Enslaved and indentured workers generated that value, and Europe accumulated wealth at the expense of the Third World, drained of its resources and labor. Those imperial processes of conquest, colonization, the exploitation of resources and labor, and capital accumulations comprised and advanced capitalism and "the problem of the twentieth century."

Imperialism and colonialism are thus aspects of nationalism and capitalism. Those features appear in the move from nation-state to imperial or extraterritorial nation-state. In the encounter with Third World peoples, nation-based races, like the German race, the English race, became Europeans or whites. Taxonomies supplied the discursive scaffolding for those essentializing, generalizing human types. Carl Linnaeus (1707–78), Swedish physician and "the father of taxonomy," grouped humans into varieties, later called races, according to the four continents, which were also social, not scientific constructs. Europe was the home of Europeans (whites), Asia, of Asians (brown), Africa, of Africans (blacks), and America, of Americans (red). He later described Asians as yellow in color and assigned natures or traits to each group that descended from the ideal type, the European. White supremacy, realized in the imperial spread, conquest, and colonization of peoples of color, affirmed the (European) discourse of race. And conversely, a justification for imperialism involved the conversion and uplift of pagan, barbarous peoples mired in backward, stagnant cultures—peoples without history or the ability to move.

In 1895, at the height of European imperialism, Kaiser Wilhelm II of Germany commissioned a painting entitled *Yellow Peril.* "On a plateau of rock bathed in light radiating from the Cross—the symbol in which alone Christians win their victories—stand allegorical figures of the civilized nations," read the explanation that accompanied the painting, copies of which the Kaiser sent to several European heads of state and the US president. Led by the archangel Michael, women in martial garb, wearing the names of European nation-states, look with varying degrees of interest and resolve toward an approaching "horror" and "calamity which menaces them." Beneath them stretches "the vast plain of civilized Europe" through which flows "a majestic stream" with cities and churches dotting the peaceful landscape. But "dark pitchy vapors obscure the sky" and "clouds of calamity are rolling up" in the wake of "invaders" with "hellish, distorted faces." Positioned above a burning city are the figures of the Buddha and a Chinese dragon, symbols of the "yellow peril," and inscribed on the painting was the legend: "Nations of Europe, defend your holiest possession."

European civilization and Christianity were the sole possessions of Europe that united the competing and conflicting national interests over empire. To meet the forces of darkness, the invasion of uncivilized, barbarous, and heathen peoples, the civilized nations of Europe must win their victory under the banner of (European) civilization and Christianity. That conflict has a deep history. The Greco-Persian Wars of the fifth century B.C.E. threatened ancient Greece, the font of European civilization, while the eleventh through thirteenth century C.E. Crusades waged "holy" wars in the name of Christianity against paganism (Islam). White and Christian nationalisms and supremacies in the United States grew from those European roots, which some 400 years of imperialism nourished and strengthened.

Third World studies locates the subject-self within society. Foundational to the constitution of civil society is the nation-state based upon sovereignty. Property rights and the relations between rulers and subjects comprise nation-states, which, to rule, interpellate and police race, gender, sexuality, ability, and nation. Sustaining those state powers is the economy, which, under capitalism, involves the expropriation of surplus product by owners from workers. Rights and privileges accrue from those social hierarchies and relations, even as subjects and workers can resist and thereby alter the forms and outcomes of oppression and exploitation.

Social formation theory purports to explain the subject-self and society as the locations and articulations of power to oppress and exploit, involving the formations of race, gender, sexuality, ability, class, and nation.

Those organizations and exertions of power comprise discourses that the material and social relations make real; that is, the discursive enact and shape consciousness, experiences, and lives. Formations are structures, institutions, forms that move; they are in formation, in process. Power (the state and capital) creates and deploys those as single formations, race for example; as multiple, race and gender; and as intersectional, gendered sexualities. In those ways, subjects might be oppressed and exploited singly as nonwhites, multiply as nonwhite and disabled, and intersectionally as the alien, which today might conjure a nonwhite, poor, criminal, sexually deviant threat.

Intended to behave as closed systems, the formations of and relations in society are designed by their creators, those who hold and wield power, to function as a whole to actualize control (rule) and privileges and poverties. But because of human agency and ceaseless contestations, the social formation is not a closed or self-regulating system. Neither is its future and direction predetermined. Rather, the social formation is historical or specific to time and place and is subject to change and transformation.

To visualize the social formation, imagine separate spheres of race, gender, sexuality, ability, class, and nation that converge to overlap and share features and diverge to differentiate; they are elastic, expanding and contracting over space and time. Think in terms of singularities and multiplicities, meetings and departures, stasis and change. In addition, intersecting spheres can result in a third category, neither "a" nor "b" but "c." That is, an intersectional Black woman is oppressed and exploited not as a sum of race ("a") and gender ("b") but as a racialized gender or a gendered race ("c").

The social formation rejects degrees of suffering that measures oppression and exploitation. Quantitative analyses are not only simplifications and misleading; they segregate and rank victims and fail to detect continuities and commonalities that can promote solidarities. Instead of "most oppressed and exploited," the theory posits the qualities of oppression and exploitation. Race, gender, sexuality, ability, class, and nation comprise the varieties that oppress and exploit as single, multiple, and intersectional discourses and material relations. They, then, render subjects susceptible to their powers, accounting for qualitative, not quantitative contrasts.

Moreover, oppression and exploitation differ in contexts of place and time. Colonialism, for instance, served imperialism from the fifteenth through twentieth centuries; it had a beginning and an end. After independence, another form of colonialism called neocolonialism held in bondage Third World nation-states. Former colonial masters and global institutions like the World Bank direct Third World states and economies toward capitalist "development." And following the pattern of European and settler nation-states, Third World versions installed privileged elites to rule over and profit from their oppressed and impoverished masses. If national self-determination was the solution to imperialism, colonialism, and racism, "the problem of the twentieth century," neocolonialism kept intact the locations of power in the core but also distributed it to the periphery in what some have called the "new imperialism."

Social formation attends to the multiplicity of forces at work in the exercise of power. It demands a complexity in our thinking and politics to ascertain how social categories overlap, interact, conflict with, and interrupt each other. Social formation is not solely the intersections or sum of oppressions; it accounts for those variances and meeting points but also their resistances (and accommodations) and the mutually constituting and shifting relations between discourses and the material conditions. Finally social formation theory supplies a rubric for affiliations among discourses of racial formation, feminist, queer, critical (dis)ability, and critical theories and for solidarities in political insurgencies from oppressed and exploited peoples across the imposed divides of race, gender, sexuality, ability, class, and nation.

In the movement against police profiling and violence as we witnessed in Ferguson, Missouri and New York City in 2014, thousands marched chanting "Hands up, don't shoot!" and "I can't breathe" across social divides. That cause and movement surged anew in 2020 after the police murders of Breonna Taylor and especially George Floyd. And in the largest single-day protest in US history, the Women's March on January 21, 2017 amassed between three and five million women and men, white and nonwhite, straight and queer, abled and (dis)abled, rich and poor, citizen and alien to affirm that women's rights are human rights. Those mobilizations attest to the single, multiple, and intersectional features and powers of oppression and exploitation and their resistance—the social formation.

The social formation examines power as discourses and material relations. It apprehends oppression and exploitation as the workings of power to rule and profit from its naming, describing, and ranking race, gender, sexuality, ability, class, and nation. Those taxonomies and their policing impose order through divide and rule even as transgressions erode their borders. Single, multiple, and intersectional formations add complexities to resistances, but they also provide opportunities for mobilizing solidarities for liberation.

Third World studies is a conversation about liberation. As such, it is open, subject to adoption and resistance. It is a work in progress. Liberation suggests necessarily an opposition. It exists in resistance to oppression, exploitation, or the curtailment of agency and expropriation of surplus product. Liberation thus is a form of abolitionism and emancipation from confinement, the prisons of power, discursive and material. Such enclosures limit space; isolation prohibits connections across divides of the subject-self and society. That compression, that restriction of boundless possibilities affects us all. Our imaginations must approach the infinite. Third World studies poses to us that challenge.

Gary Y. Okihiro

Acknowledgments

We, the editors, wish to sincerely thank the many people who have been involved in the production of this book. We would like to thank the editors at Wipf and Stock for all the email correspondence they have had with us in the preparation of the text. We would especially like to thank George Callihan in the ongoing communication of the writing process. His patience, wisdom, and kindness were deeply appreciated. Emily Callihan was incredibly helpful and attentive in answering specific questions regarding copyediting. We would like to thank Joshua Little (editorial content manager), as well as Matt Wimer (editorial production manager) in their assistance with this book project. Everyone at Wipf and Stock has been so kind, supportive, and encouraging in this publishing endeavor.

Emmanuel would like to acknowledge the work of Brother Ishmael Tetteh and the Etherean Mission in Accra, Ghana. Bro Tetteh's courageous meditative and spiritual practice, aspects of which I write about in the first chapter of this volume, have been deeply inspirational. I would also name my Professor Kofi Asare Opoku, whose work on a consciously African approach to the study of religion and spirituality have been seminal in my own work.

Hellena has had multiple correspondences with each of the contributors to this volume. This book project *was* a spiritual practice. I am grateful for the conversations and journeying together in the organic evolutionary process of this book. This volume came together because of the ideas each of you shared. The ideas in the volume demonstrate the power of togetherness and how everyone helped shape it—from the sequence of the chapters to the content. I got to know many of you better through our conversations. Lori Klein especially helped set the tone of "togetherness" with her vision for a multi-authored chapter. Namju Cho was wonderful in our ongoing conversations about the book and our early morning/late night talks as the book was in its final stages. Thank you for being on this journey with me and for helping me complete the book.

Hellena would like to thank Gary Okihiro whose academic work in Ethnic Studies has been revolutionary. I am grateful for the many conversations we have had and his openness in seeing the relevance of a Third World Studies curriculum to spiritual care—and to Religious Studies overall. Loretta Ross was especially generous with her time, scholarship, and mentorship for our joint chapter. I am honored to have had the opportunity to co-write a chapter with you, Loretta. Pamela Cooper-White was extremely gracious in sharing her own work on forgiveness (her unpublished paper) and in writing her epilogue for this volume.

Hellena would like to thank Tom Painting for his passion for teaching and birding. Your love for humanity and all creatures is inspirational. I want to thank you for your compassionate care, brilliant mind, and creative, fun-loving spirit. This COVID-19 year was better because our family learned from your heart. Thank you for the gifts of teaching, birding, poetry, and care.

To my co-editor, Bishop and Professor Emmanuel Y. Lartey, I would like to express enormous gratitude for your words of wisdom and guidance on this project. Indeed, our conversations on liberative practices of spiritual care have shaped this volume. Your work on interculturality and spiritual care is the groundwork that has outlined a new path for many of us in the field of pastoral care. Thank you for your pioneering work, as well as your academic and spiritual integrity.

Most importantly, Hellena would like to honor her family. Madeleine and Benjamin, you are my greatest teachers in life! I learn by listening to you and hearing your many thoughts. Our nightly dinner conversations are like seminars (sometimes serious) or comedy shows (many times hilarious)! We have so much fun in our talks and chatter. Julyann, you are always the greatest model for practicing care. Your empathy and compassion are transformative. I would like to honor my mother (*ohmma*) Theresa. Your joyous, youthful spirit at age 78 is amazing. Your practices of care are what taught me to see that there is no sacrality separate from the quotidian practices of life. Lastly, I would like to thank my life partner, Elbert Chun, with whom I engage in the daily practices of care work and connect in the routine renewal of our energy through play. Together, we make everything special in its practicality.

Introduction

Postcolonial Practices of Care: A Project of Togetherness During COVID-19 & Racial Violence

Hellena Moon

Images & Practices

Gary Okihiro's foreword is a conversation about liberation from the various forms of power that exploit and oppress us. We invite such conversations of liberation—and the meta-discourse of liberation *itself*—as a spiritual practice. As such, this book is also part of the ongoing conversation for liberation that Okihiro describes. To practice our agency for liberative ends, Okihiro challenges us to expand our imaginations. Our first co-edited book, *Postcolonial Images of Spiritual Care*, did precisely that.[1] It was an anthology that was inspired by my (Hellena's) children's queries about images of G*d. My then seven-year-old son asked why G*d was depicted as a white man in the Sistine Chapel painting [of God and Adam]. "If the first people were African," Benjamin asked, "and we were made to look like God, then God should be Black. Why is God made to be white?" My then nine-year-old daughter stated that it was about power. White people, she stated in her age-appropriate way, had the power and wealth to control what God looked like and whose paintings got to hang in art museums. "So, they painted God to look like the white men who painted them," she told my son.

1. Lartey and Moon, *Postcolonial Images.*

1

Our conversations further underscore the unsettling power of images and its impact on gender, culture, and religion. The dominant stories reveal how images have discursively controlled who is considered valuable or closer to divinity—or who even *gets to be* divine. These conversations with my children demonstrate the ongoing power of visuality—and the resulting discrimination and oppression—of the racialized, gendered, and sexed body. Such conversations about liberation expose the imbrication of our materiality with the spiritual care of humans, as well as underscore the power of racialized images in religion and spiritual care to reify bodily vulnerability.

The images that have produced our racist epistemologies have, in turn, instantiated the practices driven by their biases, hatred, discrimination, and fear. Images are shaped by our practices. This implies that practices—or what practices are considered legitimately spiritual— are controlled and dictated by those in power. What *becomes* the normative or dominant image is controlled by those in power. Images are heuristics that construct our theories, histories, and epistemologies. The stories are shaped by those who have the power to control what/who is represented. Our first book, then, has been significant in *revealing* the problematic meta-image of our US Protestant ethnocentric monoculturalism, but also in *challenging* issues of equity in pastoral care's hegemonic white Protestant assembly. Our volume exposed, not necessarily the shortcomings of our field, but rather the field as an appendage of the white Protestant assumptions and worldviews of the dominant group in our institutions, churches, seminaries, and schools.

Despite the predominant milieu of a monocultural ethnocentrism in the field of pastoral care, there has been an intercultural community of practitioners, academics, chaplains, and others of the periphery that have had very different perspectives, experiences, and lived practices that have been critical of the images representing a monocultural ethnocentric worldview. Our book, *Postcolonial Images of Spiritual Care*, disturbed the collective image of a white Protestant assemblage in pastoral care, as well as unsettled the hegemonic power of those images to elide certain stories and variegated practices of care.[2] The meta-image for our previous book, then, is a postcolonial paradigm of kaleidoscopic hybridity, multiplicity, and relationality that more accurately reflects the undercurrent of what was—*and is*—happening on the margins of pastoral care.

2. Lartey & Moon, *Postcolonial Images.*

Images tell stories, so our hope is for more images that shape practices and practices that evoke renewed images. Our *Postcolonial Images* book underscored the important *practice* of telling our story as one of the first steps of healing from complex and harmful manifestations of white supremacy in our society. We hope that more books are forthcoming that illustrate the complexity, diversity, and hybridity of who we are as scholars, practitioners, theologians, and chaplains. We desire to further refine a postcolonial methodology that addresses and engages the various societal problems in our ongoing conversations for liberation.

This volume seeks to deepen the conversation on liberation by redefining and critiquing "spiritual" practices of care during the dual pandemics of COVID-19 and racial violence of 2020–21. Our methodology incorporates practices that help give life to the theories of postcolonialism, decoloniality, biomimicry, and Gary Okihiro's Third World Studies curriculum. We share practices of "radical spiritual care," not necessarily within a corporate or monolithic faith, but rather as part of a praxis-oriented framework that transcends/transgresses Enlightenment-era European epistemological categories of religious, cultural, political, and/or national boundaries. Our work is part of the critical interrogation of the colonial origins and meanings that constitute the sacred and secular that have validated certain practices (practices that are legible to the colonizer's worldview), while deeming other valuable practices and rhythms of care as barbaric or "primitive." Thus, a secular/sacred binary has distorted what/who/where is valued and what/who/where is not. We, the co-editors, seek to highlight practices and engage conversations of decolonializing spiritual care in our desire for liberation.

"Study" as an Interdependent Process of Becoming

This book project adopts the subversive praxis of "study" as part of the genealogy of Third World Studies that Okihiro describes in his foreword. Fred Moten and Stefano Harney see "study" as a discourse, a conversation that can happen at a picnic, a barbecue, walks, and so forth.[3] Harney and Moten state that study is not just sitting in a library. "Study" is organic. Life *is* study. They describe "study" as subversive practices that are grounded in our quotidian life with others—as part of the "consent not to

---

3. Harney and Moten, *The Undercommons*.

be a single being."[4] That is, we are interdependent, connected, and reliant on each other to disturb and rattle normative methods of seeing, hearing, reading, and knowing. Moten emboldens us to do similarly through study. Daily conversations constitute study. Study inhabits our work, ideas, relationships, community-building, and vision for sustaining our humanity and the planet. These practices, conversations, and dialogues are ripe with the potentiality for creating new theories and epistemologies—ideas and imaginings—for our liberation.

"Study" involves a Paulo Freirean method of liberation from oppression, dehumanization, and objectification. Such a method involves dialogue, not dogma; critical thinking, not memorization; relationality, not hierarchy; sharing of power, not a concentration of it. "Study" poses problems and inquiries of the incomplete human being as a "process of *becoming*—as unfinished, uncompleted beings in and with a likewise unfinished reality."[5] This book project is such a "study" of liberation. Our liberation, that is, our humanity—and our becoming—*insists on* the human spirit practicing "study." Decolonial spiritual care requires praxis of our humanization—to *continue on* with the emancipatory projects initiated by W. E. B. Du Bois, Frantz Fanon, Aimé Césaire, Albert Memmi, the Third World Liberation Front, feminist and disability movements, and many others. Decolonial spiritual care also sees nature as inextricably tied to our humanization and liberation. We cannot survive without Earth; therefore, planetary care and well-being is intimately part of our praxis of "study."

A starting point for our practices of liberation, then, is to address the admonition of Du Bois regarding the color line. He states, "The problem of the twentieth century is the problem of the color-line—the relation of the darker to the lighter races of men in Asia and Africa, in America and the islands of the sea."[6] Du Bois later acknowledged that the "problem of the color-line"—as he initially observed in the United States—did not manifest itself identically across the world. Though discrimination

4. "Consent not to be a single being" refers to Fred Moten's trilogy. See Moten's three books which constitute, "consent not to be a single being": *Black & Blur, Stolen Life,* and *The Universal Machine.* Moten adapts the phrase from Edouard Glissant, but I have used it in reference to how Moten has understood it as an ontological desire not to be a "single being," or not to be "alone" because ontological awareness is normatively understood in a liberal subject framework of autonomous singularity. See El-Hadi, "Ensemble."

5. Freire, *Pedagogy of the Oppressed,* 65.

6. Du Bois, *The Souls of Black Folk,* 9.

existed everywhere, Du Bois expanded this challenge to include discrimination beyond that of Black versus white. While the "color line" was
used by many as a reference to the racial problem in the United States, he
saw oppression and violence as crises cutting across much of the world in
Asia(s), Africa, and the islands of the sea.

Du Bois lamented the deaths of Jews, the oppression of the disabled,
the young, and widows. In a letter to his friend, Gabriel D'Arboussier,
Du Bois urged him to encourage others to "reassess and reformulate the
problems" of such interwoven oppressions that continue to uphold forms
of white supremacy. He later revised his understanding of the "color line"
following his visit to Poland in 1952 when he realized the imbrication
of religion, liberalism, imperialism, and power within discourses of race
that helped him to complexify his earlier understanding of racism and
colonialism.[7] Du Bois engaged in a more thorough observation to articulate oppression and violence from a sociological lens of "racial formation" that involved culture, class, liberalism and bodily autonomy, and
its coeval materialization with "religion."[8] We argue for a deeper *critique
of religious discourse as a process of racial formation*, as it was elided in
the original vision of the 1960s Third World Liberation Front and Third
World Studies. This very important analysis of religion and racial formation continues to be left out in emancipatory work (discursive or activist)
or treated additively.

The color line reveals that the spiritual *was* and *is* political (that
people's spirits—our practices and ways of practicing care—have been
politicized, manipulated, and altered from its socio-historical contexts).
It also *necessitates* a "relational way of seeing"—of using a critical lens
that helps us build our own nodes of relationalities that subvert imbricated power structures that continue to use colonial epistemologies.[9]

Decoloniality & "Studies" as Praxis

A central idea of this volume sees decoloniality as a framework for understanding practices of care. This book situates itself within the meta-project
of decoloniality, which refers to the "undoing" and the "undisciplining"

7. Du Bois, "The Negro and the Warsaw Ghetto," 45–46

8. Omi & Winant, *Racial Formation*.

9. Mignolo & Walsh, *On Decoloniality*, 17.

of the epistemological devastation of colonialism.[10] It refers to Aníbal Quijano's proposal of "epistemic reconstitution" which explores the rich sources of native epistemologies and ways of knowing that were deemed superstitious or barbaric.[11] Decoloniality means discursively building a new world on top of the colonial ruins, centered on radical theories— epistemologies that are grounded in native cultures—and practices that repurpose the tools that were used to colonize the Third World/Global South. It requires re-examining the relationalities and relationships that helped build colonialism(s), such as epistemologies, structures of oppression and privilege, class and spiritual hierarchies, and power structures.

Extending our critique of the theories, epistemologies, and practices of pastoral care; we argue that the term, "spiritual care" is not without its problems. The term has become a substitute for pastoral care. Or, it is used as a demarcation—a division—between the pastoral and spiritual. We articulate a method of decoloniality as a project for spiritual care, which engages renewed ways of thinking radically about the coeval development of Christianity, pastoral care, and colonialism. It was precisely because of the resistance to the oppressions of colonial rule that such creative practices of decoloniality and repurposing strategies of care emerged. In that sense, we seek to interrogate and rehabilitate the term, "pastoral" care, as certainly not oppressive or colonialist in and of itself. While Christian colonial tools of cultural obliterations have been critiqued and excavated in postcolonial theory, the pastoral practices of decoloniality and the ongoing work of subversive care that have been an important narrative have not been explored to its fullest. This project delves deeper into subversive spiritual practices of care that were—and are—avenues of liberation. What we problematize is the monocultural ethnocentrism within the work of pastoral care. We invite practitioners to support and practice the interculturality, inter-religious practices, and innovative disruptions of white cultural superiority and unconscious white supremacy within dominant Christian narratives of pastoral care.

Aligned within Okihiro's Third World Studies method, our vision of spiritual care practices articulates the importance of critiquing how colonialism and imperialism brought about the devastation and destruction of individual lives and communities. It also highlights the turmoil that such forms of oppression continue to wreak on a global and systemic

---

10. Mignolo & Walsh, *On Decoloniality*, 11.

11. Quijano, "Coloniality of Power."

level—epistemic violence, destruction and demoralization of people's daily practices, abuse of animals, and lands. Part of the ongoing racism against the Black, brown, and Asian communities is a denigration of indigenous roots of cultural beliefs and practices. It is the continued disavowal of the decolonial roots of "religion" and the colonizing discourses that privilege white European cultural Christianity that prevent our liberation from the harms of epistemic and psychic violence.

Decoloniality of the Sacred and Secular During the Pandemic

March 13, 2021 marked the one-year anniversary of the US—as well as near global— shutdown due to COVID-19. We were quarantined in our homes for most of 2020, uncertain of what our future would be like. The few months thereafter were precarious times, and many of us were reading the news vigilantly for updates on how to stay safe from the virus that was devastating the global community. For those of us non-white bodied beings, we were also experiencing heightened racism. We were overwhelmed by stories and media coverage of the racial violence and brutal, inhumane murders of George Floyd, Ahmaud Arbery, Breonna Taylor, as well as many other Black and brown bodies in 2020. The demeaning representations of people of color are further exacerbated when we are inundated with social media images that depict racial violence. The images of George Floyd's murder on May 25, 2020 became the tipping point for demanding accountability against racial injustices, as the barbaric killing of Floyd sparked the largest protests in our nation's history. The racial violence, hate crimes, and killings continued throughout the pandemic, with a new wave of fear shattering communities of color with the targeted shootings of six Asian American women in Georgia on March 16, 2021.

Spiritual practices (confessions, genuflecting in prayer, fasting, self-flagellation, etc.) can easily shift to modes or apparatuses of state power and control (interrogations as forced confessions, kneeling on people's necks to control them and kill them without accountability, targeting people in the justification of shepherding—that they are providing safety for the community—when it is a form of racial profiling or targeting of those referred to as "sheep" in pastoral care).[12] Genuflection as a practice

12. Foucault, *Discipline and Punish.*

in prayer, then, can easily slide into definitions of torture, as the heinously disturbing image of Derek Chauvin's knee on George Floyd's neck for nine minutes and twenty-nine seconds exposed.

The milieu of systemic racism, ongoing police brutality against Black and brown bodies, and anti-Asian hatred and violence revealed the physical precarities of white cultural superiority for people of color. Many of us, nevertheless, inaugurated rituals to repair the harm. We engaged in practices of protest, created justice-building platforms that addressed the heinous crimes against people of color, as well as maintained routines and rituals of self-care and communal well-being. In conjunction, we established the habitus of masking, social distancing, and constant hand-washing as the procedures and practices that would keep us safe and keep the virus at bay. These have become interconnected "religious" practices in that they have become ritualized in our quotidian lives that have kept us together.[13] Systemic racism highlighted our bodily vulnerability; at the same time, it showed forms of resilience we human beings have from harm. Violence—and the so-called sacred—is implicated in the ordinary. Sacrality is not outside the ordinary. Violence is linked to the "sacred" and vice versa. There is a convergence of the secular and the "religious," as the year of 2020-21 has exposed.

Scholars of religion have constantly altered their ideas and theories on what has constituted religion, what is superstition, what is secular, sacred, etc. Since the "invention" of religions in the sixteenth century by European explorers and missionaries, life practices of non-European peoples have intrigued and piqued curiosity that drove scholarship about religions. Such religious formations created hierarchies and categories of superiority as to what even constituted religion. Religion has been a boundary marker manipulated to discern what cultures and peoples are primitive and what practices are "modern." Religion itself is a discursive tool of power in who gets to control spirit and what constitutes spirituality. As Mignolo and Walsh have argued that "there is no modernity without coloniality" (modernity/coloniality),[14] religion itself is a necessary component of modernity and coloniality: religion/modernity/coloniality. "Religion"—imbricated with race, gender, sexuality, and bodily normativity—was an invented methodological tool of the imperial/colonial categorization of peoples. A conversation about liberation, therefore, is

---

13. *"Religare"* in Latin means to tie, bind, bring together, so we use "religious practices" in that communal sense.

14. Walsh and Mignolo, *On Decoloniality,* 4.

not complete until we talk about how religion and monocultural ethno-centric practices of pastoral care were—and are—integral tools in shaping coloniality, (i.e., the colonial matrix of power).[15]

Such categorizations and hierophanies—expressions or materialization of the sacred—were used by Christian colonial explorers who searched for nodes of similarity with Christianity in what they defined as "religion." This search for "hierophanies" was a colonial tool and a prominent characteristic of the "empire of religion."[16] Hierophanies, according to Mircea Eliade, organized space and separated the sacred from the mundane and profane.[17] In connection with his far right politics, antisemitism, and associations with fascism, Eliade's work on hierophanies is now deeply critiqued as ahistorical, colonialist, and entangled with theosophical comparative religion.[18] Laurie Patton, former student of Eliade, notes, "Fascist thought often longed for a purity of culture outside of time, for the grand system that connected all truths in a single cultural insight. Eliade's thinking was no exception."[19] Hierophanies are more of an epistemological invention and myth than reality or "discovery" of uniqueness within cultures and religious truth.[20] Eliade's work on hierophanies, then, helped construct the colonialist package of myth-making and fantasizing of the peoples of the two-thirds world, thereby creating "Africa" and "Asia" in the imaginations of Europeans within the field of religion and religious practices. Religious practices themselves became confined—and defined—to colonialist-era understandings of rituals that helped to reify Western cultural superiority.

To interrogate hierophanies and to understand religious epistemologies in the context of Eliade's fascist connections is not only socially responsible practice; it is immoral not to do so.[21] Rather than a "Christianization" of other society's cultures and practices, ideas and theories need to be seen in the social context of their origins. The "sacred" and "secular" need to be further explored in spiritual care within the context

15. Quijano, "Coloniality of Power."
16. Chidester, *Empire of Religion*, 276.
17. Patton, "Mircea Eliade," 385.
18. Chidester, *Empire of Religion*, 276.
19. Patton, "Mircea Eliade," 390.
20. Chidester, *Empire of Religion*, 276.
21. Patton, "Mircea Eliade," 390.

of Eliade's ahistorical, fascist, theological framework.[22] Employing a method of historicism and understanding the demise and fallacy of his work from such a critical social justice lens is part of the practice of decolonial spiritual care.[23] Decolonial spiritual practice is a descent into the ordinary and mundane, not an ascent or a transcendence into the otherworldly or unique. In that regard, the spiritual practice of justice work is the underlying thread of establishing ongoing harmony in the relationships we have with each other, our communities, and our environment.

As a meta-project of decoloniality and the "undoing" of the epistemological destructive aftermath of colonialism and the fascist underpinnings of hierophanies, we reassess the importance of nature and the re-suturing of the chasm between the ordinary and the sacred. A radical, decolonial spiritual care paradigm upholds the "radicality" of African spiritual practices and places our care within a porous paradigm of relationality, nature, intercultural mimicry, and biomimicry (i.e., exploring/being inspired by nature and what nature teaches us).[24] Rather than reify the religious demarcations that a project of modernity/coloniality has constructed; an epistemically reconstituted understanding of care underscores the nexus of care practices that highlight the amalgamated togetherness of who we are as humans. This understanding of biomimicry is not modern, nor is it new; it is the roots—or the radicality—of humanity that African religions maintained despite its attempted obliteration by forces of modernity/coloniality. Radical care, then, literally refers to the care that is vital to life. And that originates in the ground. That is, as all life starts with Earth and goes back to Earth, nature and humans cannot be separate. We garner wisdom from nature.

As Lartey has stated, African societies had no divisions between the sacred and ordinary.[25] Every aspect of life was revered. While recent Western scientists have referred to inspiration from nature as biomimicry, African religious practices have known and sought wisdom from nature for centuries. As Brother Ishmael Tetteh has underscored, nature is the inspiration for African religious practices. In that regard, we reassess the relationship between religion and science. The similarities of our human

22. See Moon's forthcoming book, *Mask of Clement Violence.*

23. Patton mentions this is part of the "undeadness" of his work. Patton, "Mircea Eliade," 393.

24. Etymology of radical is roots, originating in the ground. Radical means "that which is vital to life."

25. Lartey, "Be-ing In Relation."

practices to that of the natural world is an attestation to the importance of practices we adopt from the natural world. The concept of dignity and care implies reverence for all of life as a habitus of life, as has been part of the precolonial practices of many cultures and communities. Flourishing of humans entails harmony with the natural world and the flourishing of our nonhuman and infrahuman designations. Forms of life (or the Western understanding of it) mask the spiritual political struggles. The social nature of who we are means that our agency—of becoming who we were meant to become—is to be revered and respected in our ethnic, gender, sexual, racial, class, and bodily differences.

Included here are stories that value the importance of daily life, creating space for the voices that articulate ordinary rituals and our relationships with one another and how nature becomes a medium in cultivating practices of care. Veena Das highlights the importance of giving life to words. Voice is not necessarily speech. Thus, this book is about the practices that "give life to our words"—giving life and dignity to the ordinary, daily practices of living. Das argues that relationships are those life-affirmations that help give life to our words. Relationships are also the root of human African spiritual practices. Relationships are the connectors, the ligation (the religion), to our subjectivity.

Decolonial spiritual care, then, focuses less on "belief" in the many definitions and meanings of religion. Instead, it highlights and affirms the *practices of care and our relationships of—and with—the everyday*. Quotidian practices and relationships shape our agency and ethical subjectivity. We understand COVID-19 as an event—as an emergence of a series of violence, deaths, disruptions of life, and fear—that was overlapped with variegated forms of trauma. While violence disrupts the everyday and the routine, violence sometimes *is* the routine. And life itself is repaired through the various forms of healing we find in the everyday. Life is "recovered . . . through a descent into the ordinary."[26] Relationships require ongoing attention to the most ordinary of rituals, objects, and events, as Jeremy Lewis so eloquently encapsulated in his work in our earlier volume.[27] We reinforce our agency, not by escaping the ordinary and searching for the sacred, but by spiraling into the mundane. Our agency is part of our circadian rhythm and the circuitry of life. Veena

26. Das, *Life and Words.*
27. Lewis, "Organic Rituals."

Das states, "The blurring between what is human and what is not human shades into the blurring over what is life and what is not life."[28]

We are reminded of Michel de Certeau whose work on relational practices and agency reveals the problems of having—or maintaining—a sacred/secular divide.[29] A meta message of de Certeau's work is relevant to the "disciplines" themselves, as it reveals the need to break down the barriers and boundaries of disciplines—the modes of power that control knowledge, as well as our agency. While Audre Lorde warned that "the master's tools will never dismantle the master's house,"[30] we argue for a subversion or repurposing of oppressive practices of divides and boundaries. We can and do have agency to circumvent institutionalized practices and structures of power to enact more liberative practices. Throughout history, we have seen people subvert the structures of power to make meaning of laws or rituals for their own use or self-determination. Michel de Certeau understood the daily practices of people's lives as creative resistance to hegemonic forms of power established by the ruling class. Ordinary people—or the colonized—destabilized structures of power and challenged the tools produced by the ruling class (or colonizers). Tactics of subversion were everyday activities such as walking, reading, and socializing that became forms of political resistance.

Certeau's work discusses the strategies that are linked with institutions and structures that are producers of power. He uses "the city" as a model to demonstrate how the space is mapped out and determined by strategies of governments to control and maintain power, but how the people walk or navigate their way around cities to make use of the city to their benefit. "Religion" could be traversed in this similar way. There is a road map—an outline—of what is "religion" and how it has been defined via epistemologies and institutions, which become reified as fixed, institutionalized identities. Most of us have circumnavigated or transgressed the fixed identities of religions to engage in practices that may be ambiguously understood as secular or as "belonging" to another "religious practice."

In a way, COVID-19 has shaped the routines of where we can and cannot go—and the rules of how to navigate that map. This limitation of where certain bodies can go has always been precarious and limited

28. Das, *Life and Words*, 16.

29. De Certeau, *The Practice*.

30. Lorde, *Sister Outsider*, 110.

because of the violence targeted against Black, brown, Asian, transgendered, and "dis/abled" bodies."[31] The "map" of Certeau was further limited because of COVID-19, but also because of rising violence and threats against communities of color. The limits of where we people of color and other bodies can feel safe makes those spaces of nature and the natural world even more valuable as part of "our city." Gardens, mountains, rivers, fields are the paths on which we have engaged in the routine practices of hiking, biking, walking, gardening, protesting—albeit in a limited way because of safety concerns for people of color. Even the central practices of masking, using social media, and communicating have been contoured by COVID-19. COVID-19 has re-shaped and destabilized the rules and tools of what is "religious," what spaces are "sacred," and what practices are cherished.

In conjunction with a decoloniality of hierophanies, we critique the heterotopias of pandemic life. Heterotopias of the "other space" were "simultaneously mythic and real . . . an 'enacted utopia.'"[32] Foucault hypothesizes that European colonialism produced 'heterotopias of compensation,' i.e., the ordered construction of spaces to counteract the blurred non-boundaried European spaces motivated by "religious zeal."[33] Our understanding of private/public/ secular/sacred has automatically been displaced, reconjoined, and repositioned due to COVID-19. We have held many more outdoor events—whether church services, music concerts, yoga/art/ballet classes, sports, etc. What "sacred" spaces meant has had to be reconsidered and reinterpreted. We can witness a church service being held outdoors in a park, followed by a music concert in the same spot, and then that space used as a place for a picnic meal, napping, or Tibetan Buddhist monks playing soccer—and later meditating together—in the same space.

Sacrality and the boundaries that held the sacred are being reconfigured. Such designations of what/who/where is sacred have been redrawn over the centuries to privilege the Christian position of who has power and hierarchy over sacrality. This year, we see how "space" and the location of where we practice "sacrality" has been similarly negotiated for

31. The term, "disability," needs to be historically unpacked. Jen Ham, in this volume, problematizes the ability/disability binary. She reconfigures the boundary, as "dis/ability," calling into question the politics of power in naming and deciding the porous boundaries of ability and inclusion. See Ham, "The Facemask."

32. Leezenberg, "How Ethnocentric?" 97.

33. Leezenberg, "How Ethnocentric?" 98.

the sake of public health and safety. The "geographical space" of spiritual care has shifted from "sacred space"—to that which is practiced in Foucauldian understandings of heterotopias as "safe" space. Negotiating such spaces, then, requires us to shift the epistemologies that structure the spaces of safety-as-sacrality (or reverence for safety from racial violence and COVID-19). Practices have moved from the private, inner "sanctuaries" to the public outer realms of the great outdoors or online.

Pastoral Power

The routines and rituals developed during the COVID-19 pandemic have shaped who we are as individuals, as well as what constitutes "living" in our communities. This book centers conversations, questions, and "study" around what constitutes life—who, what, whose life is valued and seen as worth living, where we can be without feeling devalued, and why—and who has the power to construct such boundaries of life and living. In that regard, we find it necessary to interrogate the concept of pastoral power as it relates to decolonializing hierophanies and heterotopias that have limited power and agency of the people. It takes community care, not one shepherd. And it takes reciprocity and mutuality, thereby disputing the top-down hierarchical heuristic of a shepherding paradigm.

We all contributed to forms of care for one another (the doctor, baker, teacher, and others, and that has been more evident during COVID-19 since our roles of parenting, teaching, working, and cooking were blurred).[34] Pastoral care as outlined by Foucault in understanding pastoral power was via "it-takes-a-village" practice of communal care. Foucault states, "All may lay claim to being shepherds (*pasteurs*) and are therefore rivals of the politician."[35] Foucault's work reveals the problems of unitary power within a shepherding paradigm. It limits what "care" is and who provides care. Hegemony of pastoral power by one leader (i.e., the shepherd) does not support the democratic flourishing of societies via the levels of care that persons and communities receive on a given day, nor does it support the levels of care needed to make and create systemic changes to have a just society. Coalition-building with multiple types of care and levels of leadership are essential: we need to listen to the ongoing needs of our communities—and to make good use of the

34. Foucault, *Security, Territory, Population*, 143.
35. Foucault, *Security, Territory, Population*, 143.

available resources—to make democratic praxis a reality. The flourishing of democracy does not happen in a pastoral care paradigm with one
shepherd, i.e., one leader. Such flourishing of democratic praxis—of the
demos—is spiritual care work.

Chapters

In this volume, we explore the practices, rituals, and stories that have sustained people during the year 2020–21 and the subversive practices that
they have used to counter the myriad forms of violence we experience
every day. Here in this anthology are stories of care—care of self, care
of others, and supportive communal practices that have sustained people—during this past year of the dual pandemics of COVID-19 and the
unsettling racial violence against communities and individuals of color.
The contributors to this volume are lawyers, parents, students, chaplains,
educators, as well as other professionals. Stories here speak of relationality, nature, pilgrimages, cooking, etc. that are practices grounded in our
humanity.

Even under quarantine, we found ways to connect and communicate with one another in renewed and repurposed ways (outside, masked,
socially distanced, telephone, zoom). We also found it necessary to find
solitary respite in practices of *self-care*—so that we could continue with
the care work of our professions and care for family members. Like the
mycorrhizal fungi and the wisdom of forest communication, we are always learning how to build networks and connect with each other (via
zoom, telephone, emails, texts, talks, walks, etc.).[36] Scientists are learning
about the "social nature of the forest and how this is critical for evolution," and how we humans are "mimicking" nature.[37] We learned how to
make new connections with people, imagining new ways of togetherness:
via the facemask, protests, zooms, dinners, walks, hikes, etc. It reaffirms
the importance of our "consent not to be a single being."

In his foreword, Gary Okihiro shared his model of reinvigorat-
ing/repurposing Ethnic Studies as a way of theorizing liberation. He
describes his method, "Third World Studies" (TWS), as a conversation
about liberation from the powers that oppress and exploit. The name of
TWS derives from the Third World Liberation Front, the students who

36. Simard, *Finding the Mother Tree.*
37. Simard, *Finding the Mother Tree,* 5.

protested in the 1968 student strikes who, along with the Black Panthers, desired a Third World curriculum that would be a praxis-oriented study, united with Third World struggles in Africa, Asia, and the Americas. Okihiro argues that the genealogy of TWS begins with W. E. B. DuBois and includes Frantz Fanon, Amílcar Cabral, and Eduardo Mondlane. It incorporates the work of Black liberation theologians, feminist thinkers, disability scholars, and others. We see our work of decolonializing spiritual care as part of the trajectory of a Third World Studies curriculum. Our hope is that we continue to work towards a vision of a decolonial community that honors each person, respects the diverse communities of which we are a part, as well as cares for the global society which inhabits Earth. Our lives are a *habitus* on Earth. That is, we are practicing "socialized subjectivity, an active and creative relation with the world."[38]

Part One: Decoloniality & Repair of the Harm

In part one, we commence with Emmanuel Lartey's chapter, "Soul Processing: A Postcolonial African Path to Well-Being," which seeks to repair the psychic wounds and harms of colonization and imperialism by invigorating the core dignity and goodness of human beings from coloniality/modernity. In using a framework of decoloniality, he foregrounds a key spiritual practice of restoring and centering human dignity that continues to devastate formerly colonized peoples. Self-healing is an important step in the healing of trauma work.[39] His chapter explores a spiritually based mind-science promulgated by African mystic Ishmael Tetteh that offers a means of transformation through cleansing of the mind and stimulation of thoughts and attitudes that release persons from this debilitating captivity. Lartey's chapter explores spiritual, mental, and physical well-being that results in and is related to communal and ultimately global transformation. It represents a thorough and careful exposition of *soul processing*, a therapeutic modality which in true African fashion begins with the spiritual core of all human beings, and proceeds through mental, physical, and the social realities of existence.

A project of decoloniality understands that the colonial matrix of power continues to impact our world in the structures, patterns, and practices of ongoing forms of "violences—racialized, gendered, physical,

38. Mignolo & Walsh, *On Decoloniality*, 42.
39. Mollica, *Healing Invisible Wounds*.

civilizational, cultural, linguistic, ontological-existential, epistemic, spiritual, cosmological, and so forth...."[40] Religions are part of the life histories—the reconstructed life/lives—that were built on the ruins of colonized society. My (Hellena Moon's) chapter, "Decoloniality of the Shared Wounds: Forgiveness as a Refusal of Ownership," is a critique of the idea that somehow "Western" practices are unique or more "authentic" than that of Third World/global South cultures and spiritual practices. As the practice and understandings of reconciliation has been so vital for this year of racial violence and COVID-19, I critically interrogate the idea of forgiveness and that it is a concept unique to Christianity. Contrary to the opinions of many Western scholars, pastoral theologians, and practitioners; I show the limits of forgiveness as a tool for healing. I argue that for healing to occur, we need to interrogate and problematize forgiveness and incorporate other spiritual practices to repair the harms and restore justice in selves and in society.

My chapter (Hellena Moon) seeks to deconstruct ideas of "uniqueness" in pastoral care as such ideas are part of the legatees of Western particularist, colonialist, and nationalist historiography that helped construct a white Christian nationalist identity. That there is something "special" or "magical" about pastoral care is colonialist—and questionable. Rather, care needs to be "rescued" and excised from its hold of neoliberal markets that have destroyed humans and the natural world. Care—quotidian life practices, habits, and imaginations that are imbricated in the fabric of the everyday—needs to be reinvigorated and valued. The rootedness and grounded-ness of our traditions and cultures are entangled with movements of people, our circumstances, and our histories. Our practices shape our evolving traditions, which are hybrid and malleable to our lived realities.

Next, Loretta Ross and I (Hellena Moon) explore the tools allegedly "belonging" to the "master." That is, we challenge the methods that constructed the borders and boundaries of what practices and concepts are considered sacred/secular, profane/holy. Such boundaries are part of the "construction of religions" as global, cross cultural objects of study that has been part of a wider historical process of Western imperialism, colonialism, and neocolonialism. We show the complexities and paradoxes of what constitutes religion or sacrality in one epoch might be seen as profane or vulgar in another. We expose the blurred lines of what is

40. Mignolo & Walsh, *On Decoloniality*, 23.

"distinct" religions but also what is considered to "belong" to the master. Forgiveness, alone, is not a model of healing for people of color. There are other methods to repair harm than empty apologies—or acceptance of words—that may have little depth. Ross and I explore practices of empathy that shape structures of justice. In our co-written chapter, "Repair Through Practices of Care: 'Calling-In' as Justice Work," we see "self-healing" as an integral pre-requisite of the care that is needed to do human rights and justice work of calling-in, not calling-out. Reproducing justice is part of the racial restorative justice work of Fania Davis.[41]

Together, Ross and I (Moon) understand this work as a "canceling-debt" culture that foregrounds a sense of sharedness. No one religious tradition or culture owns forgiveness—or any practice of forgiveness, as the previous chapter explicated. Instead, we value the shared interdependence of ideas, thoughts, and practices that bring communities together to build on the human rights work of the beloved community and repair the harm. We can practice radical love and generosity because we know it is necessary for the togetherness and the well-being of human beings and our planet.

Part Two: Transgressive Boundaries, Bodies, & Liberative Practices of Care

Jen Ham's Chapter, "The Face Mask as Affective Agent of Transformation: COVID-19 and Beyond," explores the emergence of the COVID-19 facemask as an "affective agent" of transformation—transforming bodies, impressions, and orientations. Working with an understanding of impressions that Sara Ahmed develops in *The Cultural Politics of Emotion*, she explores how the practice of masking creates new impressions on our social bodies. Ham engages in a practice of repair for how the mask has been repurposed during the pandemic. She scrutinizes the transformation—or a decolonial Eliadean "hierophany"—of the facemask from a symbol of violent crime and fear into a contact point of community and conviviality. It has been an agentive heuristic for disabled folk, dismantling borders of healthy/sick, abled/disabled. Whereas masking was seen as a renegade practice of banditry, it is now a signifier of a type of loyalty to community, to building the beloved community. There is no magic or hierophany—just good public health practices and

41. Davis, *The Little Book.*

community-building—in transforming and challenging necropolitics and bodily vulnerability.

Jen Ham's chapter is a perfect segue for the next few chapters that transgress religious borders and destabilize disciplinary boundaries in practices that help bodies to matter and be revered. That is, practices that were shunned as not "belonging" within certain traditions are embraced as needed for human bodies, such as intercultural meditative practices that welcome—and not disdain—the body. Richard Rohr has described liminality as the space "where we are betwixt and between the familiar and the completely unknown."[42] In that regard, the authors' practices have negotiated the liminality of COVID-19 territory. It has been a time for which new beginnings have happened with others—and *for* others— as their work is reshaping the field of spiritual care. Our project of decoloniality interrogates how to repurpose "spiritual" care as a meaningful concept for decoloniality that can be reframed as a discursive "working" in the space of the liminality. We share some of the renewed practices that have emerged for the body—even when the body cannot be with other bodies—as discursive sites of coalition building and mutuality.

Inter-religious, intercultural, inter-generational practices of care have been repurposed and have organically emerged in a response to arenas of struggle due to the dual pandemics of racial violence and COVID-19. As Milan Kundera mused, our emergences are not single events.[43] The work of our authors in part two is a rejoinder of how care should be approached as a revolutionary practice. Audre Lorde stated, "Revolution is not a one-time event. It is becoming always vigilant for the smallest opportunity to make a genuine change in established, outgrown responses."[44] The authors demonstrate how creating allied emergences of mutuality with other cultures, people, and lived experiences creates new modes of practices.

In Lahronda Little's chapter, "Virtual Practices of Care: Rituals of Hope for Inner Peace and Communal Wholeness During the Pandemic," she describes the processes of adapting to the transformed ethos of the entire globe due to the pandemic. Her chapter explores her adapted spiritual practices as a source of healing and embodied *knowing* for the purpose of communal awareness. Little draws on the work of African

---

42. Rohr, "Liminal Space."
43. Kundera, *Laughable Loves*.
44. Lorde, *Sister Outsider*, 140–141.

traditionalists, philosophers, and healers for insights to the phenomenon of adaptation when traditional ways of being are no longer accessible. She creates rituals and meanings—not as "episodic events," but as ongoing natural pulses occurring throughout the day—that draw us deeper to our ancestors, others, and ourselves, highlighting the importance of nature and our responsibility to Earth.

Next, Won-Jae Hur's chapter, "COVID-19, Violence, and the Rupture of Contemplation: A Theological Reflection," addresses the limits of Christian contemplative practices for nonwhite-bodied people to provide meaningful and effective resources that interconnect the somatic (including the racial), the contemplative, and the socio-political for people of color in the present context. Both Christian and non-Christian practices have been important for Hur's care of self and care of this violent world. It is as if the practices themselves need one another and are welcoming to its own respective shortcomings. The intercultural mimicry of practices instantiates the idea of "consent" not to be a single practice.

Lori Klein and her team of chaplains (Sarah Lapenta-H, Kafunyi Mwamba, Anna Nikitina, and Samuel Nkansah) have helped to put into practice, "consent not to be a single being" and "consent not to be a single practice" that supersedes all expectations within bioethical frameworks of care. The team of chaplains at Stanford Hospital co-produce a narrative paradigm of healing in their chapter, "Spiritual Care in the Shadow of Loss and Uprising: A Year in the Life of a Team." Their quotidian practices and ethics of care are interwoven in the narrative story—the conversation—they share. The voices of several members of the Stanford Health Care Spiritual Care Service reflect on the professional and personal challenges, losses, and innovations of autumn 2019 through autumn 2020. Lori's team of chaplains shows the importance of collaboration in delivering novel practices of care for patients and their families. Their practices of care demonstrate *religare*— to bind, to tie together—and the power of the *habitus* of assembly, of generating networks of interdependent communication. By engaging in teamwork and adapting to global changes that necessitate new rhythms of care, they transform and recreate practices that provide pathways for growth and professionalism in the field of spiritual care by listening to the stories, as well as engaging in the work of repairing harms and restoring justice.

Part Three: Fugitivity & Escape in Our Heterotopic World

"Caring for myself is not self-indulgence. It is self-preservation,
and that is an act of political warfare."
Audre Lorde

In part four, we draw attention to the stories of self-care and how our authors have articulated and experienced meanings of joy amid deep grief
and anxiety during the pandemics of COVID-19 and racial violence. The
narratives reveal how much we have relied on nature for self-care during this pandemic and how we have sustained and enriched relationships
and our togetherness. Fred Moten, in *Stolen Life*, writes about fugitivity. He writes, "Fugitivity, then, is a desire for and a spirit of escape and
transgression of the proper and the proposed. It's a desire for the outside,
for a playing or being outside, an outlaw edge proper to the now always
already improper voice or instrument."[45] In subverting our discursive
captivity, we evoke an image of fugitivity, as Moten has so creatively described in his work. The authors express a spirit of escape, a constant
unsettling, or a transgression to upend forms of violence and repair the
wounds in ourselves, communities, and Earth. Being "outside" refers as
much to our social marginality or allyship with those who are on the
margins—and creating our own space "outside" malestream society—as
it also refers to the freedom of creating our own joy and our *becoming* in
our heterotopic world.

Jillian Eugene's chapter, "Creative Escapes: Finding Peace Within
the Grounding Rhythms of Life," delves into the heightened year of racial
violence of 2020. Her chapter focuses on what it means to be Black not
only during this year of racial violence during COVID-19, but the routine
impact of racial and systemic violence on the Black body. Her chapter addresses various self-care practices as an act of promoting mental wellness
and healing during such trying times.

Yukiko Takeuchi's chapter, "Patriotic Drag and Performance in the
Time of COVID-19," explores the practices of trying to perfectly balance safety, mental health, ethical priorities, and sensitivity to external
perception as daunting to accomplish simultaneously. She ruminates
on her Asian American identity, the issue of performance, the struggles
of parenting during the pandemic year, and the ways in which play and

45. Moten, *Stolen Life*, 131.

fugitivity in nature brought her some healing care. Time spent in nature is medicine.

In, "Root Systems: Community and Gratitude as Self-Care," Miranda Dillard takes the reader on a journey through a forest community which provided her support during COVID-19. She was able to rely on tools she developed in the same way trees grow—from the root systems of trees to the protective environment they create—and reach out to others. She relied on self-care practices and sought out new ones. Social justice activism, singing, taking courses, and practicing gratitude sustained her and her community find ways to reach out to each other, building community as if we were plants and trees growing from the Earth.

Namju Cho describes her experiences of what care—of self, kin, friends, and ancestors—looks like to her in her chapter, "What's Cooking: Food, Love, and Community During a Pandemic." She is happiest when harnessing her own intercultural, multi-national background in fostering deeper intergenerational and intercultural connections between people. That is what care looks like to her. She shares with us her passion for bringing people together through her cooking. She repurposes Confucian practices of ancestor commemoration with an intercultural feast that mandates a forthcoming cookbook!

Jackie Weltman explores her convivial practice of reproducing goodness in her chapter, "The Front Yard." During COVID-19, the garden became the meeting place of practicing inter-relational care, love, and "study." Neighbors and visitors alike took joy and interest in the vegetables and wildflowers, and Weltman shared fresh vegetables and exchanged seed with them. She gave some of the neophyte youngsters seedlings and tempted them into gardening, while the old-timers taught her things they knew. Taking their sweet time together, sitting in the sun, masked and six to ten feet away, she got to know the stories of her neighbors' lives.

In her chapter, "Things Seen and Unseen," Anne Gardner describes parallels of the Episcopal ordination process and the emergence of COVID-19. In the ordination process, there is a thorough examination of the major influences that have shaped the prospective ordinand's life. Similarly, there has been deep discernment of what is needed to have emotional and spiritual stability in times of crises. She describes how the pandemic has forced her to alter her own spiritual practices, her understanding of pastoral care, and the vision of her own ministerial future.

Her contribution to this anthology speaks of these challenges and the lissome response they both required and inspired.

Part Four: Conversations, Reflections, & Poetry: "Study" From the Community

Commencing on the date of March 13, 2020, we had been under quarantine. More than a year has passed; restrictions have been lifted, but the variant strains of the virus continue to thrive. The authors in this section reflect on that past year of 2020 under quarantine, and how they used the tool of writing and conversation as a method for healing. We share the creative, intercultural, inter-generational stories told through art, poetry, and revolution narratives. We believe in the power of poetry as an experience of our whole being, as a rhythm and cadence of our creativity. Aimé Césaire saw the revolutionary power of poetry. He saw poetry as critique and construction of new epistemologies.[46] Writing poetry was a spiritual practice, an experience of rising up. It was also a subversive tool, a weapon, to be used to uproot colonial structures of oppression. We share some of the revolutionary power of poetry, prose, and conversations, reflecting the myriad types of revolutionary restorative racial justice work and practices of care being done during COVID-19.

Lahronda Little's powerful tribute to Breonna Taylor in honor of Black Lives Matter is a meditative pause that also reminds us of the collective trauma our nation has yet to fully acknowledge and address. We want to honor and commemorate the many Black and brown people who were killed while living their daily lives during the COVID-19 year, once again, exposing the racial violence woven into the everyday.

Phebian Gray, Taylor Powell, and Jetta Strayhorn provide brief reflections and poetry in their collaborative chapter, "Fighting for Change & Inclusion: Tools for the New Generation." Three Black female high school students describe their experiences over the summer of 2020 pertaining to Black Lives Matter, COVID-19, and attending a private school in Atlanta. Their work has been part of a revolution, a third reconstruction, in our country. We can only hope for the needed changes in education and society that their prophetic work has exposed. It gives us hope to know that our younger generation will move on with the justice and healing work.

---

46. Césaire, *Discourse on Colonialism*, 17.

In "Caregiving and Contemplative Spiritual Care Practices in the Age of COVID-19," Leenah Safi shares personal reflections on the beautifully rich Muslim practice of preparatory ritual washing (*ghusl*) of the deceased in which she took part for the burial of her mother who died during the pandemic. In relating her story of *ghusl* and its communal practice of togetherness, she reflects on the limits of a shepherding paradigm and opts for a more inclusive and connected Qur'anic image and metaphor of the "steep road." That is, she highlights the mutual caregiving practices of the Prophet Muhammad—and what she herself experienced in caring for her mother—and how mutual engagement of community is overshadowed in the shepherding paradigm.

In seeking solutions to the racial animosity towards Asian Americans during COVID-19, the Paideia Asian American high school students had a "conversation" with Russell Jeung, co-founder of the "STOP AAPI HATE" movement.[47] Jeung reflects on the long-term racial trauma from this COVID-19 year, his visions for youth and racial justice, and his own ongoing work of self-care in the midst of difficult racial justice work as a spiritual practice that ultimately desires restorative justice–or a practice that seeks to repair harm to the victims and to lift up—and highlight— their stories so that the healing process can begin for them.

We then feature some poetry and prose written during the COVID-19 year by high school student, Sophia Huynh, junior high student Madeleine Moon-Chun, and elementary student Benjamin Moon-Chun. Throughout the anthology, we showcase the haiku[48] poetry of Tom Painting and Madeleine Moon-Chun.[49] The Japanese poetry form has deep relevance for this volume because of the intimacy that haiku has with nature and humanity. According to the Haiku Society of America, haiku are defined as, "A moment keenly perceived, linking nature to human nature."[50] As Tom Painting states about the Japanese poetry form, "haiku happen— if we are attuned to ourselves, aware of our natural surroundings, and

---

47. The high school students posed questions for Dr. Jeung, which I (Hellena) asked him on a telephone conversation with him. Because this phone conversation occurred after the conclusion of the school year, we were not able to have the students ask Dr. Jeung directly.

48. "Haiku" is the singular and plural for the Japanese poetry form.

49. Madeleine's featured haiku in this volume were all written under the guidance of Tom Painting in his Junior High humanities class. Thank you, Tom, for your lovely mentorship.

50. Haiku Society of America, "HAS Definition." I want to thank Tom Painting for pointing out this definition/quote I used for the Introduction.

in the moment. Life is full of haiku surprises."[51] In Japan, many argue there is no definition of haiku. Haiku are fluid and creative art forms that relate—or tie (*religare*)—images from nature to our emotions. In that regard, haiku are important components of the stories we seek to share in our volume. Haiku are interspersed throughout the anthology as emotive images in our conversations for liberation and our practices of care. Haiku are part of our project of the decoloniality of spiritual care.

Epilogue

Pamela Cooper-White's epilogue, "Reflections on Irony and Eschatological Hope," brings heartfelt closure to our anthology. She reflects on the paradoxes of postcoloniality: the "post" has not happened in the reality of ongoing neo-colonial struggles, because we are still not living postcolonially. She explains the collective trauma we have inherited in our country, and why US white supremacy is so virulent and tenacious. There is a lot of work to be done in the decolonializing pastoral practices of care that address—and tend to—our spiritually dehisced wounds. Her own personal work of a "postcolonial way of living" reveals the importance of owning/claiming our own racism as a practice towards shared collective healing. If we extend the meaning of belonging, we can think about it in terms of what it is we want to claim ownership of. Do we want stories of harm to be parts of our current lived identities, or can we excise them? Rather than dismiss or forget the racist stories in our memory closets, Cooper-White shows that owning our racist past and sharing these stories can help all of us to do anti-racist work with honesty. We cannot expunge our past, but we can excise how that past impacts our becoming. Belonging and inclusion begin with owning and including our own racist histories so that we know how to heal collectively. It is the decolonial "undoing" of our ideas that moves us towards renewed beginnings as a sort of spiritual reconstitution that contributes to epistemic rebuilding.

This decoloniality project of the practices of care during COVID-19 is inspired by Moten's "consent not to be a single being," signifying the kaleidoscopic assemblage of our shared practices and togetherness. Our book is also motivated by Chakrabarty's "conviviality"—to engage in conversations and daily chatters—that sustain and enrich our lives of

---

51. Email exchange with Tom Painting on July 17, 2021.

community through the practices of the mundane.[52] Through our conversations for liberation, our contributors demonstrate that our shared commonalities are more powerful in binding us together than unrelenting differences that would keep us divided. Our project of decoloniality commences with the words of Brother Ishmael Tetteh, "we are not better than one another, we are better with one another." In other words, we "undo" the "we are better" western colonialist superiority that strived to establish hierarchies of difference that have further entrenched the reifying power of divisions. We aim for practices that reflect the "better with one another" ideas that refute pseudospeciation and reflect the agentive strength of collective projects. Liberation sometimes means being connected to the practices that bind you to the discourses—or images—of freedom.

Hellena Moon
July 2021

---

52. Chakrabarty, *Provincializing Europe*, 189.

waning moon
on a deserted road
taillights fade into black
  —Madeleine Moon-Chun

PART ONE

Decoloniality & Repair of the Harm

1

Soul Processing:
A Postcolonial African Path to Well-Being

Emmanuel Y. Lartey

> In whatever direction you throw light on an object, it casts a
> shadow unless the light flows from the center of the very object.
> (Ishmael Tetteh)[1]

SOUL PROCESSING IS THE name chosen by contemporary African mystic Ishmael Tetteh for a form of treatment he has fashioned to restore
well-being to persons hindered in their functioning and flourishing.[2]
Soul processing is founded upon a holistic anthropology that sees the
human person as a "composite of spirit, mind, feelings and body."[3] In this
conceptualization, the center of human personhood is spirit which is the
origin of body, mind, and emotions and is "the animator of the bodies."[4]

---

1. Tetteh, *Soul Processing*, 88.

2. For an introduction to Brother Ishmael Tetteh and his Etherean Mission see
Lartey, *Postcolonializing God*, ch. 4.

3. Ishmael Tetteh, *Soul Processing*, 13. Brother Tetteh's usage of the term "Man"
has been changed to "human being" to reflect the translation of the term more ad-
equately from Tetteh's mother language, Ga. Ga is a Kwa language spoken in Ghana
in and around the capital Accra. Brother Tetteh has translated "Gbomo adesa" which
means 'human being' and refers to both male and female. As such, where Tetteh has
translated "gbomo adesa" as "man" or "his," I have adhered to its original meaning of
"human being" and translated it as such. The Etherean Mission is very clear in the
non-sexist nature of its teaching and practice.

4. Tetteh, *Soul Processing*, 13.

Soul Processing entails an undoing—an epistemological, spiritual, bodily restoration—of the harmful philosophies of colonial, imperial, and white supremacist teaching. It is a decolonial practice that affirms the dignity and spirituality of all persons, and is especially suited for the colonized, oppressed, or downtrodden. Undoing the collateral damage of white supremacy is crucial to address the deep psychic wounds inflicted on the colonized. Much of the self-hate, self-harm, and anti-social behaviors in communities of color can be traced in many ways to the ongoing harms inflicted upon them by their oppressors. Religion is often the vehicle by which such devastation is inflicted and unquestioned among colonial devotees.

Soul Processing understands how the pain-filled stored pictures and sense-realities that lie deeply embedded in our minds originate. Our present bodies re-play the trauma of our past experiences. The goal of Soul Processing is to heal the self, the community, and ultimately have justice and peace in the world. I explore Soul Processing as liberative spiritual care work using many quotes to capture the rich images Tetteh's words evoke.

The Goodness and Infinite Possibility of all Humans

A truly exalted image of the human person—equipped with God-given capabilities—is central to the therapy that Brother Ishmael Tetteh espouses.[5] Unlike many religious anthropologies that present the human as flawed at core, for Ishmael Tetteh, the human spirit "is of God and is ever perfect."[6] Each human is "the holy individualized breath of God, the immaculate child of God."[7] One of the cardinal teachings of Tetteh's Etherean Mission, is the divinity and divine nature of humanity, a belief that is stated in their core beliefs.[8] Tetteh's underlying metaphysical anthropology, then, is founded on the principle that the human "is a perfect being, clad in garbs of innocence, who still wants to unfold into a perfect being in full consciousness."[9] For people whose very humanity has been at best questioned and at worst explicitly denied through colonization

5. Tetteh, *Soul Processing*, 14.

6. Tetteh, *Soul Processing*, 19.

7. Tetteh, *Soul Processing*, 45.

8. Tetteh, *Fountain of Life*, ix.

9. Tetteh, *Soul Processing*, 22.

or enslavement, this reaffirmation of their human dignity is incredibly invigorating.

White supremacist scholarship as adumbrated by some of the greatest minds of western philosophy and theology such as G W. F. Hegel and internalized by many of the colonized and enslaved and their descendants, has delivered such wounds to the psyche as to make such elevated truths concerning their humanity hard for many to embrace.[10] This assault on the humanity and dignity of African, Asian, and other non-white persons is the severest and most traumatic wound to the soul of humanity, one from which many to this day have been unable to recover. The fact, however, is that the African person—as all human beings, far from being inferior, uncivilized, or undeveloped—is pure and glorious, a divine and unique emanation of God, yearning to unfold into full perfection. This fact constitutes the key that Tetteh uses to unlock the treasures of humanity through the practice he calls Soul Processing.

In elevating the fact of humanity's creation in the image and likeness of the divine and making it foundational to his therapeutic endeavors, Tetteh's approach is an assets-based, strength-recognizing model much needed within communities that have for centuries been trodden down and considered inferior psychologically, spiritually, and emotionally.

All Humans Are Spiritual at Core

In teaching that resonates with classic African philosophic and religious thought, Tetteh affirms that human beings are "essentially spirit beings."[11] For Tetteh, "Spirit is formless and infinitely expansive: spirit does not live wholly in the body it has created and robed itself with. The physical, emotional and mental bodies dwell in the expansiveness of spirit as attributes and tools of spirit."[12] Tetteh explains the origins of the mental, emotional, and physical bodies of humans as a descent or materialization emanating from an essential spirit.

In the human's descent into material form, just as one puts on diving suits to descend into deep waters, the human took on various "bodies." First, Tetteh would argue, human spirit took on a mental vehicle just as one would put on underwear. Next, they would put on an emotional

10. See Lartey & Moon, eds., *Postcolonial Images*, 4–5.

11. Tetteh, *Soul Processing*, 41.

12. Tetteh, *Soul Processing*, 15.

vehicle as one would put on a shirt or dress, and finally humanity put on a physical body vehicle, like one would put on a coat. The universe, Tetteh would argue, is created by God through human (spirit) and formed to be a space within which experience and experimentation take place. For these purposes, our bodies are creative laboratories.

We took on emotional bodies, giving attention to our thoughts, images, and creations. We took on material bodies in order to reify our creative energies.[13] Elaborating further, he argues that "these three bodies serve as the medium through which the spirit's attributes are differentiated, just as the cloud or prism breaks out and differentiates the spectrum of transmitted light energy. Through these bodies, the real [hu]man (spirit) communicates with and receives communication form other spirit units as it lives in this self-discovery and evolutionary universe."[14]

The Primacy of Mind

The mind, per Tetteh, is the first creation of spirit. It provides the forms and the pictures that the spirit assumes. In Tetteh's framing there are three levels of mind, namely—the conscious mind, the subconscious, and the unconscious mind. The conscious mind refers to that faculty by which we engage the world through sensing, analyzing, making inferences, and drawing conclusions. The subconscious mind executes and automatically reacts to whatever is programmed into it. Tetteh refers to it as human's "automatic creative motor" (ACM). It is largely reactive. The unconscious mind functions as the repository and record keeping storehouse of all experiences, especially painful ones. Tetteh sometimes refer(s) to the unconscious mind as the 'cud-mind' because it collects data of painful experiences "just like ruminants store their food and chew their cud." The primary data here is pain that—when triggered—hinders our daily living.[15]

To Tetteh, "mind is nothing but energy imbued with creative and discriminative reasoning."[16] Our human individualized spirits and minds are units of the vast expanse of God's infinite wonder. All of humanity is therefore united in a beautiful and complex way. All minds are

13. Tetteh, *Soul Processing*, 14–15.
14. Tetteh, *Soul Processing*, 73.
15. Tetteh, *Soul Processing*, 18.
16. Tetteh, *Soul Processing*, 43.

individualized yet interrelated. Through the mind and its senses, we receive as well as transmit information from and to our environment. Tetteh sees the centrality of our mind, and that mind and thought are key to the work of Soul Processing. He elaborates, "when the mind is beleaguered with painful thoughts, life becomes a pain. A healthy life must first have a healthy mind. Thoughts provoke feelings. A happy or unhappy life depends on the thoughts you allow your mind to nurse."[17] Sin, for Tetteh, lies in a movement away from the pure, perfect, and true nature and core of human being. Tetteh argues that human beings at present are living a life of sin, where 'sin' refers to diverging from our true nature of humanity.[18] Tetteh concludes that what is sorely needed therefore is conscious awareness of one's true nature.

The Rationale of Soul Processing

Tetteh teaches that we merge with what our mind gives attention to. Thus, prayer or spiritual practice engaged in from a place of negativity or fear only amplifies that same negative emotion. When prayer is partaken from an awareness of purity, it augments the positive capacities of our connection with God. To achieve this, Tetteh develops an approach that facilitates the filtration of the mind of all its impurities. Spiritual practices such as prayer and meditation for Tetteh need to focus on expanding the true nature of the human being which is good and full of infinite possibility.[19] Tetteh insists on the pure and perfect mind of all human beings and that we should not let our minds wander into areas of pain, which cause unreasonable and self-destructive actions. Our minds are liberated when we can challenge and transform the negative stored images to allow for serenity of prayer.[20] Tetteh sees that the most effective way forward for us all is to cleanse the mind of all pain images. This is exactly what Tetteh's therapy seeks to do. He therefore explains its goal as follows: "*Soul Processing is the spiritual mind science for the restoration of the full God potential*" and the many spiritual opportunities for humans.[21]

---

17. Tetteh, *Soul Processing*, 23.
18. Tetteh, *Soul Processing*, 47.
19. Tetteh, *Soul Processing*, 50.
20. Tetteh, *Soul Processing*, 52.
21. Tetteh, *Soul Processing*, 55 (italics mine).

The "Process" of Soul Processing

In accordance with the high esteem of the human being as spirit being, Tetteh's therapeutic modality is based upon strength and capability, not on a deficit model of human weakness or inability. Humanity is by nature pure, able, and imbued with divine attributes. Tetteh's therapy then is solidly based on humanity's God-given ability to handle all things. He asserts: "The premise of Soul Processing is that whatever a [hu]man can confront, they can handle."[22] Soul processing, it seems to me, proceeds sequentially through three phases, the first of which is preliminary, and as such could be termed pre-soul processing proper.

Pre-Stage: Affirming Ego-strength

1. Removal of evil

2. Activation of spiritual abilities

Pre-stage: Affirming Ego-Strength

In the preliminary phase of the process, persons' self-esteem and ego-strength are established, affirmed, and built up. Through processes of education, meditation, affirmation, and declaration; the truth about human potentiality, creativity, intelligence, and what Tetteh calls "God potential" becomes firmly established within all who embark on the journey of Soul Processing. Teaching helps people affirm their creation in the image and likeness of the divine, their divine nature, and the beauty, purity, and power of the spirit that lies at the center and core of their humanness. Soul Processing is described as an Etherean Mission Application Technology (EMAT) which is embedded within and operates out of the educative and restorative social environment of the Mission's life and ethos. The Etherean Mission is one of the most wholesome, empowering, positively life-affirming, and uplifting environments that I have had the good fortune to experience and be involved in. Meditations, prayers, services, and activities all help to surround all who participate in them with a socially uplifting and spiritually empowering communal nexus. The community epitomizes and enhances the dignity and divinity of the human being, one of the central tenets of the Mission. As a result, persons are strengthened and uplifted, both individually and socially. They

---

22. Tetteh, *Soul Processing*, 55.

begin to embody the reality that they can face and overcome whatever challenges they may encounter. Such social and personal empowerment are what is needed, without which, much of the soul processing activity would likely flounder.

There clearly must be a process by which a person gauges their strength and readiness for the confronting of the unconscious mind and "cud" processing prior to any engagement in this form of treatment. It seems to me that this preliminary stage of Soul Processing, in which persons discover or recover their ego-strength and a secure understanding of the power of their spiritual core, is a *sine qua non* in Soul Processing.

Phase 1: "Cud" Processing & Removal of Evil

Tetteh identifies the major problem to be addressed in life as lying in the imprints of pain that remain in our minds, what he refers to as "cuds." Cuds are "the pictures of mental, emotional, and physical pain perceived through the senses."[23] Tetteh makes this abundantly clear in his writings. He declares: "The simple cause of sin, evil, irrational fears, madness, psychosomatic diseases etc. which cause about 90% of the woes of [hu]man[ity], is PAIN."[24] The source of evil is from the harms that are inflicted and how we respond to them.[25] In no uncertain terms, Tetteh argues that the origin of evil is in our minds, and since our minds are our greatest tools, we can eradicate the evil with our own tools. In other words, we can practice self-healing. Our thoughts backed by the emotions of the heart is what crystallizes as our outer revelation. Tetteh uses the scriptural quotation of Proverbs 23:7 ("as a person thinks in their mind so they are") to demonstrate that good or evil is perceptual and based on our thinking.[26] We are "the sum total of all the thoughts which have been banked by [your] feelings and actions of yesterday."[27] In Soul Processing, we have to encounter our own cud images and reflect on reimagining those images more constructively. Every harm has the potential to teach us how to heal. Self-healing is crucial, or we recycle the pain.[28]

23. Tetteh, *Soul Processing*, 78.

24. Tetteh, *Soul Processing*, 78.

25. Tetteh, *Soul Processing*, 77.

26. Tetteh, *Soul Processing*, 79.

27. Tetteh, *Soul Processing*, 60.

28. Tetteh, *Soul Processing*, 55.

With such a high view of human goodness and abilities, what are we to make of the many mistakes and misdeeds that are evident in our lives? Tetteh reframes and re-characterizes mistakes as natural occurrences along the road of discovery and development. They are part of the journey of life. There is no perfect journey, but each situation teaches us more about the potential for growth and change. He declares, "New scientific discoveries, time after time, have proven past scientific theories and postulates wrong. The disproved theories were once the heralded discoveries. Each mistake in science, however, is used as a basis for new scientific discoveries."[29] In that regard, humans are constantly learning and growing, using what they experience to improve their previous experiences as foundation for improved discoveries of their infinite capabilities. When there is "evil" or harm, it can be interpreted as humans' learning how to approach a situation and use that experience as growth. This refreshing view of personal and social misdeeds is very much needed within societies in North America wherein members of minoritized communities are the targets of labeling, misrepresentation, stereotyping, and strong censure in which every minor infraction is not merely severely punished but also viewed as characteristic of every single individual who shares the ethnicity or social location of the culprit.

Tetteh argues that the presence of a personified devil is the result of the unconscious mind. He argues that harm enters the mind as a

> picture frame, capturing all the perceptions recorded by the five senses (within Time, Energy, Space and Circumstance (TESC)) and equates each element within the pain as equal to the pain. In this manner, any of the elements can, in future, trigger the pain. A painful incident which caused the evil of hate, for example, can be re-stimulated by anything seen, heard, touched, smelt, or by the time within which the incident occurred.[30]

To deal with pain and its deleterious effects, Tetteh encourages Soul Processing to make the person more aware of our capabilities and abilities to renew and transform the mind, Tetteh argues, with reference to New Testament language, that, "through mind renewal technology, you are rehabilitated into your true self, which was created after God in righteousness and in true holiness (Eph 4:23–24). The former conversations of the old person are the filed information of pain, which when remembered

---

29. Tetteh, *Soul Processing,* 72–73.

30. Tetteh, *Soul Processing,* 74.

or triggered, result in sin, worry, anxiety, stress, sorrow, disease and even madness."[31]Convinced of the existence of pain and evil within the mind of human beings, and of humanity possessing the innate capacity to confront and deal with it successfully, Tetteh raises and responds to the question of evil. The goal of Soul Processing is to engage in the ongoing practice of cleansing our minds of this self-harm that the image of evil can do to our psyches and our bodies.[32] In addition to our five senses, Tetteh describes a sixth sense, which he describes as the "sense of imagination within which all of the senses can be summoned to function at the same time." [33] The sixth sense can be used to help liberate the unconscious mind.

While self-processing is effective, the Etherean mission offers training to people who are dubbed "Liberators" to facilitate their work with clients referred to as "Liberatees" in the process of Soul Processing. He explains that in Soul Processing, clients use their inherent spirit energies to uproot causes of their problems by *reliving it*. When we relive it, we are eventually able to discharge it from our minds.[34] The first formal phase of Soul Processing can therefore be summed up in the following assertion of Bro Ishmael Tetteh: "Confront your inner demons and pains, *within you is the wisdom of God to dissolve these elements of pain with knowledge*."[35]

The *Re-living* Technique

Brother Ishmael Tetteh explains reliving as "the practice of returning to a past event and recounting it in present or present continuous tense as though the event is happening in present time."[36] He continues,

> through a gentle process of re-living, present pains are uncovered and reduced, opening us to the root or primary causes of the pain. When the primary cause of the pain is removed, the entire tree of the pain and its effects are removed, and the

---

31. Tetteh, *Soul Processing*, 81.

32. Tetteh, *Soul Processing*, 63.

33. Tetteh, *Soul Processing*, 60.

34. Tetteh, *Soul Processing*, 56 (italics mine).

35. Tetteh, *Soul Processing*, 57 (italics mine).

36. Tetteh, *Soul Processing*, 56.

individual becomes free. This process is known as *Cud Process-ing*; it is the processing or chewing and removal of the Cud.[37]

But is 're-living painful experiences' which is seen as the key to the re-moval or dissolution of the problem, not dangerously re-traumatizing, especially when the painful experience was devastating in its occurrence? Does it not run the risk of aggravating the problem by re-enacting the trauma?

Tetteh explains it metaphorically, that humans typically "chew" the cud of our emotional and physical pains. We can therefore "replay" the pain that has been stored away when we have the strength and energy to do so, thereby removing the "sting" from the pain.[38] He argues what many in Western psychotherapy have also argued, which is that we re-live the traumas in our bodies and that of our ancestors: "Nothing in life is ever forgotten, . . . Everything that happens in one's life is filed in consciousness and can be played back in vivid colors with all accompany-ing perceptions through the science of re-living in which the faculty of recall is used."[39] Reliving is akin then to the painful process of cleaning a wound and applying the medication which may sting but ultimately removes the infection. Tetteh pays attention to characteristics necessary for cud-processing in the following instruction.

> The ideal way to practice this science is to work or team up with someone you can comfortably face with that past or current incident. This person plays the role of your soul *Liberator* and you in that instant the *Liberatee* (on the road to liberty). The Liberator goes through the incident with you and assists you with straight non-suggestive questions to experience and re-ex-perience the very painful moments with all of their perceptions. They also assist you to keep yourself in present time instead of relating everything as an incident in the past.[40]

Tetteh cautions Liberators to not influence the Liberatee with their own thoughts or suggestions. Instead, there needs to be utmost mutuality of respect, trust, and care in using the re-living technique. Tetteh admon-ishes, "*As a Liberator you are walking into the secret areas of somebody's*

37. Tetteh, *Soul Processing*, 56.
38. Tetteh, *Soul Processing*, 57 (italics mine).
39. Tetteh, *Soul Processing*, 58.
40. Tetteh, *Soul Processing*, 58.

soul and so must be gentle, patient, and trustworthy."[41] Some information that has been negatively stored might be "erased," and this potentially contributes to physical and spiritual well-being.[42]

Communal Practices of "Re-living" Painful Experience for the Healing of Communities.

Re-living typically occurs as an individual encounter in the Soul Processing experience. However, communal re-enactments have been created that facilitate this for whole communities of people. Two examples of social re-enactments of tragic historic occurrences which ultimately serve the purpose of healing are the Maafa Commemoration started in New York City and the Pilgrimages to West African slave dungeons organized by the non-profit organization, African Pilgrimages Inc.

(1) MAAFA COMMEMORATION[43]

The Maafa Commemoration is an annual weeklong remembrance of the Transatlantic Slave Trade and experience of the Middle Passage. It was started in 1995 by New Orleans-born preacher Johnny Youngblood, pastor of New York City's St. Paul Community Baptist Church in Brooklyn, N.Y. Youngblood organized the first *Maafa* Commemoration to help African Americans heal from the psychic and spiritual damage that he felt had gone undetected and untreated for centuries. Since that time, the annual *Maafa* observance, held each year during the third week in September, has grown considerably. Other religious communities have recognized the value of the event, and the practice of commemorating *Maafa* has spread to other locations in the U.S.

The word *Maafa*, a Kiswahili word meaning catastrophe, great disaster, or terrible occurrence, has come to refer to what many call the African Holocaust—the transporting of millions of Africans in the holds of ships through the Atlantic Ocean to lives of slavery. Dr. Marimba Ani is credited with appropriating the word, *maafa* to collectively commemorate this historical occurrence. Dr Ani has argued that only by going

41. Tetteh, *Soul Processing*, 58–59 (italics mine).

42. Tetteh, *Soul Processing*, 60.

43. For a discussion of this commemoration by a pastoral theologian, see Johnson, *Race, Religion, and Resilience*, 113–14.

through the pain and the grief of the past can persons find an acceptance of their being and spirit.[44]

The commemoration at the St. Paul Community Baptist Church in Brooklyn, N.Y., centers around a dramatic presentation put on by the church's drama ministry titled "Maafa Suite: A Healing Journey." The drama depicts the history of African Americans, from Africa to the Jim Crow South. As many as 100 performers in music, dance, and theatre contribute to the Maafa Suite. The work's creators describe it as a transformative psychodrama that aims—through drama, song, rhythm, and dance—to educate and heal the collective memory of African Americans.

Various activities occur throughout the Maafa Commemoration. There are repeat performances of the theatrical production, "Maafa Suite- a Healing Journey," that is aimed at educating, reconciling, and healing collective memories. In addition, there are worship services, lectures, tours of the Maafa Museum, workshops on resisting institutional racism, special programs for both seniors and youth, and a ceremony on the shores of the Atlantic. These ritualized re-enactments—and the participation in them by members of the community—serve as communal re-living or cud-processing activities that are necessary in the journey towards healing for all.

(1) API's Journeys to the Slave Dungeons of West Africa.[45]

African Pilgrimages Inc. has since 2007 organized sacred journeys of remembrance and rediscovery of roots for African Americans. In Ghana, participants on pilgrimage visit the dungeons where enslaved Africans were held prior to their being transported through the "Middle Passage" to the New World.[46] Time spent in the dungeons offers opportunities for historic re-enactments and re-living of the pain, suffering, and horror experienced by the ancestors—pain which lies deeply embedded in the psyches and collective unconsciousness of all descendants of the enslaved.

44. See Ani, *Yurugu.*

45. For information on African Pilgrimages Inc., see their website: www.african-pilgrimagesinc.com.

46. For a fuller account of one of these pilgrimages that occurred in the bicentennial year of the abolition of the Transatlantic Slave Trade, see Lartey, *Postcolonializing God,* ch. 3.

Such re-livings conducted carefully and sensitively as a part of journeys of Soul Processing can be crucial steps towards cleansing of minds and recovery of wholeness.

In this crucial 'removal of evil' - phase of the process, then, an essential principle of Soul Processing is fulfilled. The principle is "to confront the unconscious mind, free it of filed pains and restore to it all its abilities lost through lack of use."[47] Re-living is confrontation with the pains filed and stored with all the dimensions of the senses within the unconscious mind. It is through this courageous engagement that the powerful spirit at the core of all humans is enabled to free the mind and begin to restore persons to health.

Phase 2: Activation of Spiritual Abilities

The final phase of Soul Processing is dubbed "ability processing" and entails the activation of the vast resources of Divine and natural energy present and available for and in all human persons. For Tetteh, this phase is a period in which participants focus on the positive and divine potentials manifest in their own persons and in all humanity. Ability processing helps us understand that "this major part of Soul Processing is for the activation, reclamation and actualization of your forgotten God abilities. Tetteh encourages us to nurture divine images of beauty and goodness within us.[48]

Conclusion

Soul Processing reverses the denigrating philosophies of colonial, imperial, and white supremacist teaching and practice by affirming the dignity and spirituality of all persons, not least the colonized, oppressed, or downtrodden. Such reversals are crucial to address the deep psychic wounds inflicted on the colonized. Much of the self-hatred, self-destructive, and socially devastating behaviors evident in minoritized communities can be traced to the negativity inflicted upon them by their oppressors. Religion is often the vehicle by which such devastation is inflicted upon hapless

47. Tetteh, *Soul Processing,* 63.
48. Tetteh, *Soul Processing,* 176.

devotees. Tetteh is deeply critical of such religion and argues instead that, "religion must be the science of spiritual well-being."[49]

Soul Processing encourages courageous confrontation with the pain-filled stored pictures and sense-realities that lie deeply embedded in our minds, bringing them to present consciousness through creative whole-body practices of re-living. The final phase of soul processing re-focuses persons on the vast good that lies within them and re-stimulates the image of God in which humanity is created. The ultimate outcome is the creation of communities of people who actualize the God-given goodness within persons for justice, peace and flourishing of the whole world.

49. Tetteh, *Soul Processing,* 82.

forest fire
violets sprout
through the ashes
        —Madeleine Moon-Chun

2

Decoloniality of the Shared Wounds

Forgiveness as a Refusal
of Ownership and Belonging[1]

HELLENA MOON

Introduction

PASTORAL THEOLOGIANS HAVE DEFINED the field of pastoral care with the understanding that reconciliation and the shepherding paradigm make it unique from the spiritual practices of other religions. If forgiveness is uniquely Christian (and pastoral care prides itself on being exceptional in comparison to the spiritual care practices of other religions), who is doing the forgiveness and who are we asking to forgive? Where is the healing? Is it the responsibility of non-Christians and those oppressed to practice the forgiveness if it is exceptional to Christianity? If forgiveness is a distinctively Christian concept, are those of other spiritual traditions *forced* to practice that which is not their tradition? And this raises the question of whether forgiveness *is* distinctively Christian, and if not, is

1. I want to thank Professor Pamela Cooper-White and Dr. Won-Jae Hur for reading an earlier version of this chapter and providing important feedback. I also want to thank Professor Robert Buswell for our email exchanges on forgiveness. I am fully responsible for any errors in this chapter.

pastoral care so unique? Why do pastoral theologians insist on different language—Judeo-Christian practices are referred to as "pastoral," while other care is referred to as "spiritual?" I raise these aporias as critical antinomies within pastoral care.

In 1969, founder of Black liberation theology, James Cone articulated prophetically that reconciliation cannot happen on the terms of white Americans. That would only further entrench racist structures and white supremacy. To ask the Black community to practice racial reconciliation on white terms is tantamount to a cease-fire whereby the injustices committed would be left unaddressed and unabsolved. Cone states,

> White people have short memories. Otherwise, how are black people to interpret questions about reconciliation, love, and other white values? Is it human to expect black people to pretend that black parents were not chattels in society? Do they really expect black people to believe that their status today is unrelated to the slavery of the past? Do they expect black people to believe that this society is not basically racist from top to bottom? And now white religious people want to know what can be done about the "wall of hostility" between blacks and whites.... First, let me say that reconciliation on white racist terms is impossible, since it would crush the dignity of black people.... White oppressors are incompetent to dictate the terms of reconciliation because they are enslaved by their own racism and will inevitably seek to base the terms on their right to play God in human relationships.... It is this fact that nullifies the "good" intentions of concerned white religious people who insist that they are prepared to relate to black people as human beings.... Therefore, the real question is not whether Black Theology sees reconciliation as an end but, rather, on whose terms we are to be reconciled.[2]

A decade later in 1979, Ed Wimberly lamented that the goal of healing, the heart of the clinical paradigm of pastoral care, is too premature to be addressed when we have not yet resolved or fully discussed the racism and Euro-centric practices extant in pastoral care.[3] He stated that we have yet to heal the wounds of spiritual and material violence, so we cannot talk about reconciliation.[4] Forgiveness as whites have outlined is not liberation; it is a further entrapment that instantiates more forms of

2. Cone, *Black Theology*, 163–64.

3. Wimberly, *Pastoral Care*.

4. See Lartey, *Postcolonializing God*. Also see Lartey & Moon, *Postcolonial Images*.

violence and "thingification" of human beings. The crimes of racism—
and those who committed them—are exonerated, while the people who
experienced the racial violence continue to suffer.

James Cone's and Ed Wimberly's sentiment about reconciliation being a premature goal still echoes loudly today in 2021. More than fifty
years since Cone's statement, the ongoing objectification—"killing, or
caging all who refuse to cooperate with the laws against humanity"—
and oppression persist.[5] When Black, brown, and Asian bodies are killed
and murdered as if they were sheep, we need to catechize the pastoral
power, sovereignty, and the accountability of the shepherd. If, as Carrie
Doehring states that the twin goals of healing and storytelling lay at the
heart of pastoral care,[6] I argue that herein persists the dehiscence of the
pastoral wound,[7] the hubris of the zero point for pastoral care. Walter
Mignolo aptly summarizes the phrase coined by Santiago Castro Gómez,
"hubris of the zero point," which refers to how "the knowing subject maps
the world and its problems, classifies people and projects onto what is
good for them."[8] The dehiscence of the pastoral wound renders healing
a difficult process because we have yet to theorize and decolonialize the
stories and myths that have prevented true reconciliation and healing to
occur. Edward Said stated that narrative is crucial to hegemonic discursive power, and that "stories are at the heart of what explorers and novel-
ists say about strange regions of the world; they also become the method
colonized people use to assert their own identity and the existence of
their own history."[9] Pastoral care theologians and practitioners have repeated and reproduced the colonialist narratives of Christian superiority,
thereby exacerbating the wounds we purport to heal.

In her metaphor of the "living human web," Bonnie Miller-
McLemore states, "we must hear the voices of the marginalized from
within their own context to have reconciliation and healing in our personal spirit, in the field, and in greater society."[10] Miller-McLemore insists
that those within the web who have not yet spoken must speak for themselves. She contends, "if knowledge depends on power, then power must

5. Cone, *Black Theology*, 165.

6. Doehring, *The Practice*, xix–xiv.

7. See Fred Moten's language of dehiscence in Wallace, "Fred Moten's Radical
Critique."

8. Mignolo, "Epistemic Disobedience," 2.

9. Said, *Culture and Imperialism*, xii.

10. Miller-McLemore, "The Living Human Web," 46.

be given to the silenced."[11] "Speaking up" has meant access to a platform that has transformed the field—and the potentiality to cause deeper epistemic ruptures—as part of the work of decoloniality. Prior to demanding reconciliation and healing, we need to interrogate the epistemic violence imbricated in the narratives, histories, and myths that have shaped white, androcentric Christian privilege in society, as well as within the field of pastoral care. We need to reassess the pastoral hubris of the zero point that romanticizes the epistemic mythic fantasy of Western cultural superiority and benevolence. If categories of religions were created by European Christian colonizers practicing "pastoral care" in Africa and Asia(s) to establish such categories, thereby labeling *their* "care" as unique or superior, then the decolonization of such hubris shows that rather than argue its exceptionalism, pastoral care needs to assess its participation and cooptation in the myths of modernity/coloniality and its colonial projects.

In this chapter, I provide a brief genealogy of pastoral care and forgiveness. I also engage Jacques Derrida's deconstruction of the concept of mercy in Shakespeare's *The Merchant of Venice* and show how the concept of forgiveness has been misinterpreted or misunderstood as particular to our neoliberal cultural context, and not necessarily particular to Christianity. Not only is "forgiveness" about issues of cultural and linguistic translation, power, and Western Christian hubris; feminist theologian Pamela Cooper-White has argued that it is a theological misreading of the original language that actually refers to a "canceling of a balance due."[12] It refers to a release from economic debt. Despite the connections that forgiveness has had to forms of debt clemency, forgiveness has become an emotional and psychological trademark of neoliberal Christian devotional practice.[13]

Finding "essence" or uniqueness is a problem of colonial, nationalist historiography that was used to set imperial rulers and their societies apart from the countries and peoples they subjugated.[14] Forgiveness has been a hierarchical, mercenary tool that perpetuates colonialist practices. Rather than be liberative for communities of color, bring healing, or be meaningful in its true contextual meaning of a canceling of an economic

11. Miller-McLemore, "The Living Human Web," 46.

12. Cooper-White, *Cry of Tamar*, 257.

13. Cooper-White, *Cry of Tamar*, 257.

14. See my forthcoming book for a detailed argument on colonialist historiography in pastoral theology. Moon, *Mask of Clement Violence*.

debt; on the contrary, forced forgiveness has brought on spiritual debt or burdens and reproduced the harms by demanding forgiveness in situations where the forgiveness is premature or superficial. I argue for engaging in "epistemic reconstitution" as an important postcolonial practice in the field of spiritual care and pastoral theology that can help transform and upturn some of the colonialist narratives in the field.[15]

Genealogy of Pastoral Care and Forgiveness

A genealogy of the modern pastoral care paradigm focused on "therapeutic" work with individuals. Anton Boisen, pioneer of the Clinical Pastoral Education (CPE) movement, placed more emphasis on the person in crisis, rather than the minister.[16] Seward Hiltner, a student of Boisen, did the opposite and placed the minister as central in the pastoral encounter. The dominant image of the 1950s and 1960s has been Hiltner's "solicitous shepherd" whose functions were healing, guiding, and sustaining. This shepherding perspective has been criticized for its focus, mainly on the individual without locating the subject in a contextual framework. In his "solicitous shepherd" imagery, Hiltner stated,

> As we have understood it, shepherding from the biblical period to our day is unique to Christianity. Other high religions have spiritual directors of one kind or another who deal with people as individuals or in small groups. But dealing with people in terms of shepherding, the essence of which looks toward healing in a holistic sense, is unique to Christianity and Judaism, and even in Judaism its development since biblical days has been quite different from that in Christianity.[17]

Hiltner highlighted the uniqueness of Christian care by arguing that the concept of mercy, as it is depicted in the story of the good Samaritan (in Luke chapter 10:30–35), is specific to Christianity. Along with mercy and healing being interpreted as distinctively Christian, Hiltner also stated that the shepherding model itself—of attending to the one sheep that was lost—is particular to Christianity. He argued that the virtues of attending,

15. Aníbal Quijano argues that we need to scrutinize the indigenous epistemologies that were dismissed as superstitions or barbarisms. See Quijano, "Coloniality and Modernity."

16. Clinical Pastoral Education is a training educational program for people interested in providing spiritual care to patients, families, and staff.

17. Hiltner, "The Solicitous Shepherd," 48.

mercy, and healing are those aspects of Christianity's and pastoral care's distinctions. We have adhered to this colonialist story that allegedly makes pastoral care unique from other "high" religions. While not in the purview of this chapter to contest the mythic Christian exceptionalism of the shepherding paradigm, I raise this point in the context of contesting the assertion that reconciliation and forgiveness are specifically Christian practices.[18]

Edward Wimberly has been a pivotal figure who helped shift the paradigm of pastoral care from an individual-focused model to that which recognizes the importance of community and context. Writing ten years prior to the official recognition of the communal-contextual paradigm, he has been a leading critical voice of the dominant therapeutic paradigm. His work has been pioneering in examining the inter-related nature of self and society, as well as introducing concerns of racism and oppression in pastoral theological discourse. Wimberly was one of the first to be critical of the function of reconciling for the African American community.[19] Wimberly prophetically stated more than fifty years ago that a community of people who has experienced the history of exploitation in Africa (ravaging of their land, resources, people, culture, language, laws), as well as historical and current inhumane treatment in the United States (slavery, denial of citizenship and other rights, racism, etc.) cannot talk about reconciliation.[20] He argued that there was too much pain and harm that needed to be addressed before we could talk about reconciliation.

Wimberly was one of the first in the field of pastoral care to give importance to socio-cultural contexts and introduced a critical social power analysis of race and racism.[21] He argued that efforts toward reconciliation within greater society are premature and futile until the inequities between Blacks and whites have been removed. Reconciliation is not possible, he admonished, until the dominant culture has acknowledged its past injustices and found ways to atone for—and repair the harm of—the dehumanizing injustices over the last four hundred years. Wimberly lifted up the importance of the sociocultural context and the need to address issues of racism and oppression within pastoral theological discourse. He

18. I address the problem of Christian exceptionalism within a shepherding paradigm in my forthcoming book. See Moon, *Mask of Clement Violence.*

19. Clebsch & Jaekle, *Pastoral Care.*

20. Wimberly, *Pastoral Care.*

21. Wimberly, *Pastoral Care.*

openly challenged Clebsch and Jaekle's reconciling function as limited for the African American context and community. Acts of reconciling are of secondary order of ministry, he stated, for African Americans. Healing for African Americans, he argued, still awaits. He wrote,

> The racial climate in America, from slavery to the present, has made sustaining and guiding more prominent than healing and reconciling. Racism and oppression have produced wounds in the black community that can be healed only to the extent that healing takes place in the structure of the total society.[22]

He prophetically argued for the need to address these structures of marginalization before we could talk about reconciliation. His work has defined the parameters of the field in addressing social justice issues and concerns of reconciliation for us today.

Pastoral theologian Archie Smith also recognized the community and the importance of humans living in a "web of social relations."[23] "From a relational perspective," he argued, "psychic liberation and social transformation are dialectically related and interwoven."[24] He effectively demonstrated "that emancipatory struggle must seek to strengthen awareness of the interrelatedness and interdependence of human life; this includes the life of the psyche as well as social life."[25] He raised the issue of liberation from oppression and the joint transformation of person and society—inner and outer transformation occurred together, not separately. Personal, individual oppression are intertwined within systems of institutionalized oppression; they are interwoven threads of a web.[26] As the indigenous and African practices of restorative justice have revealed, we cannot repair the self without healing of society.[27] Carroll Watkins Ali added to this critique by arguing that the traditional Hiltnerian categories of shepherding (sustaining, guiding, and healing) do not go far enough.[28] She addressed the critical need for survival and liberation, which are key issues in the African American context. Very few pastoral theologians

---

22. Wimberly, *Pastoral Care*, 21.

23. Smith, *The Relational Self*, 138.

24. Smith, *The Relational Self*, 228.

25. Smith, *The Relational Self*, 228.

26. Smith, *The Relational Self*, 51.

27. Davis, *The Little Book*.

28. Watkins Ali, *Survival and Liberation*.

have critiqued this pastoral care argument of the uniqueness of forgiveness alleged by Hiltner and others.

Wimberly, Smith, Watkins Ali, and others have said that we cannot go forward as a society until the healing—of self and society—occurs. We cannot progress (we *cannot be* progressive), nor can we even think we are modern until we heal from the dehiscence of the racial wounds. Decades after Wimberly's work first came out, it is still not a current reality for UnitedStateseans[29] of African descent to talk about healing or any type of closure. The wounds never came together and healed properly. The racial wounds of oppression and the superficial attempts to suture the wounds have festered into the ruptures in society we have today. We are trapped. The aporia of forgiveness, articulated as the unique spiritual marker of Christianity, is that which we have *not had* in our society, much less in the field of pastoral care.

Forgiveness and Its Relationship to Clement Violence

If mercy is uniquely Christian as Hiltner and others have argued, are we forcing the spiritual Other to take on practices within the Christian tradition? Is it, then, an unseen problem of neo-evangelization? Or is it a problem of translation or hubris to think it is exceptional to Christianity? People who have experienced racial or sexual trauma, oppression, and spiritual marginalization are expected to forgive the perpetrator, have mercy on society, and reconcile with their pain in a private manner. Forgiveness from a Christian lens has been—and is—a hierarchical, top-down mandate. It is demanded from the top-down or expected, regardless of the actions. As Derrida stated, there is no such thing as forgiveness without power; there is no purity of forgiveness. Unconditional forgiveness without sovereignty (i.e., without power) is not possible. The more we forgive, or are told to forgive and move on, the less we become certain of what liberation means or entitlements entail. Herein lies the problem and the difficult, ongoing work of spiritual care. The racial reconciliation has yet to occur, and there is fragile trust among the various communities that are so divided. Yet, trust and mutuality are starting points for how to engage and commence in the work of reconciliation.

If healing and reconciliation are far from the reality of the stated goals of pastoral care, what does this say about the role of forgiveness in

29. Janet Halley's neologism. See Halley, *Split Decisions*.

pastoral care and its alleged exceptionalism? If the spiritual marker of forgiveness—that which differentiates pastoral care (Christianity) from spiritual care (i.e., other religions)—is far from reality in our society, does that mean we have never fully practiced pastoral care? I want to elaborate a bit more about the myth of pastoral care being distinctive to the Judeo-Christian tradition[30] and forgiveness being unique to Christianity.

In general layperson's terms, forgive means to grant mercy, have amnesty, or give clemency to an action. We give clemency to acts of violence and racism that have not been reconciled, where there has been no sense of trust, thereby producing more violence. Granting clemency to an action that is imbricated with forms of violence is one meaning of "clement violence." Clement violence also refers to the myriad forms of violence, trauma, and "fugitive aggressions" that wo/men[31] and people of color experience. By "fugitive aggressions," I refer to the mutating forms of microaggressions that escape any borders or rigid rules within the constantly evolving practices of racism. Fugitive aggressions transgress reparation or redress as it is difficult to capture subtle or elusive racist acts or thoughts. It is the morphing, transmogrifying practices and ideologies of hate and inferiority that impound the infrahuman community. We continue to pardon the violence—or are expected to forgive—as the aggressions escape and flee existing racist frameworks. The term, "microaggressions," is too benign a term for the psychic and emotional pain inflicted; such clement violence ignores the stealth image and slippage of racism's fleeing captivity. Fugitive aggressions signify the harms that defy repair. We infrahumans are expected to forgive, forget, and move on. When we realize the racism and feel the pain, the aggression has fled and moved on to escape being "seen" as racist, leaving behind a trail of wounds.

In many cases, people of color are the ones to ask for pardon for the violence that has been perpetrated against them/us because society expects us to do so! This is society's translation of the "mildness" or clement nature of the violence or trauma—the nicks and cuts of the everyday

30. Doehring, *The Practice*, xxii–xxiii.

31. "Wo/man" is a neologism coined by feminist liberation the*logian Elisabeth Schüssler Fiorenza. "Wo/man" reminds us of the limits of an essentialized or unitary category, "woman." Wo/men—or those constituted as "women" are a heterogeneous category, fragmented by multiple subject positions of race, class, religion, ethnicity, colonialist historiography, national identity, and so on. In using the neologism, I recognize and underscore the constantly shifting positions of subjectivity, agency, and vulnerability in wo/men's lives. See Schüssler Fiorenza, *Sharing Her Word*, 186.

racism and sexism—that wo/men and people of color are presumed to endure to conform to the normative white malestream society in which we live.

As part of a hierarchy of forgiveness, violence perpetuates and brings on more forms of violence, which is reproduced in numerous ways. Such a tautological aporia of forgiveness signifies its imbrication with forms of brutality and how misinterpretations and mistranslations of forgiveness—or demands to practice it—instantiate the violence. "Forgiveness" or amnesty is constantly being expected of 'ethnics' in that we are asked to move on (or are expected to give clemency to the violence), but this paradoxically produces more hostility. Amnesty itself is a form of forgetting, not forgiving. Amnesia and amnesty both come from the same Greek word, *amnēstía*, meaning to forget, not remember, erase—as if the traumas never happened.

In granting amnesty, we have not healed from the wounds of racial, sexual, economic, and spiritual violence. We have only forgotten—or told people to forget and move on—from society's collective traumas. We have not repaired the harms; nor have we transformed or healed the wounds. An image this evokes for spiritual care is the dehiscence of the improperly tended wounds beneath the Du Boisian veil of double consciousness.[32] The aporias of healing, mercy, and reconciliation—and the question of who forgives whom (or whether there can be forgiveness or healing) and what it might mean for various communities that may not have "healing" as understood in the Western Christian culture, language, or tradition—continue to plague the field of pastoral care today.

According to Hegel, the "essence" of Christianity is forgiveness, especially in relation to Judaism.[33] Hannah Arendt also claims the unique role of the Christian practice of forgiveness as a Western concept. She states,

> Without being forgiven, released from the consequences of what we have done, our capacity to act would, as it were, be confined to one single deed from which we could never recover; we would remain the victims of its consequences forever, not unlike the sorcerer's apprentice who lacked the magic formula to break the spell.[34]

32. Du Bois, *The Souls of Black Folk*.

33. Hegel, "The Phenomenology of Spirit."

34. Arendt, *The Human Condition*, 237. Arendt gives a detailed explication of her understanding of forgiveness.

Arendt states that while the genealogy of forgiveness is Christian, thereby being religious, it can easily be translated for secular usage as well.[35] Love, argues Arendt, is the healer, the path to forgiveness. Concepts such as love, forgiveness, and reconciliation are themselves problematic because we are using Western interpretations (and varying historical and cultural contexts) to have the power to label what is forgiveness and decide which religions practice it and which do not. If forgiveness can only be interpreted in a certain context, it negates the idea that forgiveness and reconciliation are uniquely Christian practices. It only reinforces and raises the problem of colonial power, European translation, nationalist historiography, and Christian myopia.

Other cultures can have variations or affections that may be forms of our understanding of forgiveness but not in the way we understand it in the West or in the English usage of it. We have not addressed this deeply enough. Historically, Western colonizers helped shape the contours and hierarchies of global spiritual practices via a comparative theological method. The creation of "objective standards" that allegedly established criteria for "religious difference" after the Enlightenment era has shaped Western moral superiority and righteousness. Timothy Fitzgerald states, "a construction of 'religion' and 'religions' as global, cross cultural objects of study has been part of a wider historical process of Western imperialism, colonialism, and neocolonialism."[36] What were deemed to be methods of "objective standards," "universal progress," and "universality," were epistemologies and theories of the white male elite and nation-states that privileged Europe and Western ideals.[37] Such epistemologies and historiographies relied on a binary split between the West and the East (Occident/Orient, modern/traditional, history/nonhistory, civilized/noncivilized, religious/nonreligious), emphasizing cultural difference and backwardness of the "East." The West and its histories highlighted the particularistic attributes that made it unique and superior.

There are variations of "forgiveness" in other cultural contexts. If love is the path to forgiveness, what of the other "religious" practices that incorporate love as healing for various transgressions? Korean Studies scholar Robert Buswell muses that most Buddhist variations of compassion (*karuṇā*) and loving-kindness (*maitrī*) might come close to an

35. Arendt, *The Human Condition*, 238.

36. Fitzgerald, *Ideology of Religious Studies*, 8.

37. Tanaka, *Japan's Orient*, 34.

English/Christian reconfiguration of forgiveness: offering love and compassion to other suffering sentient beings.[38] He further states,

> I've never really seen anything like "forgiveness" enter into these traditional explications and suspect this is a rather peculiarly Western interpretation of compassion. The closest I've been able to come are some commentarial accounts that suggest that forbearance (*kṣānti*), which purges the mind of hatred and resentment, could be a preliminary to loving-kindness meditation, since once the mind is freed from resentment, love and compassion will be more readily developed. I suppose forbearance might include some dimension of forgiveness, though I don't know that specific denotation. I also wonder whether forgiveness might derive from "non-harming" (*ahiṃsā*), in which one seeks the welfare of all beings, rather than their harm. But again, this seems a bit of a stretch.[39]

Western Christian understandings of forgiveness may be untranslatable to "fit" into every spiritual practice or community. Yet, it is far from "unique" as Western scholars and theologians have argued.

This issue of translation is one problem of the European category of religions and practices. While it is not the purview of this chapter to engage in an intercultural translation of forgiveness, mercy, or reconciliation; I raise the issue of translation as it pertains to critiquing the pastoral care claim of the distinctiveness of some of its practices from other spiritual care practices. In this year of the heightened visibility of racial violence, society sees how these unjust acts of racialized violence need to be paid—or what spiritual debt is owed. Derrida's reading of Shakespeare's *The Merchant of Venice*—on forgiveness—reveals the Christian arrogance of the need for forced translation and mercy.

The Merchant of Venice

Shakespeare's *The Merchant of Venice* is emblematic of the conundrum (and Christian hubris) within pastoral care—that reconciliation is "uniquely" Christian. That is, the story and its exemplification of forgiveness are seen as the marker of civilization that elevates Christianity above other 'religions,' demarcating its practices from other so-called

---

38. Email correspondence with Professor Robert Buswell, April 26, 2020.
39. Email correspondence with Professor Robert Buswell, April 26, 2020.

"high religions." I examine the context of reconciliation for pastoral care, employing a Derridean interpretation of Christian forgiveness. The hierarchal verticality of forgiveness that Derrida critiques is itself the problem of Christianity in relation to other religions and how Christianity establishes vertical, non-negotiable hierarchy and supremacy over other spiritual care practices.

Written around 1596, the play takes place in the city of Venice, an important seaport of trade and activity.[40] Bassanio, a businessman, asks for a loan from Antonio, his friend. Since Antonio does not have the money, he suggests Bassanio borrow from the Jewish moneylender, Shylock. As part of the loan contract stipulation, Antonio is the guarantor for the loan, whereby Shylock demands a pound of Antonio's flesh—instead of interest—if Bassanio cannot repay the loan. The contract is agreed upon. When the loan cannot be paid back, Shylock demands a pound of flesh from Antonio, endangering Antonio's life. A trial is called to save the life of Antonio. Portia, now wife of Bassanio, disguises herself as a law clerk. Portia demands clemency for Antonio. She tricks Shylock, stating that the contract argues for just a pound of flesh, without shedding even an ounce of blood—nothing less, nothing more. Shylock is tricked, and Antonio's life is saved. In return for not losing his own life in the trial, it is demanded that Shylock become a Christian. He is forced to convert to Christianity. He loses the trial, as well as his identity.

When Shylock asks why he needs to be merciful, Portia semiotically baptizes him with praise on the power of forgiveness, as the supreme power, "a superlative might, this transcendent might of mercy rises above might, above the economy of might and therefore above sanction as well as transaction."[41] Mercy is superhuman and divine, states Portia. Portia, representing the Christian community, argues that forgiveness is above the law or justice. Forgiveness is prayer, she states. Portia, speaking as a Christian, continues her panegyric that mercy falls from heaven like a gentle rain shower. Mercy, in other words, comes from above. She states that it happens like the rain and cannot be calculated or predicted. Forgiveness comes from the top, descending vertically. There is no heterogeneous, horizontal flow of mercy. The person who forgives is better than the one asking for forgiveness. There is a hierarchy of power that flows from above, not the other way (or reciprocally). Portia implies that

---

40. Shakespeare, *The Merchant of Venice*.

41. Derrida, "What is a 'Relevant' Translation?" 188.

the experience of forgiveness—to forgive—is a form of power, not only of political power, but beyond any form of human power. Derrida sums up Portia's testimonial on forgiveness, stating that "Mercy becomes the throned monarch.... It is higher than the crown on a head.... The crown manifests temporal power, whereas forgiveness is a supratemporal, spiritual power."[42] Portia then coerces Shylock to become a Christian by convincing him of the supposedly Christian interpretation that "consists of interiorizing, spiritualizing, idealizing what among Jews (it is often said, at least, that this is a very powerful stereotype) will remain physical, external, literal, devoted to a respect for the letter."[43]

Shylock is outwitted and loses everything, including his religion as he is forced to convert to Christianity. There is no true forgiveness from the Christians—there is only hypocrisy. His life was pardoned but his spiritual identity—that which gave him life—was robbed from him. His life was spared but his spirit was trapped, immured. Shylock, however, would rather die than be pardoned in these terms. The mercenary dimension of "*merci*" is well-explicated in this play: Portia, disguised as the male law clerk, is monetarily rewarded for her work. Ironically, she has transgressed from the earthly, mundane work to receive heavenly supernatural powers to "forgive" Shylock—or granted Shylock the power to forgive. Derrida points out that the Latin root for "mercy" also gives us the word for merchandise, referring to the heavenly reward we receive from exhibiting kindness. Derrida notes, "this woman in the guise of a man, that she has in some way been paid as a mercenary of gratitude [*le merci*], or mercy [*la merci*]."[44] Portia makes the ultimate con-artist deal in the story, expecting Shylock the Jew to forgive, delivering an accolade on forgiveness but does the direct opposite of forgiveness and turns forgiveness into a tool of hierarchy and power.

Derrida muses on the "power to pardon" as God-like. He states, "This like, this analogy or resemblance, supports a logic or analogic of theologico-political translation, of the translation of the theological into political."[45] In analyzing this connection between the theological and political ramifications of such an interpretation of the Shakespeare text, Derrida speaks to the heart of the problem of an image like shepherding,

42. Derrida, "What is a 'Relevant' Translation?" 193.
43. Derrida, "What is a 'Relevant' Translation?" 194.
44. Derrida, "What is a 'Relevant' Translation?" 191.
45. Derrida, "What is a 'Relevant' Translation?" 194.

whereby we are "equating" care to being God-like as in the biblical images of Jesus as shepherd. Such a translation—or conversion—masks the clement violence and deception of Christian pastoral mercy, expecting others to act like Christians or seeing Christians as superior. As Derrida states,

> This analogy is the very site of the theologico-political, the hyphen or translation between the theological and the political. It is also what underwrites political sovereignty, the Christian incarnation of the body of God (or Christ) in the king's body, the king's two bodies. . . . This analogical—and Christian—articulation between two powers (divine and royal, heavenly and earthly), insofar as it passes here through the sovereignty of mercy and the right of grace, is also the sublime greatness that authorizes . . . every ruse and vile action that permit the lawyer Portia . . . to get the better of the Jew, to cause him to lose everything, his pound of flesh, his money, even his religion.[46]

Derrida, in musing on the Christian expedient articulation of a discourse on mercy, critiques the ways in which a particular European translation has shaped what has amounted to the semiotic legatees of the "discursive, logical, theological, political, and economic resources" of mercy.[47]

The hyphen between the theological and political (or the marker that signifies a move *from* the theological to the political) is the discursive space of the immured spirit, the space where dominance, authoritarianism, hierarchy, as well as the power to control how and what is "theological" and what is "political" is determined, elected, and marked. The alleged objectivity of this theological and political designation is a deception. Forgiveness is coerced and demanded of Shylock, while Portia the Christian uses her position to manipulate Shylock and force him into converting to Christianity. Forgiveness is not a choice for Shylock, the Jewish moneylender. It is coerced on him, as he is held captive, trapped, and immured by the reinvented discourse of Christian forgiveness. The antisemitism of *The Merchant of Venice* underscores the pastoral power and the politics of sovereignty within discourses and practices of forgiveness.[48]

46. Derrida, "What is a 'Relevant' Translation?" 197–98.
47. Derrida, "What is a 'Relevant' Translation?" 198.
48. Derrida, "What is a 'Relevant' Translation?" 191.

Tolerance, Forgiveness, and Clement Violence

Seeing mercy as sublimating justice is, as Derrida states, "at the very heart of the Hegelian interpretation of mercy, particularly in *The Phenomenology of Mind*: the movement toward philosophy and absolute knowledge as the truth of the Christian religion passes through the experience of mercy."[49] When there is mercy, the human experience is elevated to the "zone of divinity." A decoloniality project of mercy, then, refers to transgressing or critiquing that which allegedly differentiates Christians to be God-like or closer to God, therefore more perfect and simultaneously more human. A postcolonial critique of mercy shows the hyphen—translating the theological into the political—to be the discursive liminal space of Christian hubris and Western arrogance. Mercy, sublimated to the level of justice via ruse or compulsion, is the zero point of hubris for pastoral care. It is the discursive dwelling space of the immured spirit.

In further theorizing the "hubris of the zero point," I explore how this theory—describing what Santiago Castro Gómez declares as European arrogance—is relevant to pastoral care.[50] In this Derridean critique, there are parallels of "forced conversion" here on the part of white Christian pastoral care. Portia (representative of Christians) causes Shylock to lose everything, even his religion. Her paean on mercy is a trick in the guise of a discourse on mercy. Shylock has experienced a force of conversion and a loss of his spiritual identity. If forgiveness—unique to Christianity—is the heart of pastoral care, then are we implying that non-Christians practicing forgiveness is a form of forced spiritual assimilation? Is the practice of forgiveness a mimetic desire on the part of the ethnic, religious Other? If the boundaries of care are so clearly delineated by religious identity, then are we saying non-Christian others do not have forgiveness? If mercy, as Derrida denotes, is a subjective theological articulation of what is political, such a spiritual erasure suggests a form of spiritual necropolitics.

Spiritual loss is more than assimilation; it is more painful than excising a pound of flesh. As Shylock conveyed when he was forced to convert to Christianity, it was spiritual loss—death—and the politics of whose spirit gets to live or die. Such coerced assimilation and loss of identity have been the greatest of human rights abuses for colonized Third World peoples. Koreans under Japanese colonial rule (1910–1945) experienced

49. Derrida, "What is Relevant' Translation?" 197.
50. Mignolo, "Epistemic Disobedience," 2.

one of the worst forms of human rights abuse in the forced assimilation policy of *naisen ittai* (Koreans and Japanese are one), a type of spiritual necropolitics. This act of forced assimilation, however, is interpreted or converted as "mercy" in the eyes of Portia, the Christian.

We assume that reconciliation (the way we choose to interpret it) can fit every person. In the play, Portia is depicted as the shepherdess, the one who saves Antonio from Shylock, the wolf. The play alludes to the greed of the shepherds who use the sheep (to eat the fat and use their wool).[51] But the cruelty of this story is the pastoral power that Christians have conferred for managing and maintaining nodes of difference—whether in religious practices and cultures or between peoples. The very heart of Shylock's identity is robbed from him due to his forced conversion, a *cura animarum*, or a form of curative violence.[52] "Cure," as Eunjung Kim describes, "appears as an attempt at crossing that can reveal the multiplicity of the boundaries that divide 'human' and 'inhuman' as well as 'life' and 'nonlife.'"[53] There is no mercy in that Shylock's clemency—his freedom of life—is dependent on his conversion to Christianity. Shylock is the Other as non-Christian and therefore not part of the flock. He is a wolf-Other and forced to convert to a sheep, forced to be a member of the flock.

Clement violence—as I described earlier in this essay—refers to the forgiveness or clemency that wo/men and people of color are expected to practice as part of the package of living in a world dictated by white supremacy. Adding to this, clement violence also refers to those forms of spiritual losses, assimilation, or erasures which are seen as "lesser" forms of violence or acts of Western benevolence. In other words, the "violences" of spiritual and identitarian erasures are allegedly clement or mild in comparison to physical death or bodily injury. Clement violence, then, is a metonymy for the forced forgiveness of quotidian racial and spiritual violences—as well as its erasures— that have been plaited into the demos of amnesiac society.[54] Such narratives or logics of care (or cure) are emblematic not only of the pastoral power of dominant white Christian society, but also how *tolerance discourse itself* is a form of power. Portia is a broker of culture and civilization who gets to decide what/who

---

51. Astington, "Pastoral Imagery," 49.

52. Curative violence refers to the forced physical, psychic, spiritual assimilationist practices in which Ethnic others engage to be accepted by dominant white society. See Kim, *Curative Violence*.

53. Kim, *Curative Violence*, 9.

54. Moon, "Aporias of Freedom," 184.

is tolerated, what is not. Tolerance becomes a mask of clement violence and a guise of justice, liberation, and freedom. Tolerance is a narrative of power, a discursive tool to *maintain* difference that sustains hierarchical structures. Tolerance manages to negotiate and transform the difference that cannot be elided and endured in public life without violating the norms at the pinnacle of that communal life.[55]

Forgiveness as a Release from Debt and Ownership

Just as the liberal subject discourse of human rights assimilates and transforms/converts the infrahuman citizen-subject from the old truncated, third world body; pastoral care "protestantizes" and "converts" those who are not Christian. The Larteyian practice of "postcolonializing"[56] pastoral care reveals that the new forms and practices of evangelization or "Christianization" are tied to capitalist, neoliberal practices. The revised practices of evangelization and assimilation collude with the secularization of society as a mask of clement violence that reproduce the violence by insisting on conversion or demanding of forgiveness as Pamela Cooper-White describes has devolved into a form of commodified individual "self-help" neoliberal practice.

Cooper-White argues that forgiveness may be unconstructive, "poor psychology," and a neoliberal tool of self-help popular cultural indulgence that has been significantly altered from its original meaning.[57] Such demands of the neoliberalized version of forgiveness could add further trauma to the victim, contributing to the onus of guilt. She shares the work of her late mentor, Krister Stendahl, who pointed out the church's focus on forgiveness and sin in modernity is not an accurate interpretation of the apostle Paul.[58] I share the following quote from her work:

> The word most often used in the Gospel accounts of Jesus' teachings on forgiveness is the verb *aphiēmi*, which means "I send away," or "let off," in the sense of forgiving a loan. This is the word for forgiveness used, for example, in Matt. 18:21-35 and in the Lord's Prayer (in both Matthew and Luke's Gospels). In Matthew 6:12, the verse literally means "release us from our

55. Brown, *Regulating Aversions*, 71.
56. Neologism coined by Emmanuel Y. Lartey. See Lartey, *Postcolonializing God*.
57. Cooper-White, "Is Forgiveness Necessary?" 32.
58. Cooper-White, "Is Forgiveness Necessary?" 42.

debts (*opheilēmata*) as we also have released those who are indebted to us (our debtors—*opheilētai*). We no longer hold them
in obligation to us. In ancient times, we would tell the judge
to let them go free from debtors' prison. There is no emotional
or psychological meaning to the original way in which Jesus
used it. It is a cancelling of a balance due. Furthermore, in Mark
11:25, Jesus is more likely arguing against *taking revenge* than
he is arguing for feeling forgiving. The Gospels and the Epistles
both advocate turning away from active vengeance (e.g., Matt.
5:38; Rom. 12:17-21). However, refraining from personal retribution does not equate to feeling emotionally warm toward
someone who has done us harm.[59]

A critique of the narrative and interpretation of forgiveness by Western
scholars reveals the misreading or modern-day neoliberal psychological interpretation of Judeo-Christian texts and traditions that has been
forced upon us as consumers of goods and services.

While the original meaning stemmed from an economic context,
and referred to the canceling of a debt, it certainly was not unique to
Judeo-Christian practices. Granting clemency of debt was used in ancient Mesopotamian societies (as early as 2500 B.C.E.) to restore balance
in society and to prevent debt peonage, slavery, bondage, and serfdom.[60]
It was not a practice advocated uniquely by Jesus's teachings, as some
have argued. Debt clemency was rhythmically practiced in ancient Egypt,
Sumer, and Babylon as a way of maintaining equilibrium and social stability.[61] Despite the deep historical roots of forgiveness as an economic
practice, the emotional and psychological dimension of the word continues to hold popular sway; and we persistently adhere to the emotional
conversion of the concept and practices of forgiveness as particular to
Christian identity.

While it is troubling that Western scholars claim unique ownership
of a concept, Derrida's own claim that forgiveness *is* a Western concept
itself shows a type of vertical sovereignty and hierarchy of cultural mimesis. Derrida brings up an important conundrum:

> when the victim and the guilty share no language, when nothing
> common and universal permits them to understand one anoth-
> er, forgiveness seems deprived of meaning; it is certainly a case

59. Cooper-White, *Cry of Tamar*, 257.
60. Hudson, *And Forgive Them*, ix–xii.
61. Kilborn, "The 5000-Year Circle."

of the absolutely unforgivable, that impossibility of forgiveness, of which we just said nevertheless that it was, paradoxically, the very element of all possible forgiveness. For forgiveness it is necessary on the one hand to understand, on both sides, the nature of the fault, to know who is guilty of what evil toward whom, etc. Already a very improbable thing."[62]

Forgiveness, as I argued à la Derrida, is a problem of translation (which itself is a form of conversion), as well as a problem of *coerced* conversion when one is forced or expected to forgive but not necessarily even understanding what is forgiven. Derrida's argument that it is a Western concept imposed onto others is itself is a hierarchical, superior claim to make. It is problematic because how and what is forgiven—or what forgiveness entails— is never negotiated. It is expected and understood as purely Christian and unique to Western culture.

If non-Christians cannot have forgiveness (if there is no translation and no conversion), do they have a debt to Christianity? Does it become a relationship of credit and debt, as well as ownership to an idea or practice? Do Christians really own the concept? How do we understand forgiveness or mercy here if it is impossible to have understanding about the Other? And if we cannot understand one another, does it become more obligatory to clear the balance due (what is owed for this lack of translation)?

Ideas or practices are collective, creative, regenerative practices that are not owned by anyone or any religion, especially when forgiveness (of debts) was used to stabilize the equilibrium of social well-being. An epistemic reconstitution of forgiveness, then, shows that it was a collective practice of intercultural mimesis that originated in ancient African and Asian (near Eastern societies) societies to alleviate people from going into debt slavery. The practice has occurred throughout history in various cultures, and it was also integral to Jewish religious practices.[63] There is no debt to repay to Christianity—especially since the practices of debt relief did not originate with Jesus.

Cancellation of debts by rulers was an ancient practice to stabilize power in society. Contrarily, canceling of spiritual debts—mounting from clement violence—abuses that power and further confers power to those with privilege to instantiate more forms of clement violence. Such

62. Derrida, "On Cosmopolitanism and Forgiveness," 48.
63. See Deuteronomy and the Book of Leviticus.

hubris that forgiveness is unique to Christianity suffocates and immures the creativity and radical love that is necessary for repairing the damage of society's wounds and harms to people.

Fred Moten and Stefano Harney describe two types of debt. They lament that people "owe" and are in debt to their parents or to a mentor. They want to rethink debt as a "principle of elaboration." By that, they want to exterminate the concept of "owing" and reinstate a more productive concept. They also argue that debt and credit refer to forgiveness and the idea of collectivity—of "consent not to be a single being."[64] By that, they mean that we are interdependent and better when we collaborate in our struggles of togetherness. There is no "owing," owning, or "belonging" to anyone. Forgiveness has become a transaction of "owing." That would, I argue, re-employ the language of human bondage, as we have seen human beings as *belonging to* a master or *belonging to* a certain house.[65] Debt is a collective social form, not hierarchical relief that is managed by a power relation of owning, borrowing, crediting, and forgiving. As an example, Moten states that jazz does not "belong" to a community of people and that such resources should collectively be regenerative.

The other kind of debt is about aesthetics and mutual care of reciprocity. Moten laments that we "owe" *quid-pro-quo* to people, because we "owe" them a favor or an amount of money. It should be organic care. Forgiveness of true debt involves such regenerative, creative love. In Moten-esque style thinking, then, Christianity does not "own" forgiveness or any aspect of pastoral care that others would be indebted to them or be seen as unique. Charles Hallisey refers to an understanding of the fluidity and the back-and-forth negotiation of cultural practices as intercultural mimesis.[66]

So even using the language of "belonging" when we speak of inclusivity is questionable because of the concerns it raises. Forgiveness does not *belong to* a faith community—nor do we *belong to* anyone. No one can own us. We need to engage in a repurposing of such language because of its ties to ownership, property, or debt. Christian forgiveness needs to be repurposed as a spiritual project of decoloniality of repairing the

64. Harvey and Moten, *The Undercommons*, 156.

65. The language of "belonging" is etched in the Zealey daguerreotypes—of human beings "belonging to" their masters. The daguerreotypes were properties of the scientist, Louis Agassiz, which were discovered in the Harvard Peabody Museum. See Barbash, Rogers, and Willis, *To Make Their Own Way*.

66. Hallisey, "Roads Taken."

harms of our dehisced wounds. Moten and Stefano have also elaborated on debt and forgiveness, *not* as mercy, *but* as mercenary. Moten laments that some damage is irreparable.[67]

The word "sorry" itself becomes a form of continued existence for Third World subjects' survival. If "forgiveness," as a literal translation of how Jesus used it, is a "canceling of a balance due," is it something we can really practice with the spiritual debt incurred in racial injustices and violence? Is mercy another form of spiritual necropolitics in our neobliberal age? Can spiritual life be restored via feigned words of apologies?

Pastoral Care, Forgiveness, and the Mercenary Coloniality of Mercy

Poet and author Ocean Vuong, in describing his mother's work in a nail salon, alludes to the neoliberal *impotent* power of forgiveness. He, too, describes the concept of forgiveness as a mercenary tool and its use as a way of ingratiating to the white customers. Forgiveness in a nail salon is *le merci* (mercenary of gratitude). Vuong confesses:

> The most common English word spoken in the nail salon was *sorry*. It was the one refrain for what it meant to work in the service of beauty. Again and again, I watched as manicurists, bowed over a hand or foot of a client, some young as seven, say, "I'm sorry. I'm sorry. I'm so, so sorry," when they had done nothing wrong. I have seen workers, you included, apologize dozens of times throughout a forty–five minute manicure, hoping to gain warm traction that would lead to the ultimate goal, a tip— only to say *sorry* anyway when none was given.
>
> In the nail salon, *sorry* is a tool one uses to pander until the word itself becomes currency. It no longer merely *apologizes*, but insists, reminds: *I'm here, right here, beneath you.* It is the lowering of oneself so that the client feels right, superior, and charitable. In the nail salon, one's definition of *sorry* is deranged into a new word entirely, one that's charged and reused as both power and defacement at once. Being sorry pays, being sorry even, or especially, when one has no fault, is worth every self-deprecating syllable the mouth allows. Because the mouth has to eat.[68]

67. Harvey and Moten, *The Undercommons*, 157.

68. Vuong, *On Earth*, 91–92.

Vuong italicizes the word, *sorry*, either for emphasis or because foreign words are italicized—and it is a foreign word to the nail salon workers. It has a very different meaning for them. To the Vietnamese wo/men who work in the salons with his mother, it has become an important word of economic transaction and survival to know. Perhaps their usage of the word is closer to the economic meaning—as Jesus intended—of a canceling of a debt. It helps them *not to be* in debt.

Vuong also quickly learned the power of *lo siento* when he worked on the tobacco fields, apologizing constantly in order to make a living. It was often used as a passport or contract for many of the workers to remain in the country.[69] "*Lo siento*" is derived from the word, *sentir*, meaning "feeling." "Sorry" eventually gets woven into our very identities as ethnic others and becomes an appendage.[70] As *homo oeconomicus*, people have become dollar signs of survival—where the concepts of forgiveness and mercy have become mercenary or necessary for survival. The etymology of "sorry" is derived from the word, meaning "pained," "distressed," or "sore." We "feel" the clement violence in our pains, sores, and wounds.

To seek or bestow forgiveness does not heal the sores—we continue to feel its pains. Any attempt to suture the wound from a place of *le merci* (mercenary of gratitude) ruptures into a dehiscence of the mercy [*la merci*]. Forgiveness becomes a mercenary, neoliberal act of survival and disavowal of liberation in a racist world. *Le merci* is not about canceling a debt; rather, it is paying a bribe when there is no debt. *Le merci* reflects the myriad ways in which pastoral care discourses are enmeshed with colonial projects and necropolitics. As Watkins-Ali and Wimberly have alluded, we cannot have healing until we have addressed the needs of survival and liberation in a world that is still divided between humans and infrahumans. *The Merchant of Venice* narrates and highlights the entwinement of mercantilism, pastoral care, and forgiveness that becomes the tie, the "religion," (*religare*) that holds us captive to forms of clement violence and an antinomial *lack of care* of the soul that ruptures any feigning to suture the wound. Venice was governed by "Christian" values of mercy (mercenary) and charity ("care of the poor," "valued")—or rather, "mercenary cure of the poor/mercenary value we place on the poor." I underscore the hypocrisy, as "religion" came into being as a problem of modernity and its imbrication with materiality.

69. Vuong, *On Earth*, 92–93.
70. Vuong, *On Earth*, 94.

In an important study of the mercenary problem of modernity/coloniality and Christianity (or the materiality of Christianity), Charles H. Long describes how the meaning of fetish came to have religious significance during the colonial era.[71] In historicizing pastoral care and materiality, I highlight the work of Long, who argued for the need to study the historical context, dynamics, and the legacy of Western Enlightenment in exploring the origins and significations of religion.[72] He mused on "the study and understanding of religion" as a "child of the Enlightenment." The context of the Enlightenment (via travels, relationships, and cultural contact) gave rise to the different understandings of humanity and religion. Long's work demonstrated how the construction of the category of religion was discursively encased within racialized classifications of the cultural forms and practices of the societies that European explorers were encountering for the first time. Long has shown how religion via cultural contact became a "route" to understand the human situation. In other words, "contact" with the colonizer/colonized produced meanings of what *became* religion. He notes that European observers of religion became intrigued with "two new sources of data": so-called "primitives" and "religions of the East." They catalogued data gathered into two groupings: rational or non-rational.

European merchant capital would later incorporate African labor similarly to how the British absorbed Irish labor. Fetish was designated by the Europeans as the religion of Africans, a "nonrational religion." Fetish came to have meaning during the colonial period as Europeans saw the Africans engaging in "fetish" worship, i.e., worshipping objects. In a subversive irony of significations, Long shows how the Westerners told the Melanesians to worship the Christian God, when instead, they worshipped the cargo or the commodities that were brought to them.[73] In a creative interpretation of cultural contact and a subversive assertion of their own spiritual care, the Melanesians noted that Western lives were centered on commodity, *not* spirit. And similarly, Long notes the subversion of fetish in seeing how the Melanesians themselves were idolized/objectified and turned into merchandise/things.

This European "signification" of African cultures (i.e., pastoral care of the heathens) which was intertwined with materiality and commodity,

71. Long, *Significations*.

72. Long, *Significations*.

73. Murakami, "After Fetishism," 57.

"burst above and around us as the ephemeral balloon that they are."[74] The mercenary means of Christianity and its implications for the origins of a discipline of religions needs to be further explored in pastoral care. I quote Tatsuo Murakami, who states, "the idea of fetish addresses the problem of materiality combined with the problem of religion. By the time the modern academic study of religion had established itself in the late nineteenth century, the theory of fetishism had come to be recognized not as false religion but 'the very beginning of religion.'"[75] The origins of "religion" were founded on the methodological "problem" of primitivism, orientalism, colonizer/colonized, West/non-West, spiritual/material. That is, the problem of a politics of verticality and sovereignty for forced conversion or erroneous interpretations of Third World people's practices is the politics of *le merci* (mercenary of gratitude) and the origins of "religions" and interpretations of religious concepts such as forgiveness.

The legitimation of colonization and the violence that was a part of modernity/coloniality overlooked—or concealed—the enchantment practices and fetish worship that the West practiced, while denigrating it in Africa. This project of re-making Africa into a Western fantasy or fetish project that initiated "religious studies" helped to shape the myth of modernity and uniqueness of Western pastoral care. While it elevated the status of the West, it simultaneously "converted" humans through a process of the objectification of peoples to control and own resources, spirits, epistemologies, and narratives. This is the spiritual debt that has never been paid—the forgiveness that turned into forgetting, as well as the decoloniality of "undoing" that never happened—and has been elided and canceled in pastoral care discourses. The mercenary zero point of colonialism, Christendom, and practices of curative violence (or a forced *cura animarum*) is the debt that is mounting when we do not address pastoral care's collusion with colonial and imperial practices that has immured the non-Western spirit. This debt—that is prophetically explicated in *The Merchant of Venice*—underscores the barbarity of the objectification and ownership of humans. The story illustrates the debt owed to infrahuman, non-Christians, via practices of commercialized cannibalism (selling human chunks in the market, as animals) that was simultaneously occurring as Western explorers demonized the peoples

74. Long, *Significations,* 149.
75. Murakami, "After Fetishism," 53.

of Africa for their alleged barbarism.[76] This forgotten spiritual debt—the clement violence—is mounting today.

Story-telling and reconciliation have both been imperialist projects that have been controlled and "owned" by Enlightenment-era white Christian theologians—or assimilated, colonized Christians. Rey Chow states that pardoning or forgiveness acts as a metanarrative of captivity and liberation: "forgiveness is a kind of rescue mission that salvages us from the hold of something exotic and foreign, like magic."[77] Forgiveness, then, is a coerced form of enchantment. It—the process of forgiving and in turn engaging in a "Christian" act—is a part of the assimilation project of "civilized" Christians since forgiveness is allegedly "uniquely Christian." It becomes part of the "myth of modernity" narrative that overlooks the enchantment and hypocrisy of Western scientists who were practicing enchantment yet denigrating the same practices in the Third world as barbaric.[78]

Jason Josephson-Storm argues that the idea of modernity in Europe—that is, a rupture with the past in terms of superstition, medieval times—as a specific epochal project is a mythic narrative. The enchantment of forgiveness is part of the myth-making project of Western superiority. Such a pastoral care paradigm that foregrounds Christian superiority promotes violence of division and pseudospeciation. I quote Erik Erikson who was concerned about the problems of pseudospeciation:

> A pseudospecies invented for itself a very special place and a movement in the 'very center of the universe' and looked upon itself as 'superior to all others, the mere mortals.' Pseudospeciation tended to harden 'mutual differentiations' among groups 'into dogmas and isms which combine larger and larger human communities into power spheres' of exclusiveness that simply became new 'examples of pseudospecies.'[79]

The shepherding exceptionalism of pastoral care and Christianity are part of this mythic narrative that has become the central story—and image—of pastoral care. Forced forgiveness, as Shylock was coerced to practice, becomes a *cura animarum*, curative violence, which is part of a

76. Robinson, *Black Marxism*, 13.

77. Chow, *Entanglements*, 117.

78. Josephson-Storm, *The Myth of Disenchantment*.

79. I want to thank Robert Dykstra for reminding me of this important Eriksonian concept of pseudospeciation. See Friedman, "Erik Erikson on Identity," 182.

hierarchy of tolerance—or intolerance. Césaire argues that colonization is a mercenary project. It is about the "gold digger and the merchant" masked in Christian pedantry.[80] And since religion is a coeval product of modernity/coloniality, constructed via the tools of Christianity and the colonial matrix of power—then the mercenary project of colonialism was practiced with the pastoral enchantment of clement violence. It is unforgiveable because the spiritual care debt will never be paid. We need to find healing in other ways.

Conclusion

Carrie Doehring articulated storytelling as the heart of pastoral care and that healing is its goal.[81] An African proverb states, "the true tale of a lion hunt will never be told as long as the hunter tells the story." I reiterate that perhaps we need to critically reflect on *how the narratives are being told, who is telling them, how they are being heard,* and *who is doing the listening.* Telling the stories from our own voice will help repair the spiritual harm and heal from the wounds of trauma, and hopefully lead to a path of liberation. The more we share our stories (via narrative, art, music, poetry, and other expressive methods) and engage in the practices of epistemic reconstitution, the more we can have reparations from the harm and be liberated from our wounds of oppression.

80. Cesaire, *Discourse*, 33.
81. Doehring, *The Practice*, xiv, xix.

as if
it never happened
firefly
    —Tom Painting

3

Repair through Practices of Care

"Calling-In" as Justice Work

Hellena Moon & Loretta Ross

> Now that we had a name, some of the fragmented pieces be-
> gan to fall together—who we were, what we were, how we had
> evolved. We began to get glimpses of what we might eventually
> become. —Gloria Anzaldúa, Borderlands[1]

Introduction

This chapter is a Ross-Moon collaborative project and praxis of decoloniality that concerns itself with some of the issues of forgiveness in
the previous chapter by Hellena Moon. In the previous chapter, Moon
employed Derrida's deconstruction of mercy in *The Merchant of Venice*
and showed how the concept of forgiveness has been misinterpreted or
mistranslated as particular to our neoliberal cultural context. She also
incorporated Pamela Cooper-White's admonition to reconsider the
impact of forcing forgiveness on victims, who argued that Christians
have misunderstood the Gospel meaning and teachings of Jesus on

---

1. Anzaldúa, Borderlands/*La Frontera*, 63.

forgiveness.[2] Rather than seeing the concept of forgiveness as unique to Christianity, Moon argued that forgiveness has been a hierarchical, mercenary tool that has not been healing or liberative for communities of color. The emotional dimension and psychological interpretation of the word continues to hold popular sway, and we persistently adhere to the emotional meaning of the concept and practices of forgiveness and not the economic, social justice meaning of "forgiveness of debt" as an amnesty of debt cancellation as was originally intended. Demanding the modern-day emotional version of forgiveness is harmful.[3]

In our neoliberal reappropriation of the original meaning of forgiveness as a canceling of a debt or a balance due, we have instead, engaged in mercenary canceling of the person. The person is commodified as if *they were the debt* to society. Practices of canceling debts in early societies (as early as Sumer in the 3rd millennium B.C.E.) were intended to restore balance in society.[4] Rather than repair the injustices, our modern-day practices of canceling humans cause further harm and damage. Neoliberal society's obsession with social media has appropriated the emotional and psychological meaning of forgiveness, thereby seeing the "debt" as the human—or the human being as sacrifice for the debt. The self-help neoliberal culture of forgiveness has gone awry, whereby we are working from the place of our wounds, harming self and other with the call-out and cancel culture. Calling out or canceling people is one form of retribution to which people have turned because we have not done the self-care or restorative justice work that is needed, further exacerbating our emotional distress.

Canceling out the cancel culture is a work of decoloniality—it refers to decolonializing the neoliberal, individual, capitalist culture that reinterpreted the original Christian biblical meaning of forgiveness of debt into a mercenary, emotional "feel good" practice that *is not* self-care. If a decoloniality of forgiveness reveals the mercenary meaning into which forgiveness has devolved into the "canceling-human" culture, then an "epistemic reconstitution"[5] of forgiveness sees the importance of undoing, restoring, and repairing the harms done to humans via neoliberal

---

2. Cooper-White, *Cry of Tamar*, 251–61.

3. Cooper-White, "Is Forgiveness Necessary?"

4. Hudson, *And Forgive Them*, xviii.

5. Aníbal Quijano proposes this term, referring to the need to explore indigenous meanings for ideas which have been colonized or destroyed by Western civilization's hegemony over spiritual epistemologies. See Quijano, "Coloniality of Power."

systems that have objectified and commodified humans. Just as canceling debts were practices to restoring balance in society, canceling the cancel culture will hopefully repair the spiritual and psychic damage and restore balance in society. This involves the work of self-care by tending to our own wounds and addressing them through our stories.

Using the practices of "calling-in," we propose a paradigm of care that can heal the dehiscence of the pastoral mercenary wound and advocate for a canceling of the cancel culture.[6] This chapter discusses the praxis of Ross's work and how the repurposing of the methods of radical love garnered via Martin Luther King's beloved community can be a method of feminist and womanist decoloniality—a genealogy of a beloved community that practices Fred Moten's "habits of assembly and being together" as a spiritual assemblage. Moten, too, argues for an end to the "nastiness" of a calling-out culture. He implores us to engage in the practices that tie our community towards a common project: it is "about the Earth to carry on."[7] If humanity wants to be a part of Earth "to carry on," then we need to practice calling each other in, not ripping each other apart.

We propose a decolonial paradigm that interrogates issues of power and vulnerability, and sees care for justice as the heart of the work of calling-in. Moon and Ross look at the practices of self-healing (individual work we need to do) and care of others as part of the project of calling-in as important to the ongoing work of social justice to repair harm in ourselves and the world. We argue that this is the work being done within the third space in-between harm and harmed. It is not a debt that is owed; rather, it is a canceling of the spiritual debt we experience due to forms of clement violence as part of the spiritual care contract.[8] The spiritual care contract is a colonial-era tool that helped establish ideologies of Western exceptionalism and white Christian nationalism that originally practiced canceling of humans of the Third world. We argue that canceling the

---

6. Bennett, "What if Instead of Calling People Out."

7. Neal, "Left of Black."

8. Moon discussed the work of Carole Pateman's *Sexual Contract*, as well as Pateman's and Mills's *Racial Contract* as elisions from the fictive story of the Lockean social contract. Moon argues that also omitted in the social contract was the spiritual care contract that denied the spirits of non-Christians and non-white Christians. Religious intolerance and belief in the inferiority of non-white bodies was woven into the fabric of political liberal and neo-liberal ideology of contractarian theories. See Moon, "Aporias of Freedom."

cancel culture is part of the project of dismantling the master's tools of spiritual debt culture that further impoverishes and harms humanity.

We advocate to strengthen forms of restorative justice that seek to undo the damage and repair harms. Instead of the language of "forgiveness," therefore, we argue for a "decoloniality of repair" of the wounds that examines our accountability and deep personal change. It is done through the lens of Moten and Harney's understanding of forgiveness as "consent not to be a single being," not as a debt owed. The spiritual and social debt we need to repay—or repair—is complex; there is much work to be done in that regard. Canceling people, however, will not get us closer to the social equilibrium of undoing the harms. We have to move forward with our goal of building a better world. Forgiveness is a refusal of ownership; it is a sharing. It is our collective responsibility to share in the spiritual and social debt.[9]

Derrida proposed forgiveness without power, and Ross practices such a model of *sharing* power—or leveraging it for those who have none—to build justice in human rights movements. In the spiritual assemblage of our "togetherness" as humans, people with or without power/privileges can practice radical love with one another by understanding to share the power—we own nothing. As Cooper-White lamented, the Christian model of forgiveness has become a form of commodified "self-help" neoliberal practice. Forcing forgiveness can be harmful and contribute to ongoing wounds.[10] Rather than a forgiveness model, Ross has formulated how to have reconciliation on the terms of communities of color that stresses accountability and deep systemic change needed to sustain the human rights movement. Radical spiritual assemblages are not top-down, vertical power practices. Rather, spiritual assemblages are horizontal "human" conversations of compassion whose goal is a radical recasting of the paradigms of power to advance the human rights movement. We need to engage in the care work of calling-in if we are to grow our sphere of care. Together, Ross and Moon understand this work as a "canceling-debt" that transforms a "demand-forgiveness" culture into one that foregrounds truth-telling and togetherness in our repair of the harms.

As this anthology highlights the importance of our relationships with nature and with one another, we employ a subversive reproductive

9. Muir and Weinstein, "The Social Debt."
10. Cooper-White, *Cry of Tamar.*

justice praxis. In a practice of biomimicry (i.e., being inspired by practices in nature), we explore the care practices of the Maculinea alcon butterfly and how they have adapted complex relationships of living with their enemies. We first examine the history of a call-out culture and provide some definitions.

Logistics, Vocabulary, and Nuances around the Calling-Out/In Culture

The practice of canceling replicates the carceral system of punishment by exiling and disposing of people who could become potential allies. It creates a discouraging atmosphere for activists in that they have to walk on eggshells, frightens others into not speaking up to tell the truth because they are afraid of being bullied, and most critically, it drives people away from the human rights movement. Joreen (Jo) Freeman, who founded the first rape crisis center, says the following about the cancel culture:

> Trashing is a particularly vicious form of character assassination which amounts to psychological rape. It is manipulative, dishonest, and excessive. It is occasionally disguised by the rhetoric of honest conflict or covered up by denying that any disapproval exists at all. But it is not done to expose disagreements or resolve differences. It is done to disparage and destroy.[11]

Ross shares anecdotally how she was constantly courted by the leftist white groups and was amused by the arguments they made about trivial intellectual distinctions. They were arguing over minor points. Such ivory tower discursive battles mask privilege while weaponizing language. It makes accountability difficult, and it increases harm rather than healing. It devalues —and renders invisible—people's lived experiences. If a white person says they have not noticed racism before, attacking and shaming them only splinters the movement, rather than strengthening it. It creates a culture of cynicism and hopelessness. It would be more productive to show them how to recognize the racism than critique them for not seeing it. That is, to "undo" the harm, they must know what the harm is or have conversations (calling-in) around the incident for which they are being criticized.

With regard to a calling-out culture of the left, here is a phrase to keep in mind: "I may be wrong, and you may be right, and by an effort,

---

11. Freeman, "Trashing."

we may get nearer to the truth."[12] Calling out refers to criticizing others' social justice practices while not self-critical of one's own. It is publicly using knowledge as a weapon against others, banishing others because they are not "woke" enough. It refers to the use of social activism to boost one's ego or their standing in the community, as well as seeking political purity of opinions through shaming and ideological bullying. We are teaching students radical knowledge and theories that are important for the social justice work we are doing, but we are not teaching the skills of radical love to go along with the knowledge that is being taught.

Natalie Wynn speaks of the seven stages of a calling out/cancel culture magnification.[13] She states that we have a "presumption of guilt" and automatically presume the person is guilty in a call-out culture. What gets called-out, gets abstracted and attached to their moral character. People are then reduced to their flattened, essentialized identity. Pseudo moralism/intellectualism is attached to the call-out culture. By that, Wynn refers to the practice of people demanding an apology, but they will attack the person out of revenge and anger. There is a culture of "unforgiveability" and how apologies seem insincere. Yet, when the canceled person does not apologize, they are told they are avoiding accountability. There is the stage of contamination/infection of others. If we agree with the toxicity of the call-out culture, we are accused of supporting the right. Finally, the dualism/false binaries reinforce the problems of identity politics.

"Calling out" refers to the public demands for people to change their behaviors, speech, or thoughts. "Calling out" is like bombing a village to keep people safe. Calling in" refers to the private or public skills for having difficult dialogues with others while respecting their human rights and differences. Calling in with love is a practice of care. Loretta Ross provides definitions in some of the language she uses for the practices of calling-in as follows:

1. Privilege: advantages one is not responsible to or accountable for certain advantages in our life.

2. Weaponizing privilege: using knowledge, identity, or status to dominate others (when we can own our own privilege, we can point out others).

---

12. Popper, *The Open Society,* 225.

13. Wynn, "Takeaways from Natalie."

3. Victimized violator: we are all capable of having our human rights violated while violating others simultaneously. Imagine a battered wife who beats her child or someone experiencing racism while they're homophobic.

4. Performance activism: symbolic actions that seek to improve one's status, standing, or approval from others.

5. Identity bullies: those who use their identities to silence or dominate others or claim a particular victimhood stance to gain power. For example, men may receive credit for something while the woman gets shamed. Using victim mantle and causing harm because they're hurt.

6. Pivots/deflections: changing the subject to avoid discomfort or accountability. They're made uncomfortable.

Ross also defines differences between punching up, punching down, and punching sideways:

1. Punching up: holding people or other entities accountable who have more clout, privilege, social and/or economic power, or celebrity status who are unreachable by other means, and who refuse previous chances to change. Call-outs are only criticized by the right when the previous victims of oppression protest against the powerful by punching up.

2. Punching down: taking advantage of your power, privilege, status, knowledge, or celebrity status to harm people who are vulnerable and can't hold you accountable.

3. Punching sideways is taking shots at those who are relatively at the same status as you, despite differences of identity such as age, race, gender, sexual orientation, gender identity, class, abilities, citizenship, etc.

Right and Left of the Call-Out Culture

People on both ends of the political spectrum are using the cancel/call-out culture. The 2020 Republican National convention said "cancel culture" was a top priority. People on the right excoriate the "political correctness," stating that it is a new witch hunt, a new McCarthysism threatening free speech by conservatives and Trump supporter. They allege that their academic freedom is being infringed upon by the left's intolerance of their ideas. The "right" argue that historical and contemporary hierarchical power structures should not matter because everyone should have the right to say whatever they want. They argue that people should not be punished for making sexist, racist, homophobic, transphobic, or xenophobic comments or jokes. Leftists should not be so "thin-skinned," "coddled" snowflakes who are too sensitive. They allege that white, heterosexual men are the principal victims, but all conservatives are vulnerable to leftist outrage. Rightists argue that they should have freedom to discriminate because of religious freedom and Christianity is under attack. Leftists have been accused of "unfairly" using call-outs to criticize US allies or corporate human rights violators. Perceived attacks on political correctness are primarily motivated by the desire to hold onto white supremacist power and maintain unjust hierarchy. In that regard, words do have the power to wound and reinforce social inequalities.

With regard to the left, criticisms of the cancel/call-out culture escalated in the 1960s when leftist professors were fired or silenced. Prominent feminist activist Angela Davis was fired from UCLA in 1970 due to her ties to the Community Party and after a lawsuit that ruled this was illegal, was fired again for her radical politics and language. McCarthy anti-communist persecutions began in the late 1940s until late 1950s that accused hundreds of Americans of being communist or communist sympathizers costing them jobs, families, and sometimes, their lives. There has been an ongoing campaign to rid liberal universities of professors like Steven Salaita who supported Palestinians (University of Illinois job offer was withdrawn) or George Ciccariello-Maher, who was fired from his tenured position at Drexel for challenging the existence of white genocide and was accused of anti-white bigotry. Lisa Durden was also fired from Essex County College for saying that "Black Lives Matter" on Fox News. Free speech, therefore, is not a consequence-free speech. Movies like "The Passion of Christ," (2004), "Chronicles of Narnia" (2005), or "Harry Potter (1997-2007) were targeted by Christian nationalists for censorship. Rock and Roll, as well as Rap music were hypocritically targeted for censorship by right with legal punishments.

Examining the History of the Call-Out Culture

The Merchant of Venice, the Shakespearean play discussed in the previous chapter by Moon, is an example of cancel culture whereby a hierarchy of forgiveness was a mask for the exploitation of power, antisemitism, and the human canceling of Shylock.[14] It was the early modern-era equivalent of selling human flesh in the markets. A Chinese slang: *renrou sousuo* (translation: "human flesh search") was used—initially as a nonchalant way to refer to the new social media accounts in the 1990s.[15] Now, it literally refers to "human flesh indeed: a pound of it, exacted."[16] Such a "human flesh search" was apparently an Asian cultural trait of shaming, something that could not possibly happen here in Western individualistic society.[17] Yet, it was the Western culture of colonialism that wielded cancel culture in the form of censorships to silence individuals.

Cancel culture, then, becomes mandated as a method of wielding power to cancel a human being, as one would cancel a debt. It becomes a type of hierarchy of forgiveness, as Derrida described.[18] Human beings become the debt owed to society. Cancel culture has become another form of commodification and is closely linked to forgiveness in many ways. It might be a modern-day, neoliberal method of forgiveness—rather than canceling of a debt, it is the canceling of a human (because in a neoliberal society, humans are the bargaining pieces. In order not to be "canceled," the perpetrator gestures apologies or feigns remorse in order to be forgiven. "Cancel" is a form of eradication, elimination, erasure. As forgiveness has been misconstrued as an erasure (and in the case of Shylock, an erasure of identity and personhood), so too, cancel is a deletion, an act of disappeared persons, a human rights violation. In critical theory, pharmakon refers to a remedy, poison, or scapegoat. Canceled people become modern-day scapegoats, according to Charles Taylor. They are the pharmakon. We quote Ligaya Mishan at length here:

> The modern scapegoat performs an equivalent function, uniting otherwise squabbling groups in enmity against a supposed transgressor who relieves the condemners of the burden of wrestling with their own wrongs.... What is lost, the Canadian philosopher Charles Taylor argues...is the ambivalent, numinous duality of the sacrificial victim. ("*Pharmakos*" comes from "*pharmakon*," which is both itself and its opposite: medicine and poison at once, healer and killer.) No longer is it acknowledged,

14. Shakespeare, *The Merchant of Venice*.
15. Mishan, "The Long and Tortured History."
16. Mishan, "The Long and Tortured History."
17. Mishan, "The Long and Tortured History."
18. Derrida, "What is 'Relevant' Translation?"

however tacitly or subconsciously, that the scapegoat, whether guilty or not of a particular offense, is ultimately a mere stand-in for the true culprits responsible for a society gone askew (ourselves and the system we're complicit in). Instead, the scapegoat is demonized, forced to bear and incarnate everyone's guilt, on top of their own.[19]

The canceled or the disappeared person becomes a public placeholder—and reminder—of our society's ills, thrown into the pit of our open, dehisced wound, further perverting our collective wound.

Canceling is a punitive practice and representative of our culture of violence. The practice of canceling perpetuates the violence we seek to eradicate. *Cancellare* is derivative of the Latin, "to cross out," but also a form of *carcer*, from which we get the word, "incarceration." We use violence as a practice of achieving purity or "good." Instead of eradicating the violence, practices of canceling eradicate the human being and perpetuate the violence. In ancient "religious" rituals, a slave, criminal or disabled person was selected to be expelled from the community as a form of purifying/cleansing the community. They were the *Pharmakoi*, the sacrificial lambs or sheep. This objectification, dehumanization, and public shaming of people is the equivalent of our modern-day "human-flesh-in-the-market-place" medieval era practice in the renewed social media *renrou sousuo*. It is punishment, "flagellation"—of others and self—according to Mishan, which is an outdated form of religious practice.[20] Modern-day social media cancel culture underscores Bruno Latour's assertion that "we have never been modern."[21]

Colonial-era Cancel Culture

Cancel culture was used by the colonizers to stratify society. When Korea was under Japanese colonial rule (1910- 1945), Koreans were censored and wrote fiction partly to write about the oppressive situations under which they lived. Literary scholar Choi Kyoung Hee notes how "censorship itself was a disabling force that impeded a liberal ideal of literary freedom."[22] She challenges us to see "the relationship between

19. Mishan, "The Long and Tortured History."
20. Asad, *Genealogies of Religion*, 116n.
21. Latour, *We Have Never Been Modern*.
22. Choi, "Trope," 433.

the representation of disability and the disabling conditions under which writers in the colony had to work."[23] The trope of disability reflected the psyche of Koreans who lacked control over their lives and were dislocated by multiple forces of colonialism, growth of capitalism, urbanization, changes of values, and so on.

Traditionally, disabled bodies in Korea were seen as shameful and disgraceful. Disability was associated with "fatalism" (p'alchasol, p'alchajuui),[24] "ascribed to the individual's wrongdoings in his or her previous life or to some fault of the parents."[25] Those shamed, disabled bodies were hidden from public view. During the colonial period, communities and families were dislocated due to changes in society, and many of these individuals were found wandering the streets without care. They were referred to as the "wandering sick people" and were then taken in by the Japanese police to be penalized, incarcerated, and canceled.[26]

As part of the stratification of society, then, many Koreans collaborated with the Japanese and participated in the censorship of their fellow Koreans. The culprits of cancel culture were the capitalists, colonialists, Koreans colluding in colonial power structures—not just the Japanese colonizers. It is not a unified understanding, because those who had the power or sought to collude with those in power, were in alignment with causing the sickness. Censorship—or a canceling—was interpreted and seen, then, as a disability. Bodily weakness translated into national weakness.

Korean literary activists critiqued the practice of disabling and limiting the full movement of humans. Disability literature flourished in the colonial period as a metonym for the nation in need of repair. This linking of the canceling of bodies with the censorship of writing as disabling is a powerful connection that Korean literary activists made to shift the situation and politicize the trope of disability, not as limiting or fatalistic but as a treatment of the loss of full humanity. Disability literature temporarily "disappeared" in colonial writing during the darkest period of Japanese colonial rule, known as the Period of Police Rule (1910-1919), but it reappeared in the 1920s. Choi notes the changes after the hiatus. She states, "the allegorical type was replaced by a subject with

23. Choi, "Trope," 434.
24. McCune Reischauer is used for the transliteration of Korean words.
25. Choi, "Trope," 436.
26. Choi, "Trope," 436.

full interiority, and the often naively optimistic, constructive hope for reform and change that marked works from the earlier period was replaced by a more naturalistic portrayal of grim colonial reality," whereby the unequipped person[27] in need of repair came to represent most of the population, as the unequipped person came to stand as a metaphor for the unequipped nation. And what is important is the emphasis on care for the disabled (and in turn, transforming *their situation*, not their condition), underscoring the importance of social justice and social transformation. Healing, then, is not curing. The unequipped person had rights, just as the nation had rights, to overturn their situation. In the context of the rights discourse, the equipped person uses the power of social media to cancel humans vs. the unequipped subject (disabled, fully human and in need of resources)—who represents the canceled, shamed person.

When Call-Outs Are Practices of Justice

Ross argues that calling out can have its benefits and be useful to the human rights movement. Ross points out the benefits of call-outs that do not result in a canceling of the human being but promote in the eradication of injustices. Most importantly, it is crucial to hold human rights violators and those who uphold structures of white supremacy accountable for their actions—or lack thereof. Those who are complicit with structures of injustice need to be held responsible for the harms and abuse towards individuals and society. Calling out is effective in protesting individuals, organizations, corporations, or governments abusing their power over others and hold them responsible for their crimes. Those who ignore human rights violations as bystanders or accomplices should be called-out as a method to expose the complicity of their actions. It is effective as a method of going beyond impotent legal remedies for relief and cessation of harm, such as the BlackLivesMatter movement. Calling out is an important strategy for increasing accountability for elected or appointed officials who violate their oaths of office. Using public shaming is the best (and often only) way to reach these "inaccessible" political officials who engage in a breech of power. The goal of such call-outs is not to cancel the person; rather, the goal is to achieve justice and repair the harm done to the person or community.

27. *Bul-gu-jah* is the term for disability and the literal Sino-Korean translation is "the unequipped person."

While call-outs are not recommended as a first choice, it can be the last resort in addressing power differentials, such as workers holding a corporation accountable or students challenging schools when other efforts have failed such as the "black@private schools" initiatives that hopefully have implemented the necessary changes in addressing systemic racism and institutional abuse. Calling out helps in defining the boundaries of acceptable behaviors, articulating what needs improvement or elimination, and achieving reparations for harms and for the prevention of future injustices. It is instrumental in setting higher standards for words, behaviors, and deeds (gently calling each other out and call each other in to do the human rights work).

Call-outs, therefore, have had a place in society and are appropriate when addressing structures of power and power disparities. There are situations when people committing the harm are inaccessible to those being harmed, except in a public way that helps protect the subaltern voices. It is also a method to avoiding increasing harm through private means or equalizing power, such as hearing from those who are historically silenced. Colin Kapernick's act of taking a knee to address police brutality was a call-out that promoted awareness and social justice. The movement at various independent schools throughout the country ("black@privateschools") has been a way of naming unmarked or hidden structures of privileges, publicly confronting trauma that has gone unaddressed for decades at various schools, as well as helping to build community for students and faculty of color to prevent future harms. Such social justice call-outs help to build community and cultivate what Jennifer Nedelsky calls a judgment community.

Black students around the country discussed their experiences at their respective private schools and then created Instagram pages that shared their stories with others. They courageously came together, thought about, and deliberated on their own experiences of racism and marginalization. When they created the Instagram posts, it sparked a plethora of responses that have been uncannily similar across the country in other elite private schools. Legal human rights scholar, Jennifer Nedelsky, discusses the importance of marginalized communities having opportunities to create their own communities of judgment.[28] Nedelsky developed this understanding of a judgment community (based on Hannah Arendt's theory that helped transform feminist consciousness-raising

---

28. Nedelsky, "Communities of Judgment."

during the 1970s among housewives that helped theorize a community-based judgment), as well as based on the theory of John Rawls, whose work established the legal foundation of an overlapping consensus in a community). Other human rights scholars (such as Abdullahi An-Na'im) have highlighted the importance of how these discursive spaces of judgment communities can help to dismantle white supremacist structures in our communities, allowing for marginalized voices (that have emerged from the overlapping consensus of a community) to be heard and working towards justice from the grassroots—not from the top-down.

With regard to the Instagram "Black@privateschool" pages, it was clear that all of the students, teachers, and alumni/ae could not be "wrong" in their feelings of objectification, marginalization, dehumanization, and oppression. As Jennifer Nedelsky, John Rawls, Abdullahi An-Na'im, and other human rights scholars have described as to what constitutes a judgment community,[29] the posts underscored the communal voice of dehumanization and marginalization to which we need to listen, have compassion, and move with proactive change so that we can address the racial, sexual, and classist forms of violence in our institutions and communities. Such a social justice calling out made visible the invisibility of people of color and the workings of power in schools. People need to be held accountable for injustices. On a meta-level, the commonly used acronym of DEI (diversity, equity, and inclusion) refers to the work of decolonializing the structures of oppression that have created institutionalized structures and practices of racist assimilation, invisibilities, and marginalization. DEI work can be done through a lens that helps our community to address the legatees of colonialism in our communities.

As the philosopher who first theorized about a beloved community, Josiah Royce wrote about the wounds and cuts on a tree that will never disappear.[30] The wounds (that students posted on Instagram) are acts of violence that Josiah Royce have named philosophically as scars that stay with a community. The Rawlsian "overlapping consensus" of the shared posts reveal that the racial wounds are actually harmful scars that are significations of the violence and dehumanization of the Black students in our community. In that regard, *not* calling-out only further perpetuates the cycle of violence and the dehumanization of students of color.

29. See the concept of overlapping consensus by Rawls, *A Theory of Justice*; also see An-Na'im, *Islam and the Secular State*.

30. Royce, *The Problem of Christianity*. For a genealogy of the concept of a beloved community, see Herstein, "The Roycean Roots."

This prophetic work of our young people who created black@private-schools movements throughout the country has revealed and exposed the human rights abuses inflicted on a community. We have much to do as a community to address the harms and racial trauma that have been highlighted in the posts.

While the scars may heal over time, Royce mentioned that they are permanent reminders of the ugliness in a community. The scars remind us of where we need to go and the ongoing work that remains undone, signifying the pain and hurts in a community. When the wounds are tended to and cared for, the pain can be transformed, just as we see beautiful knots on a tree as a reminder of the harms inflicted on the tree. In that regard, we are reminded of the Sankofa bird, the symbolic Ghanaian bird that persistently looks back while moving forward. History reminds us to always be troubled and never complacent in our successes, what feminist theorist Donna Haraway has referred to as "staying with the trouble."[31] Harney and Moten explain that the objective is not "to end the troubles but to end the world that created those particular troubles as the ones that must be opposed."[32] The goal is not to just heal the wounds; rather, the desire is to end the system of abuse and epistemologies that created the wounds. Social justice call-outs can be wakeup calls for getting in "good trouble," as John Lewis would say.[33] In doing "good trouble," we need to be reminded that we as individuals are all capable of harming others as much as we are likely to be harmed. We are all vulnerable as human beings to wound and be wounded. Ross understands justice-oriented call-outs as ways to achieve justice, not as a hubristic means of practicing hierarchical forgiveness.

Vulnerability Analysis of Calling Out

Vulnerability—as we are using it here—is not about weakness or protection of the weak. The Latin, *vulnerare* ("to wound") refers to our wounds and the wounds we inflict on one another when we are wounded. Vulnerability, then, describes the aspects of harming and being harmed. Hurt people hurt others, and we cannot do justice work in our fullest capacity if we are wounded. As Ross has pointed out earlier in this chapter, the

31. Haraway, *Staying with the Trouble.*
32. Harney & Moten, *The Undercommons*, 9.
33. Ray, "Five Things John Lewis."

culture of calling-out has divided people within their own movements. Paradoxically, we desire healing in the world but are wounding others along the justice journey. Our own wounds prevent us from doing the deep healing work. Wounds left unattended lead to dehiscence. As Henri Nouwen stated about the wounded healer, "Open wounds stink and do not heal."[34]

The decoloniality project of care insists that we need to heal from our own wounds and engage in the constantly changing ways in which we care to build on to the genealogy of justice work. Like the care work of the alcon butterfly and the ants, "calling-in" means "sniffing" out the people who can help build on the movement and care for those people— and subversively working to build the movement, not tearing it down. It means adapting and changing our strategies for staying united and expanding our movement. Human beings make mistakes; owning up to our own mistakes prevents repetition. Who are we to have the power to forgive or not to forgive? The understanding of forgiveness itself is hierarchical. We should not allow someone who may have power over us to hurt us and think we can call out people to ruin their lives or harm them when we are not any better. Understanding the origins of our own wounds may help us not to inflict them onto others. We are all complex. We are never the worst of the evil acts that we have done.

Our vulnerability and woundedness causes a lack of appreciation for a truly shared learning community, as well as a lack of discernment about threats. Instead of seeing social justice work as a service to others, it is engaged in for selfish reasons. That is, they bring their emotional needs and wounds to the social justice movement, not to be of service, but to stand out and for the movement to serve *them*. It becomes narcissistic desire and self-gratification whereby they merely seek attention or recognition. The purpose of the human rights movement is to end oppression, not be a space of public therapy. Ross suggests for these hurt people to "get a therapist!" There are places to go work on resolving our trauma. We have glorified the "wounded healer" metaphor and elided the emphasis of self-care, self-healing, and self-love. We have not fully understood the importance of the practice of self-care and the healing of our own wounds before we can heal the wounds of others—or those of society. Not tending to our dehisced wounds has contributed to a calling out culture. We cannot heal if we ourselves are wounded.

34. Nouwen, "The Wounded Healer," 80.

The problem of binaries (black/white, good/evil, etc.) is that most of us exist in-between the binary Manichean spaces of good/evil, black/white, wounder/wounded. Handling the daily violence—from this space of the in-between—is more important than the Manichean ideologies that have *actually elided* the quotidian violence. Ocean Vuong eloquently stated, "Because freedom, I am told, is nothing but the distance between the hunter and its prey."[35] If freedom is the space between the hunter and the hunted, then discerning the discursive space of where and how the violence occurs is important. If the hunted goes into hiding, that does not mean the problem has gone away. They just delay addressing the real issues. Just because we shut down someone's thoughts by calling them out does not mean the thoughts or the ideologies do not exist. It means we ignore the real problems that exist. Loretta Ross points out this issue in her work. We are fighting the small battles that keep us exhausted—hunter searching for its target-in-hiding—when we should be tending to our own wounds. The healing cannot happen until genuine care—for self and other—is truly practiced as a mutual process.

Maculinea Alcon Butterfly: Biomimicry of Care

In highlighting the importance of our relationships with nature and with one another, we explore a subversive reproductive justice care praxis of biomimicry. In a quick encapsulation of the brilliant decolonial ruse of the Maculinea alcon butterfly and its parasitic relationship with two ant species, we argue that the pupa stage of the Maculinea alcon butterfly truly embodies a praxis of subversive care.[36] In a decolonial analysis of the subversive structures of power, the butterfly manages to trick ants into rearing its young by masking them with the ants' own scent. The butterfly's caterpillars begin life feeding off a plant, but they then descend to the ground and get picked up by passing Myrmica ants, who unknowingly carry the caterpillars back to their nests and care for them.[37] The caterpillars have developed an outer sheath that mislead ants into thinking that the young are their own; they also make sounds that its host would make (acoustical mimicry), further engaging in tricking the ants to think they

35. Vuong, *On Earth*, 4.

36. I want to thank my daughter, Madeleine, for introducing me to these creative butterflies. I also want to thank her biology teacher, Aklima Ali, for teaching her about such evolutionary adaptations.

37. Brahic, "Parasitic Butterflies."

are one of their own.[38] The butterfly has tricked the would-be predator by being taken into their colonies to feed, nurture, and care for their young so that they can survive and thrive. The caterpillars who perfectly imitate the ants are taken in more quickly by the "adoptive parents" back to their nest. Interestingly, the ants fed the caterpillars more than they fed their own, perhaps because the caterpillars were larger than their own.

Scientists theorize that perhaps the exploited ants have somehow adapted a defense against the butterflies—chemical mimicry—and are engaged in an "evolutionary arms race." Alcon butterflies have developed a very similar chemical signature in their waxy outer coats. In contrast, ants from colonies that are often parasitized have evolved a much greater diversity in their chemical signatures. This suggests that the two species are constantly evolving new signatures to trick and evade being fooled. Is this exploitation or subversive survival of the alcon pupa? The butterfly larvae must constantly adapt to new chemical styles in order to survive such precarious parasitic lifestyles.[39]

This model of metamorphosis is not without its subversions, strategies, and its own masking *of t*he mask in order to flourish. It navigates a culture of vulnerability that is subtle, but it helps the pupa to survive. Instead of dying, the butterfly has learned how *to work with their enemies/* their predators and traverse precarious territory to paradoxically benefit from the situation. Humans may need to adapt similar strategies of care if we are to push through the ongoing work of social justice and human rights activism. Loretta Ross and others who have been calling people "in," and not canceling them, have done this subversive care work.

In critically reflecting on the human rights work of her Black elders in the civil rights movement, Loretta Ross believes that we need to engage in practices of "accountable" care that can allow us to move forward with the justice work that she learned from them. Ross discusses the importance of why the call-out culture has been problematic since the activism of the 1960s, such as in the Black Panther movement, where people would gossip and speak badly of one another and create more divisiveness. She sees the importance of incorporating a social justice praxis of radical love. Radical love embraces a human rights framework of *reproducing justice*—not reifying the master's tools to further entrench white supremacy—that repurposes the tools of hatred into tools of

38. Hurd, "Butterflies Behaving."
39. Hurd, "Butterflies Behaving."

radical love that *build up* justice. COVID-19 and the racial violence of 2020/21 have amplified the divisiveness in our communities, judgments of one another, and our practices of blaming, retaliating, victimizing (self-victimhood and others), ostracizing, etc. Ross laments that we are not just fighting with the "enemy;" we are fighting amongst ourselves to create more enemies—even with those allied for social justice. Her social justice practice of calling-in desires to overcome that. She believes we need to build calling-in practices among those who are *not* our enemies.

Like the alcon butterfly and their creative strategies of adaptation; so too, do we have to keep evolving our strategies for surviving, getting along with our "enemies," and practicing a culture of restoring justice. Nature needs care, and it constantly reinvents and reproduces ways to receive care in a way that mimics a "calling-in" culture. Creating unity for survival means readapting and repurposing that which did not work and calling in those who try to sabotage the work of reproductive justice and human rights. What we critique, then, is the dominant image of a "wounded healer" in the arena of care work. We advocate a decolonial feminist/womanist model of human rights care that practices the *"undoing"* of human flesh searching, eradicating, and censoring of human beings. While such canceling of human beings has certainly occurred prior to colonial-era destruction, it has been an important recent component of our twenty-first century neoliberal social media methods. We advocate a "relational way of being" that subverts practices of dividing humanity that causes harm. An important component of Ross's reproductive justice framework is the right to be cared for and care for others in a way that reproduces structures of well-being, not structures of ruin.

If, as Ocean Vuong stated, true freedom is the distance between the hunter and the hunted/ predator and prey, how can we navigate our own precarity when those whom we see as our allies become our enemies as well? How can we share and expand the human rights community and the work by better blurring the bifurcation of humans into victims and perpetrators? How can we create enough discursive space between us as to enact and enlarge our freedom, at the same time exercise our agency? When we create enemies even within our human rights circles, we narrow the distance between hunted and prey, thereby curtailing our own freedom. Ross is passionate that a decolonial praxis of calling-in actually gives us the distance to ensure our freedom.

Ross states that as long as we are fighting our own, we will not see the real enemy coming. To maintain our freedom, then, we need to unite in our struggles and not fight amongst ourselves. We also need to gain support from those who seek to harm us by subversively being fed and be nourished by them, like the alcon butterfly. The healthier and more robust we are in our coalition-building, the better we engage in the daily practices of justice-building. Instead of being so divided in a struggle of identity politics, it is crucial to remember that there is only one race: the human race. We need to be united in the race for our humanity against structures of white supremacy and the race for our own survival against the forces of climate change and planetary well-being. While we tediously stay busy in our canceling and dehumanizing of one another, the true victors continue in the oppression of our rights—laws enacted to limit our voting, restrict immigration, teach false ideologies that perpetuate racism in schools, promote anti-abortion laws, etc. Ross reminds us of the words of Joseph Lowery, her mentor and elder in the human rights movement, who stated, "we have to *turn to* each other and *not on* each other."

Our own emotional vulnerability–our woundedness—prevents the self-care we need in being empathic towards others. Ross argues that there are emotional reasons for people using call-outs. People do not forgive themselves; they do not practice self-healing. Lack of self-compassion leads to lack of compassion, empathy, and positive energy for others. Calling-out is sometimes a form of seeking approval from others in ways they may not receive otherwise. Hurt people end up hurting others—a victim/trauma (wounder/wounded) lens is the only way they can view others. So, if they are the victim, and the wound is inscribed onto their psyche, they will expect everything to hurt them more acutely if the others are saying not the perfect thing. Ross calls this, "involuntarily drafting others for emotional labor."

Practices of Subversive Care as Reproductive Justice: Growing Our Circle of Influence

Care is not a top-down, hierarchal practice. Unless we have the "care" component to a theory of vulnerability, it just becomes another binary or antinomy of dominance and subordination. Vulnerability can be understood within a power spectrum whereby the harm/harmed can be theorized as dominance/subordination. This power dynamic can be explicated in the words of Martin Luther King, Jr:

one of the great problems of history is that the concepts of love and power have usually been contrasted as opposites, polar opposites, so that love is identified with a resignation of power, and power with a denial of love. Power without love is reckless and abusive, and love without power is sentimental and anemic. Power at its best is love implementing the demands of justice, and justice at its best is power correcting everything that stands against love.[40]

A project of decoloniality works in the spaces of the "in-between"—within the third space of the solidus or the binaries. Working in the in-between is the movement between and across the sacred, the secular, the profane, and the mundane. Like the alcon butterfly that receives nourishment and care from the enemy for its very survival, we can engage in similar strategies that build the human rights movement. We need to employ inventive strategies that provide care and nourishment, not hate and wars.

Calling-in helps to build our circle of influence. In laying the foundations of this call-out culture, Ross underscores the problem of horizontal hostility in the human rights movement. Horizontal hostility has impeded our movement from advancing forward. If we want to build a human rights movement, then we need to understand our circle of influence. By that, Ross refers to those within our various circles of communities. We are likely to influence and not alienate when we work with them and call them into our circle. Marginalizing and canceling them only pushes them further towards the truly politically dangerous and racially hostile circle. Ross warns that building a human rights movement is not a safe space, so we assess these various levels of our circles of influence. Calling-in refers to working on your own issues before you can address the issues in others. It means developing deep empathy and compassion for people's experiences, their differences of opinion, and for where they might be in terms of political correctness. We can have differing ideologies and have arguments, but publicly shaming them will only alienate that person.

Ross understands that engaging in the practice of calling-in means that we first need to detoxify our "culture of perfectionism." She warns of alienating people with the pursuit of political purity or political correctness. We cannot take away someone else's pain by being their "advocate"—what she refers to as a practice of pivotal deflection. For example, white people say how we cannot have a meeting unless there is a person

40. King, "Where Do We Go from Here?"

of color present, but it really signifies people wanting to show how "woke" they are. She also problematizes the "savior" complex vs. helping people find and offer their own voices and perspectives. She disparages leftists who outwardly state their solidarity with indigenous people to give them their land, when they may have zero plans to give them their land back! She pleads for us to avoid the "woke" competition—fearing that we will be castigated or canceled if we say the wrong thing. People who engage in toxic "wokeness"—"down with the CAUSE"—sabotage their own happiness because they are so obsessed with their anger and the cesspool of hunting for flesh to castigate. She asks us to reflect on whether our "woke" purpose is making the world crueler than the way we found it.

Calling-in means deep listening to people with other viewpoints, avoiding toxic online communities, and certainly not destroying your own happiness with unrestrained anger. Calling-in means engaging in practices of joy and happiness, not hostility and toxicity in our desire for politically correct perfection. In summarizing the words of Audre Lorde, we do not have to be the same to engage in the same struggle. Our differences do not have to eclipse the goal of human rights care and our togetherness.

Liberals are called 90percenters. That is, we share 90% similar world views. The problem Ross sees is that we want to turn them into 100%ers. When we desire to convert people to adopt my beliefs, it is equivalent to running a cult. Trying to turn the 90%ers into the 100%ers is forced conversion. It is dangerous and harmful. Ross then names the 75%ers, who are the people that are repelled by our lexicon. An example of the 75%ers is the Girl Scouts organization who work towards girls' and women's empowerment. When we try to turn them into 90%ers, we can work in a way that does not involve shaming or calling them out, but in a way that calls them in to help with the work we can do together. 50%ers are those who may be religiously conservative or be a part of conservative institutions but have the values that the 90percenters can understand. Ross gives her parents as an example, as her father was in the military and her mother is an evangelical Christian. Her parents had values that they transmitted to their eight children, yet they could not understand the things their children did. If Loretta Ross speaks to them in a manner that contextualizes their own values, then her parents can feel she is not forcing her values onto them. We want to approach calling-in so that we stand with others without forcing others to adopt our values or feeling forced to adopt others' values. Talking to somebody does not mean they have to agree with you. What is of concern about the 50% is that they are very vulnerable to being recruited by the right because of being called-out. That is why practices of care need to involve practices of calling-in the 50percenters. In working from 90% to 50% circle of influence, Ross suggests the following:

- Don't overstate the harm
- Take their suffering seriously
- Challenge those narratives viewed only through a trauma/victim lens
- Offer factual explanations for their suffering
- Normalize a calling in culture
- Create sense of joy and belonging to human rights movement
- Use examples that resonate with their lived experiences that reinforce their positive values
- No name-calling or call-out tactics by weaponizing your knowledge or language

In laying out the diagram, Ross points out that our greatest mistake is that we do not work with the 90—75%ers who can be our allies. A strategy of coalition building is that the 75%ers can influence the 50%ers. They can possibly have the 50%ers influence the 25%ers.

Ross then defines those with whom we do not have much in common, yet who can still have hope to be "called-in:" the 25%ers. We 90%ers do not have much in common with the 25%. They are in our families, communities, law enforcement, etc. Our world views are planets apart; how we define freedom is radically different. When we start with such radically different world views, it is difficult to have any sort of common ground. We all learn from our mistakes and from our relationships, and Loretta knows from experience that the 25% group can still be "called in." We can talk to them about human rights through the values of patriotism that they understand, such as how the government uses this group and has lied to them about various issues. There is a possibility that the 25% can have an impact on the 0. At the same time, we 90%ers probably should not try to influence the 0. Ross then defines the 0%ers as the fascists, who need to be contained. With this group, the best that we can do is to neutralize their threat. Our biggest mistake is to have it go the other way, allowing the 50% and 25% be recruited by the Right.

Conclusion

Cancel culture is a barbaric practice reminiscent of the selling of human flesh and public viewings of flagellation that have been transmogrified in our neoliberal world as part of the ongoing commodification of beings and bodies. The greatest benefactors of the cancel culture are the media and social media moguls, such as the starters of twitter, facebook, google, etc.

Ta-Nehisi Coates point out:

> Thus any sober assessment of this history must conclude that the present objections to cancel culture are not so much concerned with the weapon, as the kind of people who now seek to wield it. Until recently, cancellation flowed exclusively downward, from the powerful to the powerless. But now, in this era of fallen gatekeepers, where anyone with a Twitter handle or Facebook account can be a publisher, banishment has been ostensibly democratized.[41]

We are coopted and complicit in the destruction of truly ethical practices, participating in our own devastation by neoliberal tools of "religious" rituals that have been manipulated for our ruin. Twitter seems to be the main platform of the cancel culture and in looking to nature for our inspiration, do birds chirp to cancel or shame each other? Birds chirp as a way to communicate boundaries and warn of impending danger. In that regard, we should repurpose why we use social media and what needs it fulfills in us to harm others or seek revenge. We should focus on calling-in as a type of warning or communication and concentrate on healing the wounds and reproducing practices that restore justice.

Decoloniality work in human rights does not mean dismantling your colleagues; rather, it refers to disimpacting the structures of violence that impede our human rights. Calling-in means staying connected and doing what we can to help each other so that we can grow in our work together. Calling-in is part of the spiritual assemblage of creating joy in the practices of justice work. Justice work is a life-long journey. We cannot just think the violence and ugliness will end. As Ross so wittily states,

41. Coates, "The Cancellation."

the violence has always been there. It just depends on when you landed as to how much you will see and how much you can help to restore and repair justice in the world. At the same time, miracles are not reserved for myths of enchantment.

In a *New York Times* article, Nicholas Kristof discusses the transformative calling-in and empathic listening practice of Daryl Davis.[42] Davis's work centers on the practice of compassionate, supportive listening to his "enemies," (i.e., K.K.K. members). In cultivating a respectful listening to white supremacists, he has been able to respond to them in calm ways that debunks the myths to which white supremacists have been held captive. His work demonstrates what Ross has also been doing with white supremacists and sexual offenders: calling-in the enemy with thoughtful listening and conversation. This "conversion" of ideological belief is more magical than any story involving religious enchantment. While it may sound like a miracle, Ross and Davis have proven that conversion from hate—and societal healing—does happen with the patience it requires to engage in truly deep, careful listening and concern to the story and the story-teller.

Calling-in practices can be religious (*religare*) conversions in that the practices work to bind us in our togetherness. In that regard, they are conversations for liberation within a human rights framework that reproduces and restores justice. The roots of religion, *religare*, means to tie or bind together. The *religare* of this project is a common project of all of us. No one religious tradition or culture owns forgiveness—or any practice of forgiveness, as the previous chapter explicated. Instead, we value the shared interdependence of ideas, thoughts, and practices that bring communities together to build on the human rights work of the beloved community and repair harms that bring justice to our world.

42. Kristof, "How Can You Hate?"

lingering day
the approach of spring
comes to light
     —Tom Painting

PART TWO

*Transgressive Boundaries, Bodies,
& Liberative Practices of Care*

4

The Facemask as an Affective Agent of Transformation

COVID-19 and Beyond

Jen Ham

Unmasking Fear

"Their faces hidden behind black bandannas and hoodies, about one hundred anarchists and antifa—'anti-fascist'—members barreled into a protest Sunday afternoon in Berkeley's Martin Luther King Jr. Civic Center Park," reports The *Washington Post* in 2017,[1] two years before the first COVID-19 case and the beginning of the mass co-opting of facemasks. In 2017, the most prominent use of the facemask was by the antifa movement as a part of their "black-block" uniform of unmarked black clothing and facial coverings. Antifa gained mass media attention beginning in early 2017 in response to the Trump administration's intensely divisive political climate. Antifa members were brought to action by the growing visibility and public validation of white nationalism and fascism. The *Washington Post* article (associated with the quote above) goes on to itemize antifa's violent actions:

---

1. Swenson, "Black-Clad Antifa."

A pepper-spray-wielding Trump supporter was smacked to the ground with homemade shields. Another was attacked by five black-clad antifa members, each windmilling kicks and punches into a man desperately trying to protect himself. A conservative group leader retreated for safety behind a line of riot police as marchers chucked water bottles, shot off pepper spray and screamed, "'Fascist go home!'"[2]

This is characteristic of how the media typically covers antifa, emphasizing the movement's violence and destruction. Similar news reports since 2017 refer to antifa as a domestic terrorist organization,[3] furthering public associations of antifa and their black-block uniforms with suspicion and fear.

Antifa—understood broadly as an affiliation of people activating "an illiberal politics of social revolutionism" against the Far Right[4]—use mostly non-violent tactics, which range from peaceful protests to social media posts. The media's focus on antifa's acts of violence, however, worked to strengthen fear of the facemask through its association with violence. This recent history, connecting fearful perceptions of antifa with facemasks, has been exacerbated by even more recent history whereby masked QAnon conspirators—ironically first believed to be antifa—stormed the US capitol on January 6, 2021.[5] This most recent sensational use of masks serves to further conflate facemasks with fear. Yet our negative perception of the facemask is not new but merely *renewed*.

The facemask has an extensive history of negative associations. At least eighteen states have anti-masking laws with the earliest dating back to 1845 in response to farmer uprisings involving tar-and-feathering in New York.[6] Similar anti-mask laws were enacted in direct response to the Ku Klux Klan, who typically concealed their faces when "terrorizing, intimidating, or otherwise harassing various minority communities."[7] These laws stand testimony to the nefarious intentions of those utilizing masks, foregrounding our current conceptualization of the mask's involvement in violent or criminal activities. This is not to say that facemasks have not been used by ambivalent wearers nor associated with

2. Swenson, "Black-Clad Antifa."
3. Meyer, "FBI, Homeland Security Warns."
4. Bray, *Antifa*, xvii.
5. Anderson, "Antifa Didn't Storm the Capitol."
6. Ahmed and Pauly, "Wearing Masks at Protests."
7. Ahmed and Pauly, "Wearing Masks at Protests."

non-threatening circumstances (such as by staff in a medical setting or pedestrians in a highly polluted city), but that *in the US context*, the facemask has recently (in the last five years) become associated predominantly with antifa events. If the sighting of a masked figure stimulated a sense of unease and suspicion in anticipation of a mugging, property vandalization or other criminal acts necessitating obscured identity, aggressively violent collective actions by the black blocked Antifa in 2017, and more recently by the January 6th QAnon terrorists, intensified the association of the facemask with suspicious or criminal activity. Yet, since 2017 (despite this most recent use of the facemask for violence in 2021), the meaning of and affective response to the facemask has radically shifted. In the following pages, I examine how such a shift was possible and what might emerge amidst this shift in place of fear and suspicion.

In teasing out the cause of our emotions, Sara Ahmed remarks how "feelings instead take the shape of the contact we have with objects."[8] By this, Ahmed suggests that our perceptions of objects as good or bad, beneficial or harmful, are not perceptions of the object's implicit goodness or badness but rather emotional impressions shaped by "cultural histories and memories."[9] To elaborate her point about emotional reactions to objects, Ahmed invokes the classic example used in psychology of a child's reaction to a bear. Ahmed asks why the child is afraid of the bear. She concludes that the child must already know that the bear is fearsome to the extent that the child—in encountering the bear—already has impressions of the risk of the encounter as informed by cultural histories and memories. Ahmed emphasizes that the bear is not fearsome on its own. She states, "It is fearsome to someone or somebody. So, fear is not in the child, let alone in the bear, but is a matter of how child and bear come into contact."[10] By this, Ahmed means to say that the valence of the encounter as fearsome is a product of our impressions that are, to an extent, social and citational.

Extrapolating these concepts to the facemask, we might interpret that the mask itself is not fearsome. Rather, our anxieties stem from the previous fearsome encounters impressed upon us through events and associations in the past. Where it is unlikely that we as individuals have been witness to violence or crime committed by a masked individual,

8. Ahmed, *The Cultural Politics*, 6.

9. Ahmed, *The Cultural Politics*, 7.

10. Ahmed, *The Cultural Politics*, 7.

media coverage and popular culture representation reproduce these encounters for us (more so due to heightened Antifa activity in the past few years). Through repeated exposure to these reproductions, we take on the impression of fear toward masked individuals.

Yet, our second-hand encounters with masked figures is currently being transplanted by first-hand encounters due to COVID-19 prevention regulations. COVID-19 has destabilized our lives in such a way that where we go, who we are with, and what we are doing has been preceded by the implementation of a mask. Whereas masks and facial coverings have been previously perceived as objects broadly associated with acts of violence or crime and have sparked a sense of suspicion or fear, the facemask in the context of the COVID-19 pandemic has been transformed into an agent capable of positive affect and perhaps even the re-composition of our social bodies. As COVID-19 has subverted our perceptions of the facemask (along with ourselves and each other as mask wearers), a corresponding subversion or rather softening of our bodies' boundaries and surfaces is taking place, making us more impressionable to new contact with—and new orientations—toward each other.

Vulnerability of the Mask

Our feelings and orientations toward the facemask have been reshaped as our contact with the facemask and each other take on new meanings and new practices. Borrowing from J. K. Gibson-Graham's conceptualization of manifesting positive affect through weak theory, I conduct a reparative reading of the mask to extricate what can be learned and brought into being from this process of reshaping. Here, weak theory refers to approaches that, as Gibson Graham articulates, might "welcome surprise, entertain hope, make connection, tolerate coexistence and offer care for the new."[11] Processing a new way of encountering one another as mask wearers, we have the opportunity to create new impressions and orientations.

So then, masked up, how might we address one another? Without the mask, we are vulnerable to infection. The mask reminds us of our vulnerability to each other as potential carriers of the virus, yes, but also it reminds us of our connection to community. In developing a conceptualization of mourning as community, Judith Butler explains how our attachment and vulnerability to others is fundamental to our sense of

---

11. Gibson-Graham, *A Postcapitalist Politics*, 7.

ourselves as socially constituted bodies. Butler further proposes that "a vulnerability must be perceived and recognized in order to come into play in an ethical encounter."[12] Vulnerability depends on norms of recognition. In the context of the pandemic, I find it useful to expand this formula so that acknowledgement of our vulnerability allows us to recognize the vulnerability of others. This recognition of vulnerability serves to help us recognize something deeper. Butler implies as much: "To ask for recognition, or to offer it, is precisely not to ask for recognition for what one already is. It is to solicit a becoming, to instigate a transformation, to petition the future always in relation to the Other."[13] Beyond the recognition of what is—namely our vulnerability to contracting COVID-19—the act of recognition opens up our social bodies to new potentials.

Digging deeper into the generative potentials of leaning into our vulnerability to others, Jasbir Puar invokes the idea of conviviality as an "open materiality of bodies as a Place to Meet."[14] Puar develops conviviality as an "ethical orientation" where bodies come together and dissipate through intensifications and vulnerabilities, insistently rendering bare the instability of the divisions between capacity-endowed and debility-laden bodies.[15] Puar defines capacity as the body's tendency to be affected or affecting (its capacity for change, evolution, transformation, and movement) and debility as incapacity, or the opposite of capacity.[16] She is thus reconceptualizing not only how to "ethically orient" toward others but also how to constitute the Other. Quoting Arun Saldhana, Puar describes an ethical convivial orientation as "letting yourself be destabilized by the radical alterity of the other, in seeing his or her difference not as a threat but as a resource to question your own position in the world."[17] If we can read the mask as making one present with and open to a shared vulnerability and interdependence, might the mask emerge as a force that destabilizes our sense of self in a generative way?

Butler suggests that it is precisely from this point of destabilization that we find stabilization in one another. In "Violence, Mourning, Politics," Butler asserts that grief exposes how our relations with

12. Butler, "Violence, Mourning, Politics," 30.

13. Butler, "Violence, Mourning, Politics," 31.

14. Puar, "Prognosis Time," 168.

15. Puar, "Prognosis Time," 169.

16. Puar, "Prognosis Time," 161–162.

17. Saldhana, *Psychedelic White*, 118, quoted in Puar, "Prognosis Time," 169.

others—with those we have lost or might someday lose—destabilizes the notion of ourselves as autonomous and in control. She states, "we are undone by each other."[18] The "undoing" refers to a realization that our gender, sexuality, or some other element that constitute the self are "a way of being for another or by virtue of another."[19] Therefore, there is a sense of fragmentation when we realize we are not quite ourselves without the Other and the only way to piece ourselves together is by settling into that very dependence as interdependence. Butler insists further that loss and other ecstatic states transport us outside of ourselves, making us keenly aware that we are "constituted and dispossessed by our relations."[20]

Undone as we are, especially now where loss can come from death of a loved one at the hands of the pandemic, from financial insecurity, and from the loss of social freedom due to the pandemic's public health regulations, we realize a need for the other, an interdependence. Butler articulates how community can be reimagined through recognizing that we are "living in a world of beings who are, by definition, physically dependent on one another, physically vulnerable to one another… we are compelled to take stock of our interdependence."[21] Butler suggests that to stick with our grief is to be "returned to a sense of human vulnerability, to our collective responsibility for the physical lives of one another."[22]

What shape does "living with" and "encountering each other" in interdependence take during the pandemic? In *When Species Meet*, Donna Haraway advocates opening oneself up to "becoming with others": "to hold in regard, to respond, to look back reciprocally, to notice, to pay attention, to have courteous regard for, to esteem: all of that is tied to polite greeting, to constituting the polis, where and when species meet."[23] Haraway's definition of species here includes both the proper biological sense of the word and a more abstract interpretation whereby those of a minoritized gender or race, for example, might be thought of as "reduced to type, all Others to rational man."[24] In this sense, when we encounter one another, even if of a different species in the literal sense or otherwise,

18. Butler, "Violence, Mourning, Politics," 13.

19. Butler, "Violence, Mourning, Politics," 13.

20. Butler, "Violence, Mourning, Politics," 14.

21. Butler, "Violence, Mourning, Politics," 16.

22. Butler, "Violence, Mourning, Politics," 19.

23. Haraway, *When Species Meet*, 19.

24. Haraway, *When Species Meet*, 17.

Haraway encourages us to meet the "intersectional gaze," to address the other with response, respect, and recognition across difference. During the pandemic, the concepts of response, respect, and recognition take the form of acknowledging and feeling deeply that our reciprocal mask wearing is a "becoming with [each] other." It is an act of caring for one another, manifesting a deep connection in that mutual care. Where the facemask previously signified a fearful or suspicious encounter during COVID-19, it re-emerged as an object signifying community, connectivity, and hospitality. A convivial orientation toward one another in this way—facilitated and inspired by the COVID-19 facemask—offers the potential for imprinting the radically new impressions of community, connectivity, and hospitality into our social bodies.

The emergence of the facemask here primes us to reconsider our orientations toward each other, and in persuading us to do so, it provides a new physical awareness of our bodies in social spaces. Impressions in the surfaces of social spaces (before the pandemic) were made to accommodate our pre-pandemic, non-mask wearing bodies. I find myself now thinking longingly of these impressions that allowed for freedom of movement, sociability, and intimacy. Now, as our mask-wearing bodies with new impressions try to sink into the pre-pandemic impressions, we find a sort of dissonance or discomfort. What was once comfortable is comfortable no more. The narrow aisles at grocery stores, rows of tightly packed treadmills at the gym, adjacent park benches, and dining spaces crowded with booths and tables are impressions we no longer fit comfortably into. We still occupy these social spaces, but we inhabit them differently. Whereas before the pandemic, the impressions of our social spaces encouraged orientations toward one another, we now orient cautiously away from one another so that these impressions begin to feel awkward to us. It is this feeling of awkwardness, according to Sara Ahmed, that brings awareness back to the surfaces of our bodies and the proximity to other bodies.[25] Perhaps we can consider our physical orientation away from one another as an ethical orientation toward the Other, respecting and responding to the needs of the Other in these public spaces where we meet.

25. Ahmed, *The Cultural Politics*, 148.

Legacy of the Mask

During COVID-19, our individual surfaces and impressions that once differentiated the "I," "we," and "them" are affectively eclipsed by the face-mask. The mask becomes the defining impression that de-territorializes and connects our surfaces and bodies. That is not to say that all of us who wear masks collapse into one, undifferentiated entity. Rather, we are our differentiated selves, other to each other, in our togetherness. The impression of the mask reminds us of our social responsibility to, and dependency on, each other. The mask emerges as a source of connection such that new affects of interdependence and community can circulate.

Disability justice scholars invoke interdependence to talk about accessibility and liberation. These scholars understand interdependence as a way of living that not only allows for needs to be met but also to have needs recognized and embraced. They hold sacred interdependence as "balancing autonomy while being in community."[26] Conceptualized and practiced well before the pandemic, interdependence becomes something we can imagine through the facemask.

Crip Futurity & the Mask

In this essay thus far, I have developed how the transformation of the mask potentiates interdependence and connection by collective coming into being through reciprocal recognition of our vulnerability and destabilization of our subject positions. As a disabled scholar and activist who is influenced by—and is in solidarity with—the disability justice movement, I want to consider a crip politics that might emerge in tandem with this transformative understanding of the mask and our subjectivity. In synthesizing concepts from previous sections, this space is dedicated to imagining how the mask might catalyze an opening that might contribute to crip futurity.

Elsewhere in this essay, I have brought awareness to how the mask reminds us of our bodily vulnerability. We are always in this state of vulnerability but the mask—in the context of the pandemic—brings striking clarity to our health and potential sickness (or articulated in different language: our ability and prospective disability). Teetering between these two states of health or sickness positions us in what I call the dis/ability

---

26. Piepzna-Samarasinha, *Care Work*, 28.

borderlands, which is inspired by Gloria Anzaldua's conceptual work on borderlands. The dis/ability borderland which is always present is emphasized amidst the pandemic and acutely demarcated by the facemask.

When we encounter someone who is disabled, sick, terminally ill, injured, or old, there is an othering that happens but also a recognition. When we see these people, we think "that's not me" but what lurks under that thought is the latent unacknowledged, hanging "yet." In "Living in Prognosis," S. Lochlann Jain suggests, "all of us in American risk-culture live to some degree in prognosis."[27] Here, Jain articulates that we do not live according to the prescribed timeline of normativity but rather by a sort of risk coding of death and illness. Jain emphasizes this concept by explicating how an understanding of our sense of self is constructed in part through health risk statistics: "Statistics seem to present us with a certainty, such as '1 in 207 women who are 35 years old will be diagnosed with Stage III breast cancer.' But it says nothing about who will represent the one, so it also carries the counterfactual hint that it might be somebody else ('why me?')."[28] To Jain's point, the question also extends to "it could have been me." In the same encounter between disabled and abled individuals, there is a returned recognition when the disabled or sick individual asks, "why me?" they are also thinking, "that could have been me," referring to the "that" of health or ability. The encounter holds the past and future in the present: "that could be me" or "that could have been me" implicates retrospective and expectant identification of health or illness and disability. To consider living this way, in prognosis, we begin to realize that we are never really solidly on either side of the dis/abled border: we are never completely healthy nor completely disabled/sick. Instead, we inhabit the "/" in "dis/abled," the borderland of the seemingly mutually exclusive states.

By "seemingly mutually exclusive" I mean to say, more explicitly, neither health nor disability is natural, totalizing, or stable. Disability scholar Rosemarie Garland-Thomson understands disability as—like the categories of race and gender—a cultural system that assigns privilege and resources to those of particular subject positions such as "beautiful, healthy, normal, fit, competent, intelligent" over "sick, deformed, crazy, ugly, old, maimed, afflicted, mad, abnormal, debilitated."[29] No one is one

27. Jain, "Living in Prognosis," 79.
28. Jain, "Living in Prognosis," 85.
29. Garland–Thomson, "Integrating Disability," 5–6.

hundred percent healthy or one hundred percent disabled in this sense. We hold this truth that though we are disabled or sick, that does not necessarily mean that we are also "crazy," "maimed," and "ugly," nor that we are not "intelligent," "fit," or "beautiful" (this logic holds true too for those identified as able-bodied or healthy). Moreover, our positions in the descriptors above are subject to change over time due to cures and treatments or, conversely, due to accidents or infection. Garland-Thomson further articulates, "disability is an identity category that anyone can enter at any time, and we will all join it if we live long enough. As such, disability reveals the essential dynamism of identity."[30] It is precisely in the transgression of this artificial ability/disability binary that we find ourselves as dis/ability borderlanders. According to Anzaldua: "a borderland is a vague and undetermined place created by the emotional residue of an unnatural boundary. It is in a constant state of transition."[31] Most of us are privileged enough that we never have to think about or question the fixity and rigidity of the ability/disability border or ever come to terms with its artificiality. Yet any of us who have experienced unexpected diagnoses or the strain associated with confronting constant ableist systems and structures find ourselves suddenly or sporadically aware of the artificiality of the dis/ability border and sensitive to that emotional residue therein.

There are those of us who have always been aware of being dis/abled borderlanders and there are those who are just now coming to this realization amidst the pandemic. Being legally blind, my days and nights are filled by this awareness as well as by my transgressions. My body is at once both young and old, seeing and blind, beautiful and ugly. I am light and free as I sprint with physical ease around the house until I slam into my blindness and nearly catch my death at the ledge of my family's fireplace. Or I am pretty and fashionable when I press my face up to the mirror and an amalgamated figure of broken shapes as I step too far away from the glass. I—like so many other disabled folk—did not need a pandemic to reveal the instability of my body. I have been asked how I have been changed by COVID-19, but I feel that it is not myself so much as those around me. The pandemic has opened an ontological channel for those traditionally identified as abled to a borderland where they find the dis/abled body is transient.

30. Garland-Thomson, "Integrating Disability," 20.
31. Anzaldua, *Borderlands/La Frontera*, 25.

The COVID-19 facemask has become instrumental in making these individuals realize their dual citizenship in "the kingdom of the well and in the kingdom of the sick."[32] The mask emerges as a sort of badge of passage between healthy/abled and sick/disabled. We put the facemask on to both protect ourselves from those around us who might be infected and to protect others from ourselves as potentially infected individuals. This gesture—of masking up to protect others from us and to be protected from others—positions us simultaneously as both the sick and healthy individual. The facemask, in this sense, is an equalizer in that it is concurrently worn by both sick and healthy folk alike, blurring and destabilizing the boundaries of sick and healthy. Ultimately, wearing the facemask is a physical action that denaturalizes the ideology of the sick/healthy and disabled/abled binaries. Pausing in the action of masking, the snapping of the mask's straps over ears coupled with the friction of cloth sliding over the nose and mouth, we might at times find ourselves feeling strange or awkward and being brought back to the surfaces of our bodies. Despite the ritualized habits and practices of masking for over a year, there are still pauses or hiccups in the normalcy where the presence of the mask (on our face or the faces of others in public spaces or otherwise) seems anew, incredibly peculiar. It is in these moments of peculiarity that our attention is snapped back to the surfaces of our body and embodiments such that we give pause to query the artificiality and instability of the border between sick and healthy or disabled and abled. The facemask creates a portal to the dis/ability borderland as a fluid reality.

As I have argued previously and will reiterate here, we are all borderlanders of dis/ability. Neither disability nor ability are stable in their appearance, behavior, or embodiment; yet popular imagination and social norms would have us think otherwise by projecting reductive stereotypes onto bodies that are never completely disabled/sick or abled/healthy. Stereotypes such as "disabled folk need special care" persist within mainstream culture when in truth, all humans need special care as a condition of humanness. Garland Thomson states this fact simply, "Our bodies need care; we all need assistance to live."[33] The COVID-19 pandemic has reiterated this simple truth while exposing the transient nature of dis/ability. Masking or demasking acts as a glitch that disrupts the grand narrative of the disability/ability binary, making visible and

---

32. Sontag, *Illness as Metaphor*, 3.

33. Garland–Thomson, "Integrating Disability," 22.

reminding us of the dis/ability borderland not only as a place we occupy but also a way to live with and meet each other.

The dis/ability borderland as a way of living and meeting each other brings into being new energetic orientations toward each other. Borderlands, where two or more cultures collide, have often incited conceptualizations of "conviviality." In mobilizing "conviviality" as an analytic tool for complicating subject positions, queer scholar Jasbir Puar foregrounds its conventional use as "relating to, occupied with, or fond of feasting, drinking, and good company – to be merry, festive, together at a table, with companions and guests, and hence, to live with."[34] Interpreted as an attribute and function of assembling, Puar complexifies conviviality as "the futurity enabled through the open materiality of bodies as a Place to Meet."[35] As the COVID-19 facemask has made the dis/ability borderland more visible, it is more salient now than ever to imagine how a convivial orientation toward one another might materialize at the dis/ability borderland.

As developed more fully earlier in this essay, Donna Haraway crystalizes this branch of conviviality as a "polis where and when species meet."[36] Recall that Haraway's definition of species is both the proper biological sense of the word and a more abstract interpretation. In this sense, when we encounter each other in the dis/ability borderland, we may be approaching one another as different "species" each with our own unique dis/abled embodiments. Encountering each other in this meeting place, Haraway posits, "is to enter the world of becoming with, where who and what are is precisely what is at stake."[37] The dis/ability borderland emerges as a convivial place to meet where we—simultaneously sick and healthy, disabled, and abled, intelligent and mad—come into being as borderlanders together.

Further putting into words what comes into being at this, and other borderland(s), Gloria Anzaldua expresses a sense of mysterious and generative energies manifesting at the juncture of a borderland: "I have the sense that certain 'faculties'—not just in me but in every border resident . . . and dormant areas of consciousness are being activated, awakened."[38]

---

34. Puar, "Prognosis Time," 168.

35. Puar, "Prognosis Time," 168.

36. Haraway, *When Species Meet*, 19.

37. Haraway, *When Species Meet*, 19.

38. Anzaldua, *Borderlands/La Frontera*, 19.

She explains these emerging "faculties" as "the capacity to see in surface phenomena the meaning of deeper realities, to see the deep structure below the surface."[39] Anzaldua is describing is a deeper kind of looking in a more meaningful way such that we simultaneously look at, look through, and look into each other in profound recognition. Looking in this way is both powerful and generative, activating Butler's solicitation of a becoming.

Catalyzed by this gaze of recognition, there is an opening up of the meaning of the faculties. Anzaldua states, "there is a deeper sensing that is another aspect of this faculty. It is anything that breaks into one's everyday mode of perception, that causes a break in one's defenses and resistance, anything that takes one from one's habitual grounding, causes the depths to open up, causes a shift in perception."[40] This faculty, conceived at the joining of dis/ability, tenderizes us to one another, encouraging us to soften our defenses and resistance to each other and to welcome the "open materiality" of one another's bodies as Puar so eloquently phrased it. Ultimately, meeting at the dis/ability borderland is a recognition of one another as bodies expressing various embodiments and temporalities of ability/health and disability/sickness to bring into being future conviviality.

At every encounter with one another, we become aware of our borders. Do we meet as fellow borderlanders or as neighbors across borders? When one is so totally enmeshed in their feelings of health or sickness, it is hard to hold in consciousness a dual belonging to that which is not corporeally felt in that immediate moment. Yet, COVID-19 has offered us this silver lining that is a glimpse into the fluidity of our embodiments. The facemask is integral to these snapshot realizations, providing peculiarity to the mundanity so that we might find ourselves estranged from the social norms of disability and ability. It is not too bold to hope that repeated exposure to these moments—where we are able to perceive dis/ability borderland—will gradually cultivate the sort of faculty Anzaldua refers to and which might, over time, build up a convivial orientation toward one another.

39. Anzaldua, 60.

40. Anzaldua, *Borderlands/La Frontera*, 60.

Conclusion

COVID-19 has transformed our affective response to the facemask (and one another as mask wearers) from one of fear and suspicion to connectivity and community so that each time we put on the facemask we assume (or resume) the impressions of recognition, interdependence, and conviviality. Even in an elsewhere beyond the pandemic, we might maintain our new impressions and orientations toward others, extending past the use of the mask and toward our new sensibilities to welcome crip folk, queer folk, transnational folk, other Other folk. As a thought experiment, this chapter aspired to *inspire into being*—to embed into our cell memory—new ways of orientating toward one another, with and beyond the mask.

autumn sunset
a blackbird steals
the last seed
      —Madeleine Moon-Chun

5

Virtual Practices of Care

Rituals of Hope for Inner Peace and Communal Wholeness during the Pandemic

LAHRONDA WELCH LITTLE

Introduction

HOW DO WE REDISCOVER our center in a world shaken to its foundations by a pandemic? Given the existence of the pandemic of systemic racism in the United States, some would question the existence of a "center" prior to COVID-19. While there are many reasons to examine the locus of one's "center," in a matter of months the ethos of the entire globe had changed, and the speed with which we have had to make adjustments has been, in many cases, disconcerting. I imagine that we will not know the depth of our disorientation for quite some time. Be that as it may, presently, there are signs of resilience in the creative expressions of people that provide sources of healing for the whole person—body, mind, soul, spirit—and the community. Rather than languish within the confines imposed upon our personal bodies and communities by COVID-19 and the viral iterations of systemic oppression,[1] people have created ways to tran-

1. The viral iterations of systemic oppression refer to social media hashtags, such as #BlackLivesMatter and #BreonnaTaylor.

scend the grisliness of the present moment. What is more, perceptions of borders between countries, systems, and people groups have been effectively dissolved by the twin pandemics of systemic racism and the coronavirus making interreligious and intercultural approaches to health and well-being even more vital now than in the recent past. The typical expressions, rites, and rituals of life are no longer normative, and society has been called to dig deeper into the well of consciousness to rediscover hope, cultivate peace, and promote wellbeing.

In this chapter, I draw on the work of African traditionalists, philosophers, and healers for insights to the phenomenon of adaptation when normative ways of being are no longer accessible. The theoretical concepts of practical theologian Emmanuel Y. Lartey and womanist thinker Monica A. Coleman inform the ways in which practices and ritual mediate healing and transformation in self and community. Then, I examine the ritual traditions of the Dagara community of West Africa as a source of inspiration which offer possible causeways for the arduous shift from normative, hegemonic praxes of spiritual care to postcolonial spiritual praxes. I also consider the energizing force of embodied *knowing* for the purpose of communal awareness towards the greater good and describe the development and promotion of these endeavors as virtual, virtuous, and virtuoso. Finally, I briefly discuss virtual, spiritual practices I created as sources for—and the facilitation of—novel forms of individual and communal healing. These practices are wellsprings of comfort and healing for individuals, families, and communities through the Facebook small group called "Holistic Wellness," the curated video discussions on health and well-being via YouTube channel "Be Well, Be Whole," and workshop gatherings hosted by "Per Ankh Wellness."

The Virtual, Virtuous, Virtuoso

The cadence of life is a brilliant cacophony of energy, sound, movement, and knowing. These elements are present in every cell and molecule of existence. Energy, the unseen palpable catalyst of all life functions, operates in and around us, "animating and pervasive."[2] This energy, of which Somé refers to as fire, "is in the water that runs, it is in the trees, the rocks, the earth, and in ourselves,"[3] and to ethically harness energy (or fire) is to

---

2. Somé, *Healing Wisdom,* 209.

3. Somé, *Healing Wisdom,* 209.

also understand that energy "is the element that keeps people connected to their purpose. . . ."[4] I submit that these connections are confirmed and affirmed by the sounds of words, music, nature, and more. Sound has a definite effect on matter, which is demonstrated in the study of cymatics.[5] Sound is not only about hearing. It is also about the effect and experience of sound, particularly the healing effects of sound. "Cymatics, from its widest purview, ultimately teaches us that we are limitless beings with immense creative and healing powers."[6] Further still, we are moved by sound. Lartey explains as such, "For African religious practitioners, the spiritual and the material are fused. The unseen and the seen realms are related. The natural and the divine are in constant interaction."[7] Lartey continues that our bodies contain wisdom through which healing for the community can be mediated. Embodied hermeneutics command that we "pay attention to the body and its messages to us in movement and artistic performances" because of God's presence as the Word became Flesh.[8] In the flow and movement of the body, we come to *know* our place and purpose in the world. This *knowing* is germane to the practice of ritual which leads one towards the very center of *life*. In this sense, life holds the breath of being and the substance of peace, health, and wholeness, throughout and beyond one's own existence. *Knowing* is not necessarily a cognitive practice of the mind or an exercise of logical choice-making. *Knowing* emerges out of the subconscious mind in how we connect and interact with all beings. During the height of COVID-19, by necessity, we were constrained to harness the interplay of energy, sound, movement, and knowing—the threads of our connections to self and to one another—from the physical to the virtual world.

Ways of knowing have never been exclusively physical, verbal, or written. History bears the value of dreams, visions, and astronomy as sources of knowledge which serve to propel humanity forward in the

4. Somé, *Healing Wisdom*, 208.

5. Hans Jenny coined the term *cymatics*, which he describes in the following way, "If a name is required for this field of research, it might be called cymatics (to kyma, the wave; ta kymatika, matters pertaining to waves, wave matters). This underlines that we are not dealing with vibratory phenomena in the narrow sense, but rather with the effects of vibrations. Our documentation is primarily concerned with the experimental demonstration of phenomena in the acoustic and lower ultrasonic range." Jenny, *Cymatics*, 20.

6. Beaulieu, "A Commentary on Cymatics," quoted in Jenny, *Cymatics*, 13.

7. Lartey, "Knowing Through Moving," 102.

8. Lartey, "Knowing Through Moving," 111.

interest of progress. Through this lens, "virtual" may refer more broadly to that which is unknown or unfamiliar. Navigation through virtual spaces commands creativity and calls for deep listening and courage to move through the darkness of the unknown. There is an "ethical obligation"[9] attached to one's movement through virtual spaces which has implications for not only the individual, but also the community and the environment. The process of discovering the ethical obligation in virtual spaces is necessarily a virtuous act. "Virtue," for some, is a complicated term wrought with patriarchal expectations that tend to essentialize and ostensibly oppress people to roles which do not necessarily promote the greater good. At the core of conventional virtue ethics is the belief that the performer of the virtuous act is the authority by which an act is deemed to be right. Alternatively, virtue that stems from individual and communal ethical obligation invites polyvocal, multidimensional encounters. To operate virtually and bear the stress of navigation through the unknown, virtue is requisite, and it is inclusive of the characteristics of humility, patience, empathy, and compassion for self and others. The construction of an interactive, synergistic description of virtue is to refute theological concepts such as "sacrifice, servanthood, and unmerited suffering" and the "moral instructions affiliated with them" imposed by patriarchal colonialism.[10] I employ the use of the word "virtue" as a critique of socio-eco-cultural-political-economic hegemony in favor of an inclusive sharing of communal responsibility and care.

When one thinks of a *virtuoso*, one typically thinks of a musician. The virtuoso is extraordinarily skilled and adept, some would say a progeny. Though this meaning could easily be applied to one's ability to adapt to a virtual work environment and other virtual, unknown spaces, I also employ the name 'virtuoso' to one who seeks and offers silence, sanctity, and salvation in a world that has changed in the blink of an eye. The virtual, virtuous, virtuoso creates permeable (rather than confining) spaces that foster imagination, innovation, and the transference of ritual practice. The effective care of persons amid the pandemic calls for *virtual,*

9. I borrow the notion of ethical obligation from Carl Jung and his text *Memories*. He surmises that there is an ethical obligation that evolves out of one's dreams. For Jung, dreams are not without meaning. There is an obligation to reflect on one's dreams as they may well be sources of healing for the dreamer, and consequently, the community. The broad steps to interpret dreams and learn one's ethical obligation are, 1) record the details of the imaginations, visions, or dreams, 2) critically analyze visions drawing on outside experiences, and 3) outline ethical conclusions.

10. Harris, *Gifts of Virtue*, 49.

virtuous, and *virtuoso* skill sets. Lartey describes the creative person as one who

> has inner freedom that is borne of confidence in different spheres and fields of knowledge. Such confidence comes from a variety of sources. The creative person is neither afraid of the sanctions of an authority nor has anxiety at the gaze of any legitimizing forerunner. Creativity is mature postcolonializing activity.[11]

I find Lartey's treatment of postcolonial activity insightful and helpful for the present time and all people who must survive under constraint. Our daily practices and rituals are meant to serve the needs of people and facilitate the health and wholeness of the community, not the other way around. It is the concept and purpose of ritual practice which remains static; the practices themselves must be flexible and fluid in their constructions in order to address the needs of the context and times. This became abundantly clear when we found ourselves in the throes of a global pandemic.

If rituals are ultimately for the good of the community, how do we preserve rites of passage? How do we celebrate life? How do we honor the dead and usher them into the realm of the ancestors? Out of my own reverie, I decided that in order to maintain some sense of groundedness that I must remain open to the idea of "walking in the dark."[12] Typically, darkness is not a thing to be desired. In the dark, we are apt to bump and stumble into things, especially in unfamiliar places. Our anxieties are aroused when the busy-ness of light is suddenly blown out, and we have only ourselves and our dreams with which to contend.

The unknown-ness of the dark, however, is not an indictment of our existence. Nor does it have to be a sentence to loneliness and meaninglessness. Through rituals of healing and wholeness, darkness can be an invitation to share in one another's suffering, holding on to the belief that we are never alone. Such faith opens the way for creative and faithful expressions of individual and communal health and wholeness. Though it seems I make a distinction between ritual and religious practice, I only name the two separately in order to acknowledge the nuances of differing cultural perspectives. Henceforth, I use the terms interchangeably to suggest that within our daily practices, one discerns the divine throughout

---

11. Lartey, *Postcolonializing God*, 128.

12. I borrow this phrase from Barbara Brown Taylor. See Taylor, *Learning to Walk*.

the interactions of life which can be ritualized for communal well-being and wholeness.

A holistic view of ritual practices considers a recognition of the person as an integrated body, mind, soul, and spirit; interdependency of all beings; an intention to be well and to be whole; and finally, that ritual practices are a work of the spirit. The power of ritual is in the subtle folds and movements of the practice itself which oftentimes go unnoticed until the ritual is over, and transitions and transformations have taken place. The silent participants of ritual we call time and space bear the weight and luminance of meaning—the spirit of practice. Like the trinity of Christian theology, the activities, ways of being, and ethos of an inclusive and integrated community are barely discernible. This is not to say that everyone is saying and doing the same things, quite the contrary. It does mean, however, that commonalities and differences are expected and honored which is a governing principle of what it means to be *in community*.

The cultural paradigms of western and African culture are not necessarily concrete, nor do they have to be. Somé explains that the philosophy of the Dagara is one of "inclusiveness and flexibility" and that it is better to acknowledge all of life rather than to pretend that other cultures do not exist, thereby, denying the humanity of the other.[13] The restrictions imposed upon us by the pandemics of COVID-19 and systemic racism have simultaneously revealed and blurred the lines of society to create a global collective. Inefficient healthcare systems, police violence with impunity, and inconsistent public health regulations reveal the depths of the marginalization of the Black community and other people of color. These same pandemics dissolve false transnational barriers which create multicultural modes of ritual practice and activism such as the case in the fight to #EndSARS.

The conundrums presented by COVID-19—its curses and opportunities—have thrust society into an identity crisis punctuated by swift, enforced changes in ritual practices. Our typical traditions of worship, death, birth, marriage, learning, and more have been disrupted by this invisible virus that is quickly mutating and seeking its newest hosts. The typical ways in which one makes meaning of and connections to the world have existential and epistemological implications, and how one shows up in the world and one's awareness of their alive-ness is mediated in daily

13. Somé, *Healing Wisdom*, 16.

practices and rituals. Further still, COVID-19 has called us to reckon with the constructions of socio-religious practices that have tended to govern how we engage with self, the other, and the divine, because now these same practices are potentially harmful. Now is the time for societal norms, beliefs, and ideologies to be re-examined, dismantled, and recon-structed—including the basis of our theologies. A postcolonial theology necessitates postcolonial practices.

The utility of ritual practices of people, particularly marginalized and oppressed people, is in its ability to assist in the navigation of hege-monic systems, and as it were, life under constraint. Lartey teaches that the strategies employed by those who have been forcibly colonized are strategic in nature and are, hence, a praxis which carries the intention of internal transformation first then society. Likewise, postcolonializing practices are spiritual, political, and holistic practices. Spiritual practices in the African tradition are distinctive ways of knowing because of the interconnectedness of the material and the immaterial.

Monica A. Coleman, in her text *Making a Way Out of No Way*, speaks of health and wholeness through the lens of a postmodern wom-anist theology as a strategic method that focuses on social justice in local communities. For Coleman, salvation comes through the grassroots ef-forts of communities that engage in ethical activities. Postmodern wom-anist methodology, praxis, and critique are realized, embodied creativity. Thus, postmodern womanism is a strategy for wholeness and justice that embodies a deep desire to recover or overcome that which is destroyed by evil. It also holds that while recovery is not always possible, "survival and quality of life are."[14] For Coleman, then, postmodern womanist theology is a constructive theology that seeks to counter "[evil]."[15] This is work that employs the body, spirit, and the mind—a method M. Shawn Copeland calls *critical cognitive praxis*, which is also a holistic methodology in that it effectively holds together intellect and practicality while also disrupting the status quo. Copeland explains that cognitive praxis "denotes the dy-namic activity of knowing."[16] Creative transformation along with critical cognitive praxis are in the quest for reimagining a ritualized world in the midst of a global pandemic and for creative futures.

14. Coleman, *Making a Way*, 85.

15. Coleman, *Making a Way*, 85.

16. Copeland, "A Thinking Margin," 227.

Personal, Communal, and Systemic Awareness

Every morning the elements of air, earth, water, and fire weave their way into my consciousness. In meditation, I fill my body with the moving spirit of air. On my morning walk, each step is a reminder of my own sense of groundedness and connection with the earth. Cleansing and refreshing water courses through and over my body, and warmth filters throughout my home as I open all the blinds and enjoy breakfast. Such a terreous awareness reminds me of my grandparents' garden where I spent much of my childhood watching and contemplating the cycles of life. This also calls to mind the human propensity to establish daily rhythms and rituals to maintain a sense of normalcy and to connect with that which is beyond myself. In doing so, individual practices and norms intersect with rituals of the other to create, sustain, or disrupt the ethos of a community. Said differently, one's ways of being and doing are never separate, isolated, or disconnected occurrences. Malidoma Somé reifies this reality when he asks, "Why is it that social responsibilities are insepa-rable from rituals?"[17] I am not sure exactly how to answer that question; it is rather difficult to tease apart the humanistic tendrils of intention, habit, consciousness, and their impending results. Yet, when I consider how social gatherings, such as concerts, worship services, and parties, have been upended by COVID-19, Somé's question immediately becomes an imperative. Social responsibility and ritual *must* be inseparable, and for good or bad, all community members do not perceive this obligation in the same way. Could it be that the nexus of social responsibility and ritual resides in one's capacity to create rituals that embrace an ethic of care? Furthermore, in a world of sentient beings who are forced into a state of physical social distance, can virtual spaces be a source of meaningful connectedness? And if so, how? Air, earth, water, and fire are inextricably tied to all of existence, and how one perceives their connections has deep implications for how one interacts with others.

Our daily rituals *are* religious practices which set the tone and tenor of communal life and worship and orients the practitioner towards the divine. Rituals are not merely episodic events that signal the start or end of the day, but they also have the potential to turn us towards and connect us to deeper meanings at the heart of human, ecological, and cosmologi-cal encounters. They help us to set our intentions toward ourselves and others. Somé's question about social responsibility and ritual presupposes

17. Somé, *Ritual*, 11.

an awareness of one's interconnectedness and interdependence within a community, and rightfully so, since he asks the question with respect to his familial bond within the Dagara people of Burkina Faso.[18] I submit that the Dagara have much to teach those of us reared in westernized cultures about proximity and connection with others, nature, and the divine through our daily activities. Somé goes on to make an interesting distinction between "subsistence activity," such as farming and hunting with that of ritual in that "subsistence work links humans together while ritual links humans to the gods or God."[19] Despite this distinction, activities of subsistence and ritual in Dagara culture are barely discernible from one another. For instance, Somé explains, "At least once a day we had something to say to our ancestors."

At least once a day a word is addressed to the shrine of nature, be it at home before undertaking a journey to the farm or to another village, be it in the farm before working at it."[20] The ritual of communication with the ancestors as it relates to—and in tandem with—daily life embodies the prayer and hermetic axiom, "as above so below."[21] As well, I suggest what is known in the mind and spirit is also known in the body.

Theologian Mercy Amba Oduyoye avers, "Our lives are hidden in God."[22] These paradigmatic words suggest that not only do we live life, but we are life, and we must find life. Consequently, begs the questions, what is life and how do we find it? Befittingly, the Jewish Bible creation narrative illumines a pathway for reflection. "So, YHWH fashioned an earth creature out of the clay of the earth and blew into its nostrils the breath of life. And the earth creature became a living being."[23] The beingness of humanity is intertwined with the transcendent breath of the God of creation — the imago dei. Religious practices and daily practices, or rituals as it were, help to discern the yearnings of the soul in the quest for meaning and to present ourselves as images of the divine. These rituals,

---

18. Somé describes the Dagara in this way, "They are a people whose life is determined by what the natural forces in the world require of them. Spread throughout the arid region of present northern Ghana, southern Burkina Faso and the Ivory Coast, this tribe is known by others as the Tribe of Concealment and Magic." Somé, *Ritual*, 11.

19. Somé, *Ritual*, 24.

20. Somé, *Ritual*, 24.

21. Matthew 6:10 (The Message). Three Initiates, *The Kybalion*, 16.

22. Oduyoye, *Hearing and Knowing*, vii.

23. Gen. 2: 7 (The Inclusive Bible: the First Egalitarian Translation).

mediated through the interconnectedness of the material and the immaterial, the body and Spirit, are the way of transcendence — discernment
or *knowing* borne out of one's inner being. Furthermore, as *knowing* is
experienced and expressed through the body, it also permeates the spaces
of community. Undeniably, how we typically know ourselves, one another, and God have been disrupted by COVID-19. Consequently, clergy,
educators, students, and caregivers alike have had to make sharp pivots
in their modes of working and being.

In her seminal text, *Race and the Cosmos*, Barbara Holmes offers a
brief description of Bell's Theorem of Interconnectedness, which in short
postulates, "When two particles that have been paired travel in opposite
directions, measurements indicate a correlation of characteristics that are
indicative of the pair rather than a single element."[24] This theory of "non-
locality," developed by physicist John Stewart Bell (1928-1990), provides
for the interconnection of all living things. Holmes rhetorically employs
the Theorem of Interconnectedness to demonstrate the interweavings
and networks of beings, despite the life-draining and death-dealing activities of society such as wars and systemic racism. Contrarily, by way
of the Theorem of Interconnectedness, what is also true is the efficacy of
life-giving activities that promote well-being, even at a distance. Digital,
virtual spaces of engagement invite fields of spiritual care to transcendent
creativity and innovation which, as Dr. Holmes offers, do not require direct contact. The present context, I suggest, brings into focus the ways
in which society has already existed and operated beyond the realm of
the material. Postcolonial spiritual care practices are inclusive of social
media spaces which function within a framework of a womanist notion
of a "digital ethics of care."[25]

I suggest that a womanist ethic of care is characterized as virtuous
and actionable and acknowledges the sacrality of all beings. Spirituality,
through the lens of care, denotes how we relate to ourselves, others, and
God. How we cultivate those relationships is sacred and occurs through
spiritual practices. The virtues of a womanist ethic of care include genu-
ineness, transparency, respect, equity, trust, and faith. These virtues

24. Holmes, *Race and the Cosmos*, 197.

25. Michelle O'Reilly, Diane Levine, & Effie Law address a digital ethics of care in
their research. It is a novel intellectual concept and praxis that seeks to understand
adolescent digital interactions and how they develop online relationships and friendships. Digital ethics of care uses evidence-based practice and philosophical theories.
See O'Reilly, Levine, and Law, "Applying a 'Digital Ethics of Care.'"

operate to create and fortify healthy communities, which are inclusive and familial. Re-membering and self-actualizing are the fruit of communities which employ a womanist ethic of care. Emerging examples of such communities are demonstrated in the social media platforms of "Holistic Wellness," "Be Well, Be Whole," and "Per Ankh Wellness."

Holistic Wellness

Terreous morning rituals, the traditions of the Dagara, humankind as the imago dei, and scientific theories evince a myriad of possibilities for the sacrality of virtual exploration. The creation of virtual sacred spaces is deeply consequential for the sake of the overall health of people who typically gather in public spaces for worship services, meditation, and other forms of religious ritual expressions. Virtual rituals provide spaces which allow for lament; celebration; activism, and vulnerability. Such a broad range of activities, even online, has implications for how we can cope with the emotional dissonance experienced by many while in quarantine. For these reasons and out of a sense of my vocation in spiritual care, I started a Facebook group called "Holistic Wellness." Online social media groups such as "Holistic Wellness" were created during quarantine as a pivot from physical, social gatherings to virtual communities of care and compassion which help to facilitate wholeness and wellbeing under constraint.[26] The virtual practice of posting affirmations, workout plans, or social commentary on pop culture coalesce to engender ritual creativity, community, and transcendence. "Holistic Wellness," as a ritual response, was borne out of my sense of wellness for myself and acknowledging that my wellness impacts those around me. The reality of the social and physical distancing during the coronavirus pandemic does not negate the reality of our interconnectedness.

"Holistic Wellness" promotes physical, mental, spiritual, social, and ecological health by providing community members the opportunity to participate in and support each other's creative endeavors toward wholeness and survival. For purposes other than wellness and support, the virtual group avoids solicitations, overt politicizing, and proselytizing. The primary focus is to provide support and encouragement for all dimensions of our personhood—mind, body, soul, and spirit.[27]

26. See Little's Facebook group, "Holistic Wellness."

27. Little, "Holistic Wellness."

Be Well, Be Whole

The sheer influence of social media troubles notions of fact, truth, and authority. Who is speaking, what is said, when is it said, from which platforms and perceptions of underlying agendas all have the power to shape and set forth the trajectory of our society. Dr. Holmes submits, "The importance of public discourse about difficult social issues cannot be overemphasized. Public dialogue infuses an issue with energy."[28] She explains further, that ". . . our languages construct worlds that harm and help in particular ways."[29] The YouTube channel "Be Well, Be Whole," created in the spring of 2020 by Dr. Emmanuel Lartey and me, seeks to join the myriad of voices in virtual spaces to discuss and offer spiritual inspirations that deepen one's connections with self, the other, and God. Energized by the heightened awareness of the plight of people of color who have been marginalized, particularly within the healthcare and penal systems of the United States, "Be Well, Be Whole" holds conversations with healthcare and spiritual care providers, scholars, and lay persons to share alternative perspectives on matters that directly impact their lives.

The connections provided through virtual conversations within the framework of a womanist digital ethic of care form ways of knowing in service to communal wholeness. Although "Be Well, Be Whole" is hosted by academics,[30] the platform is not divorced from the everyday rituals and practices of people. With a focus on "being," "Be Well, Be Whole" explores the ways in which people interact under circumstances that threaten *being* and flourishing. These discussions include topics such as: a tribute to Breonna Taylor; perspectives on the COVID-19 vaccination; and how to have difficult conversations with our children regarding the brutal police murders of Black and brown bodies.

Per Ankh Wellness

Prior to the coronavirus pandemic, allopathic modes of care had already begun to provide services virtually. Whereas online services were not a stretch for mental health services because online platforms already existed when the pandemic occurred, physical pre-screenings, support

28. Holmes, *Race and the Cosmos,* 52.

29. Holmes, *Race and the Cosmos,* 52.

30. Dr. Emmanuel Y. Lartey and I are the co-hosts of the YouTube channel, "Be Well, Be Whole."

groups, and complementary and alternative medical (CAM) practitioners struggled to offer efficacious and credible care to patients not stricken with COVID-19. Notwithstanding the influx of unsubstantiated claims made by some, evidence-based CAM studies offer that alternative therapies are necessary because of the prohibitive costs of allopathic drugs; the emergence of more virulent strains; lag time between vaccine development; and mass casualties.[31] Per Ankh Wellness[32] helps to bridge the gap between traditional and CAM therapeutic treatment in that it provides spiritual care in various formats with the goal of personal, communal, and institutional wellness in view.

For the individual and in small group sessions, the spiritual care of persons is addressed holistically—body, mind, soul, and spirit—through a range of services which may be conducted in person or online, e.g., movement and African dance workshops, meditation sessions, and spiritual directions services. Institutional wellness, corporate, church, and academia, is addressed in similar ways and includes workshops which focus on vocational discernment. Like small group sessions and depending on group dynamics, there is any combination of ritual, movement, journaling, workshops, and meditation. By the end of the gathering, the hope is that participants feel connected and gain inspiration and clarity of their own ethical obligations.

Conclusion

The virtual, virtuous, virtuoso transcends and holds space in the tensions between knowing and unknowing; the material and the immaterial; theory and praxis, and the ethical obligations of our times, individually and communally, are determined in the interstices of such tensions. The pandemics of COVID-19 and systemic racism have called us to reassess what we thought was the center of being, and through the elements of energy, sound, movement, and knowing we are able to construct rituals that help us to realign and reconnect with life in more holistic ways. To this end, a womanist ethic of care in a digitized world helps us to re-imagine the function of spiritual care in innovative ways even when the times deeply obscure our ability to interact conventionally. Virtual practices of care derived from our individual and communal ethical obligations

31. Arora et al., "Potential of Complementary."
32. https://www.perankhwellness.com.

foster hope and peace in an otherwise disoriented world, and as interconnected, interdependent beings, made in the image of God, we are never
disconnected from our center.

earth day
a poultice of mud
on the bee sting
       —Tom Painting

6

COVID-19, Violence, and the Rupture of Contemplation

A Comparative Theological Reflection

WON-JAE HUR

We do not pray to receive consolations; we pray in order to realize the truth.
    —SR. TERESA OK

But there is no perception of the visible that is not already imbued with value. And the body itself is a dynamic material domain, not just because it can be 'seen' differently, but because the materiality of the body itself is… volatile.
    —LINDA MARTÍN ALCOFF

MOST PEOPLE OF COLOR living in the United States know what it is like to feel their bodies jolt into sudden alertness at the sight of white bodies, or to notice a general sense of heightened danger and anxiety while living in this society as nonwhite bodies. After the pandemic hit and anti-Asian scapegoating and violence once again spiked in this country, these bodily feelings intensified for me.[1] Throughout my life, I have been grappling in

---

1. On data on COVID-19 and anti-Asian violence, see Jeung, et al. "Stop AAPI Hate National Report 2020–2021." See also Grover, Harper, Langton, "Anti-Asian Hate Crime." Also see the report by the UN Special Rapporteur, on contemporary forms of

one way or another with the trauma of racial violence from my childhood and youth. With COVID-19, I found myself once again gripped by feelings of fear and hyperarousal.[2] My body seemed on the verge of turning against me once again, tightly coiling itself for violence. It was reacting—against my will or ability to control—with seething rage, terror, or both, at the sight of any white body. My body instinctively knows all too well how such bodies can, like a plague, turn at any moment to attack it, on the street, in a park, in a store. Having children or elderly members in one's family intensifies this sense of threat, as racially motivated attackers neither regard them as fully human nor spare them the full brunt of savage force because of their particular vulnerabilities.[3]

The return of traumatic stress in my body is an awakening to the broader truths of the current situation. The context of the violence that so many Asian Americans have experienced after COVID-19 is the resurgence of white supremacist violence under Trump and his followers, anti-Black racism, and capitalist violence against the environment. It is precisely because America is founded on white supremacy, as well as the twin crimes of genocide against Native Americans and enslavement of Black Americans that we have a society and culture that enact racial violence at will against nonwhite bodies. Anti-Asian violence in the time of COVID-19 is another instantiation of white supremacy and American racial hierarchy. In a society that elevates white bodies and culture as superior and normative over nonwhite bodies and cultures, nonwhite bodies always teeter on the edge of utility and expendability. When they no longer serve white bodies' interests, they will be ineluctably reduced to fodder for blame, assault, and annihilation.

COVID-19 is also a consequence of human violence against the environment, a direct consequence of relentless human encroachment on nonhuman habitats, fueled by insatiable greed that lies at the heart of global capitalism.[4] The dramatic increases in meat consumption,

---

racism, racial discrimination, xenophobia, and related intolerance.

2. On symptoms of post-traumatic stress disorder, see Herman's classic work *Trauma and Recovery*. See also Van der Kolk, *The Body Keeps the Score*.

3. The killing of 12-year old Tamir Rice; the repeated instances of police officers using pepper spray and excessive physical force on children of color, such as the seven-year old son of Mando Avery during a nonviolent protest in Seattle; the stabbing of a two-year old Burmese toddler and his six-year brother at a Sam's Club in Texas; or the high rate of physical assaults on elderly Asian persons in places like New York City and San Francisco during COVID-19 are examples that have received press coverage.

4. Arora and Mishra, "COVID-19 and Importance," 117-18; Harrison et al., "Tropical Peatlands."

deforestation, pollution, and natural habitat loss have created the right conditions for zoonotic epidemics. Moreover, the on-going consumption and expenditure that human bodies, corporations, and nations have inflicted against the environment is intimately linked to systemic violence against indigenous peoples, with women of color bearing the brunt of it.[5] The campaign to enslave and destroy indigenous peoples and cultures has been rooted in colonialist and patriarchal epistemic violence that dehumanizes them and justifies their destruction. As many decolonial scholars and activists have articulated; environmental, gender, and racial violence go hand in hand.

Facing these truths, I often feel that I am on the verge of losing myself to rage, fear, or hate. What my body feels these days is a pervasive sense of threat, and it is not an exaggeration because encounters with white-bodied people who feel entitled to glare, verbally confront, or physically assault have been common in my experience. With trauma, there is always a high chance that such a run-in can turn violent. In this state, I am seeking a way out of the desire to embrace violence for violence. I am searching for inner freedom and the capacity for love and compassion that will both transcend this ecology of violence and strengthen me to act for others. But how?

Trauma and pain have always driven me to prayer, specifically Christian contemplative prayer and non-Christian meditation practices. Both Christian and non-Christian meditation practices have been necessary to survive and to deepen the awakening that suffering is a bridge to empathy and solidarity. Both have also been essential in my desire and effort to find a practice that I can personally contribute to addressing racial, environmental, and other forms of violence.

For many people, Christian contemplation may not be the first thing that comes to mind when thinking about Christian resources for healing racial violence. Yet, both contemplative prayer and systemic violence concern what Linda Martín Alcoff calls "perceptual practices." In *Visible Identities*, Alcoff construes racialization and racism as perceptual practices based on physically visible identities.[6] Perception of race is a learned ability based on visible differences. Perceptual practices—subconsciously and consciously learned ways of perceiving certain bodies according to specific values about race—are somatically patterned and habituated

---

5. International Labor Office, *Indigenous Peoples and Climate Change.*

6. Alcoff, *Visible Identities*, 186–8.

through cultural, interpersonal, and institutional forms. Because perceptual practices are bodily habituated within a white supremacist social and economic system and milieu like ours, they become tacit and operate subconsciously. The underlying interpretive process are attenuated to such a degree that racist perceptions become naturalized. In other words, in a society founded on and continues to propagate the supremacy of white bodies and culture, racist interpretations of nonwhite bodies and cultures become understood as natural descriptions and explanations of nonwhite inferiority in relation to whiteness.

In one sense, the whole Christian contemplative path is directed at dismantling such perceptual practices to realize the truth. Contemplative practice is different from the notion of "mysticism" that focuses on the content and nature of special individual religious experiences. Following Sarah Coakley's explanation, contemplative practice involves self-control of desires, ecclesial and liturgical participation, and progressive surrender to divine love.[7] In the influential Carmelite stream of the tradition, contemplative practice moves towards a wordless loving union with God, which is understood to be a pure gift of the divine and not something that we acquire by our effort of will. The movement toward union involves a process of "purgation." Purgation breaks down one's habituated mode of perceiving and knowing oneself and the world, which is founded on attachment to sensible objects and their valuation in terms of satisfaction of human desires, both affective and cognitive.[8]

The basic problem that the contemplative process addresses is one of priority. What determines our knowing, feeling, and loving is sense-based apprehensions, unmoored from a prior and conscious grounding in knowledge of the divine. The mode of being that emerges from this basis is determined by "attachment" to the senses and its objects. Hence, the formation of human love is always derivative of "the world"; that is, the nexus of socio-political, economic, and environmental relations, interactions, and valuations that constitute and drive our mode of being. For the Christian contemplative tradition, we are more than the sum of such factors and attachments. The contemplative process dismantles the patterns of attachment and redirects to the divine itself that impulse

---

7. Coakley, *The New Asceticism*, ch. 4.

8. From Origen onward, it has become standard to frame Christian contemplative prayer as comprising phases of purgation, illumination, and union. John of the Cross uses this framework even as he develops it in new ways. See John of the Cross, *The Collected Works*; and Louth, *The Origins*.

to apprehend an object. Precisely because the divine does not have the status of an object, the ordinary modes of apprehension falter in contemplative prayer, and that entrance into the divine leads initially to a sense of intense absence and affective aridity. Yet when the habituated patterns of attachment are broken down enough, the person begins to develop greater capacity for receiving divine love within the depth of her being (the "illumination" stage), enjoying greater freedom from the whole dynamic of grasping at and holding onto sense impressions and affective and cognitive activity. With the expansion of one's being, a person can relate to the self and the world based on divine love as the primary mover instead of "the world."

To connect this with perceptual practices of violence, contemplation entails decoupling external stimuli and habituated patterns of response, so that no social or cultural system becomes the primary giver of value and meaning and eclipses the centrality of unlimited love. Instead, contemplation aims to turn the usual stimuli-reaction pattern inside out, so that divine love becomes the primary impetus for response and the ground for perceptual acts. If racial and environmental violence enact perceptual practices that apprehend nonwhite bodies and nonhuman life forms and habitats as inferior and exploitable; contemplative practice is a potent antidote, as one of its major aims is taking apart and transforming habits of perception and cognition. Closer to my skin, contemplative practice creates space for my nervous system so that it does not become hijacked by the stimuli and reaction cycle specific to trauma and cools the fires that threaten to make rage and hatred my default way of relating to the world.

While there are some exceptions, I have found that churches and Christian groups rarely apply Christian contemplative insights to the problem of racial violence and its effects.[9] In my experience, the make-up of many Christian contemplative groups are overwhelmingly white and upper-middle class. There is almost no effort to reflect substantially on the connections between racism and contemplation. Another source of frustration that I have with mainstream Christian contemplative practice is its lack of connection with one's lived body. Despite growing literature that highlight the body in contemplative practice, the Christian tradition has broadly treated contemplation as something that happens within the

9. New Monastic movements have the right intentions and aims, but the leadership and culture are white dominated. See Walker-Barnes, "My Struggle." Important exceptions do exist, as Holmes makes clear in *Joy Unspeakable*.

"soul" and associated bodily phenomena as derivative effects that have only secondary significance.[10] The body always seems to take on the posture of a patient, and the heavy weight given to the soul, usually without any guidance on how it is concretely connected with the body, renders the body nearly irrelevant to prayer.

There are, in fact, important reasons for downplaying bodily phenomena in the Christian contemplative tradition. One is the danger of identifying contemplation with discrete experiences, bodily and otherwise. The heart and true standard of Christian contemplation is the growth of love.[11] Subjective experiences are not that important. There is always the trap of appropriating contemplation to reinforce one's sense of self or to avoid the exigencies of living in an unjust world. Yet, there is undeniable physicality that is intrinsic to contemplative practice. Where we pray, the way we breathe, how we hold our bodies make a real difference to contemplative practice. Energetic phenomena such as vibrations, subtle sensations, physical warmth, or collectedness in the lower navel region, also point to contemplation's inextricably embodied character. This character may be secondary to the growth of love, but there needs to be a better account of the body's role to truly integrate it in prayer. This is all the more necessary when we come to racial violence, as it is based on visible differences and bodily experiences.[12] White-bodied people's work of dismantling racist, violent perceptual practice requires attending to the lived body, especially the subtle levels of sensations where perceptual links and naturalization occur without conscious awareness. Most nonwhite-bodied people need to find ways to heal from the devastating long-term and continual impact of such perceptual practices and find empowering ways to re-body themselves. To draw on the full power of contemplative practice to address racist, violent perceptual practices, we need to begin contemplative practice with the body and engage the felt bodily senses throughout the process of contemplation. That work has hardly begun in the Christian community.

For myriad and complex reasons, the language found in Christian texts have so little to say on the inter-related issues of the body and racial violence that actually help me to engage my bodily being. I have increasingly turned to non-Christian meditation practices where the body is

10. See Ryan, ed., *Reclaiming the Body*; see also Laird, *Into the Silent Land*, ch. 3.
11. Teresa of Avila, *The Interior Castle*, 100.
12. Menakem, *My Grandmother's Hands*, 7ff.

better integrated. One important practice has been standing meditation (*zhan zhuang*) that is basic to *tai chi* and other internal practices (*neijia*). The fundamental posture involves standing with the feet shoulder width apart, knees slightly bent, tucking in the tail bone, relaxing the shoulders and chest downward, and the arms held out in front of one's chest with palms facing inward, as if embracing a large sphere. A key part of the practice is emptying one's body and mind, standing like a translucent body of light and relaxing the mind.[13] The practice sinks one's energy toward the ground and gives the practitioner a sense of rootedness and warmth throughout the body. The posture, emptying visualizations, and relaxation facilitate the processing of patterns of tension within the body and painful emotions. The growing sense of safety and ease that standing meditation engenders can pave the way for contemplation. The standing posture and self-emptying can quietly lead a person of Christian faith to surrender more and more to divine love in both body and mind.

Another important practice has been Tibetan Buddhist meditation on love and compassion and *tonglen*. Love and compassion meditation begins with remembrance of an experience of love.[14] Calling vividly to mind that moment of receiving genuine care, the meditation elicits a response of love and gratitude in the practitioner. As part of that loving response, the practitioner meditates on the unavoidable suffering afflicting that caring person in this world. The meditation is founded on the Mahayana Buddhist doctrine of the empty nature (*śūnyatā*), of reality, the lack of separate, independent existence of all persons and phenomena. Its understanding of suffering is rooted in ignorance of this nature and consequent clinging attachment to impermanent phenomena as if they were permanent. The stirring recollection of the caregiver's suffering due to basic human ignorance and clinging attachment engenders a powerful sense of compassion for that person as well as all beings who similarly suffer in this existence. From the Buddhist framework, the practitioner realizes that in the ceaseless cycle of rebirth and re-death (*saṃsāra*), all beings have shown such love and care to her, and they likewise suffer

13. On *tai chi* and *qigong*, I am indebted to my teachers Min-Young Jung and Shuisheng Peng.

14. The meditation is found in *lam rim* texts that explicate a graduated path of Buddhist training in the Tibetan Buddhist tradition. See Gampopa, *The Jewel Ornament*, ch. 7. The traditional visualization of loving experience begins with one's mother. Contemporary teachers like John Makransky widen the range of loving exemplars to include human and nonhuman sources that have provided care, comfort, and safety. See Makransky, *Awakening through Love*.

due to ignorance. The force of compassion generated by the meditation inspires a deep desire to relieve their suffering.

Empowered by such intense love and compassion, the practice moves into meditation on exchanging self and other (*tonglen*). The practitioner visualizes other sentient beings' suffering and its causes in the form of black tar or cloud and imagines breathing it into her own heart. She then envisions giving all her source of happiness and its causes in the form of pure beams of light that radiate from her body with her exhalation and enters the bodies of other sentient beings. She beholds these beings becoming perfectly free from suffering and attaining true happiness. It is important to note that *tonglen* practice usually begins with oneself, so that one is working with one's own suffering in the framework of empty nature before taking on other's afflictions. In this way, the practice metabolizes one's own suffering and uses it to connect with the suffering of other sentient beings. Furthermore, the meditation empowers the practitioner to use pain and suffering to generate ever deepening and widening love and compassion for others.

When practicing these meditations, I suspend any discursive thought on Christian doctrinal contents and commitments, and I approach the ultimate nature of reality as inconceivable. Instead of trying to gain some measure of cognitive mastery over ultimate reality, I simply surrender to that reality and be immersed in the steps of the practices. In the immediate moments of actual practice, what matters is the surrender and allowing the ultimate to inform me, rather than conceiving the practice as something subject to my egoic agency. When I breathe in my own and other living beings' suffering into the depth of my heart, I envision that suffering to dissolve into the inconceivable, ungraspable nature of ultimate reality. When I breathe out happiness for myself and others, I visualize pure rays of light flowing out of the inexhaustible nature of the ultimate. Continued practice has given me a sense of space within my own mind and body. It has also given me a very practical and effective way to be present to the painful sensations and feelings of anger, hatred, fear, and brokenness when they arise, and to witness their energies shifting into love and compassion.

Non-Christian meditation practices inform my Christian contemplative prayer in several ways. First, there is a convergence between Tibetan Buddhist meditations and contemplation in moving from empathy to compassion and sense of solidarity. *Tonglen* points back to the communal character of contemplation, as contemplative practice intensifies a sense of communion with others.[15] Second, standing meditation and Tibetan Buddhist practices have led me to see my physical body as radically pervaded by the mind, and what we categorize crudely as "the body" and "the mind" as always interdependent and co-arisen. In contemplative practice, I feel that divine love illumines and activates equally my body and the mind, and that the divine is holding and re-forming them in the image of infinite, prodigal love.

Both the Christian and non-Christian practices have been essential for my own survival and ability to live and hope proactively in a world beset by violence. As an Asian American, who has dealt with racial violence throughout his life and experienced renewed attacks during COVID-19, I have sought refuge in these practices in order to seek a transformative path through the challenges and to wake up more fully to the suffering of others. Reflecting on their significance during the pandemic and the country's socio-political crises, I see more clearly how afflictive times demand spiritual creativity, especially from marginalized peoples.

Part of my story has named the failure of mainstream, white-dominated Christian theological, pastoral, and contemplative communities (progressive or not) to provide meaningful and effective resources that interconnect the somatic (including the racial), the contemplative, and the socio-political for people of color in the present context.[16] This is particularly true for Asian Americans whose perspectives, experiences, and needs are consistently overlooked in most Christian discourses. For me, this has meant that Christian thought and practice in their current forms—deeply infected by white supremacist racism and Eurocentric theological and philosophical values and frameworks—must be radically expanded and reformed through a process of intentional apprenticeship to non-Christian and non-Eurocentric traditions and sources. Comparative study and practice, therefore, across religious and somatic traditions have become necessary ways for me to find a way forward to live into the vision of the divine realm (*basilea tou theou*) that Jesus proclaimed and embodied. Such deep learning across traditions, to use Francis X. Clooney's words, is the only way that I personally find viable for reclaiming my own Christian tradition to meet the spiritual demands of the present

15. Laird, *Into the Silent Land*, 12.

16. While I focus my critique on my home tradition (Christian), the same is true of non-immigrant Buddhist communities in the U.S., which are overwhelmingly white, even as Black and other teachers of color have been addressing issues of racial justice and diversity in *sanghas* for many years. See Fields, "Divided Dharma."

moment. I offer these reflections in the hope that they may benefit others who also seek a way forward through woundedness and rage to compassion and solidarity.

home from the hospital
the new father
plants a birch tree
　　　—Madeleine Moon-Chun

7

Spiritual Care in the Shadow
of Loss and Uprising

A Year in the Life of a Team

Lori Klein, Sarah Lapenta-H, Kafunyi Mwamba
Anna Nikitina, Samuel Nkansah

Prelude

Lori

Our Spiritual Care team year begins when the new Clinical Pastoral Education (CPE) cohort arrives each September.[1] The intimacy, resilience, and sorrow that have accompanied us through the year of 2020 cannot be fully comprehended without looking back to autumn 2019.

As part of our autumn observance of Spiritual Care week, our team ate at a Stanford University campus eatery featuring food from several continents.[2] Our kind of restaurant, it mirrored the offerings at our monthly potlucks, food we learned to make in our countries and cultures

1. Clinical Pastoral Education (CPE) is the accredited program by which most professional chaplains are trained.

2. Spiritual Care week is a nationally recognized time to celebrate the contributions of chaplains.

of origin. Our Cancer Care Chaplain led us on a reflective walk through a labyrinth, an art gallery, and a grove where trees mingle with sculpture. We paired off to give and receive blessings—residents, faculty, staff chaplains, an administrative assistant, and I—enlivening sacred connection.

A new hospital building opened in November 2019. Our Spiritual Care Service facilitated a people's blessing to honor hospital staff. A transporter, a patient care unit secretary, a rehabilitation services manager, an interpreter, a nurse, and a chaplain—they spoke of their pride, gratitude, and hopes for serving patients. On patient day one, hundreds of patients were moved—in their beds—from the existing hospital through connecting passageways to the new building, and from one unit to the next as the hospital transitioned to private rooms. Spiritual Care team members escorted families and accompanied nervous patients. It was a day of joyful team building among some of the staff, CPE faculty, and new residents.

The new hospital included a chapel sanctuary. To dedicate the sanctuary in December, we assembled our collective team of Buddhist, Christian, Hindu, Jewish, and Muslim spiritual leaders. They were either from or connected to our staff team. We each offered a dedication rooted in our traditions, avoiding only the triumphalist language that compares us rather than allows us to inter-inspire one another. For the capstone, the ceremony leaders circled a pottery bowl decorated with multiple religious symbols. Each of us poured water into the common bowl from a separate vessel and gave an invocation describing a sacred use of water in our distinct tradition. Many vessels, one bowl.

Throughout the year, we provide celebration, observance, activities, and food for the hospital community: Lunar New Year, Ash Wednesday, Ramadan, Good Friday, Passover, Eid, High Holidays, Día de los Muertos, Diwali, Chanukah, Christmas, and Kwanzaa. The last holiday we observed in a "normal" fashion before moving to creative, virtual adaptions with complimentary "go bags" was Ash Wednesday, February 26, 2020, the day California reported its first COVID-19 case that could not be traced to travel.[3] I find Ash Wednesday to be moving: we impose ashes on more than 1,000 patients, families, and staff. I walked the hallways that day, experiencing the visceral reminders of our collective journey—coming from dust, to dust we shall return—on Earth.

3. CDC Newsroom, "CDC Confirms."

Transforming our Practices to Meet the Moment

Lori

Santa Clara County, California, had the first known US COVID-19 death in February 2020.[4] By mid-March, hospital policies and procedures changed so quickly that I was providing daily updates to our team. At our weekly team meetings, we shared ideas about coping. Our CPE program transitioned to remote learning on class days. Everyone wore masks. Our staff chaplains with children struggled to balance work with daycare or school from home. All of us leaned on the spiritual, philosophical, or religious calling that drew us to accompany people through suffering, even as we now suffered with them.

To keep our patients and ourselves as safe as possible, the hospital suspended visits by loved ones except when a non-COVID-19 patient was at end-of-life. Months later, Stanford Health Care resumed limited visitation, and patients could designate one visitor for the duration of their hospitalization. Patients at end-of-life could have up to five carefully screened visitors. Loved ones of patients with COVID-19 still could not visit. In autumn 2020 when our numbers surged again, Stanford again suspended visits, allowing exceptions for brief visits for end-of-life patients or for other limited circumstances. These necessary shifts brought loneliness and grief to our patients and their loved ones, as well as vicarious suffering to hospital staff. This situation required us spiritual care providers to creatively evolve to best serve them. This chapter illustrates how we transformed some of our practices to fit the spiritual care needs of patients and their families. It is a collaborative project that highlights our teamwork. Each chaplain shares vignettes of their work and revised practices of care. Their practices were shaped by the "visible" racial injustices (made visible by social media) and prompted deeper listening to each other and our patients. Finally, they share how they learned to draw from within themselves and utilize their community resources to develop resilience during the pandemic.

Anna

The need of patients and their families for connection and support grew even more intense. Chaplaincy responded to these challenges by adding telehealth to in-person visits. It was important to tell myself that

4. Chappell, "1st Known U.S. COVID-19."

sacred connections with patients and families are possible virtually. I experienced that focusing on the encounter, offering reflective listening, and being present "here and now" with the person entrusted to my care created the necessary connection. The primary challenge of using tele-health is finding the right time for conversation. Spiritual care addresses topics of utmost importance to people regarding feelings, family dynamics, and relationship with the divine. We support people in the processing of emotions (fears, hopes, guilt, shame, joys). We are present for them in discussing the need for forgiveness and connections. We strive to help patients and families share their concerns about life, death, beliefs, and values. We also know the importance of memory, legacy, and healing. The chaplain explores any of these matters when—and if— the patient is ready. Also, on a given day, a professional from the hospital may call the family: the doctor to update the patient's condition, the social worker to offer psychosocial support, the bedside nurse to tell the family if the patient ate and slept well. Care of the soul is also important; yet, we must coordinate timing and messages with other disciplines so as not to over-whelm the family with too much information.

The silver lining of telemedicine was connecting with family members who live far away without their spending significant resources to meet in-person. Participating in family meetings via Zoom allowed the medical care team to be acquainted with how the family operates in its own home environment. As virtual house guests, we gained valuable per-spectives on family dynamics and decision-making processes. Telemedi-cine provided closer connections with families, which created a deeper sense of trust. While I continued to visit patients in-person, I found some could concentrate better during a follow-up telephone or video conversa-tion. Most people respond positively to compassion and kindness even when offered virtually. Healing through processing emotions continued.

Samuel

During the pandemic, I learned the power of technology via Zoom and telemedicine teamwork as a liaison of care. I also learned that fam-ily members—because they cannot be at the bedside—may expect you to call. I sometimes felt challenged to manage families' expectations for information because I could not share information with them unless the patient gave me permission. I experienced how we—through video visits and conferences —were able to resolve conflicts about a patient's care. In one patient case, we were discussing care plans for a seriously ill older woman. Her daughter would not agree to the medical team's assessment of the patient. In my conversations with the family, I learned that the patient had an adult son who might be key in helping us with better outcomes. I spoke with the daughter and son, and then I met with the patient. At the next video visit between the medical team and family, I asked the son to speak first because my conversation with him led me to believe he would better reflect the needs of his mom. I then invited the daughter to speak, who criticized and disagreed with the team's recommendations to shift to a goal of comfort care. I redirected the conversation to make it patient-centered rather than focused on the needs of individual family members. The medical team saw the family dynamics more clearly, whereby a subsequent video family meeting resolved the situation to provide the best care for the patient.

Lori

Before early March 2020, our Spiritual Care team included more than 150 volunteers. They provide religion-specific and spiritual but not religious visits, which allows our professional and chaplain learner team to focus on spiritual care assessments and more sophisticated religious interventions. In normal times, our volunteers also staff our "No One Alone" program, assist patients in completing Advance Directives, and help produce holiday and cultural events. On March 9, we suspended all in-hospital volunteer activities.

Kafunyi

Since patients were not allowed to have volunteers as visitors, Lori's wife, Irene, proposed that spiritual care volunteers write cards for patients and staff. Using Zoom, my colleagues Bruce Feldstein and Taqwa Surapati joined me in training approximately sixty volunteers to write cards that conveyed empathy and support. Staff chaplains and chaplain learners offered these hand-written cards to patients and staff, who expressed gratitude for this beautiful gesture. Volunteers appreciated the opportunity to provide care while sheltering in place.

Building on this success, we created a program for spiritual care volunteers to telephone patients who requested contact. In collaboration with Volunteer Resources, we trained forty volunteers. Volunteers were assigned to patients who shared their religious affiliation and language. Because of confidentiality around personal health information given to volunteers, we had to finetune and revisit the process several times. In autumn 2020, we began piloting a streamlined virtual visitor program on three units. In addition, chaplains and CPE learners assigned to patient care units referred patients from throughout the hospital who had been in the hospital for more than thirty days. We also began offering virtual visitors to some patients who were lonely or dying without sufficient accompaniment through a virtual version of our NOA/NODA program ("No One Alone" and "No One Dies Alone").

Volunteer virtual visits have enhanced the continuity of supportive care for patients when visits by family members are restricted and chaplains multi-tasking to fulfill numerous needs. In some cases, patients had no one who could listen to—or accompany-—them during their hospital stay. More patients can now receive support, encouragement, comfort, as well as blessings and prayers when needed. More than half of our Spiritual Care volunteers have been trained to provide compassionate care amid the pandemic. They continue to write cards and make phone calls, sometimes even singing to a lonely patient. Most of the participating volunteers feel fulfilled when they connect with patients and especially if patients ask for continued spiritual care support. Patients, families, and staff are grateful for these compassionate gestures from strangers who write cards to them or talk to them by telephone in these challenging times.

Lori

Approximately one-third of our inpatients are Catholic. While we fulfilled most of their spiritual care needs this year with interfaith providers, seriously ill and dying Catholic patients and loved ones expect a Roman Catholic priest to provide in-person sacraments. Sacrament of the Sick includes prayer and anointing of the patient with consecrated oil. To promote safety, Pope Francis issued a plenary indulgence in late March for Catholics "who, with a spirit detached from any sin," could rely on their past or current prayers and devotions to replace the spiritual benefit of these sacraments if a priest could not be personally present.[5]

Samuel

The plenary indulgence was a blessing for Catholic priests and lay people, but not all Catholics understand its efficacy since their experience and belief tell them the priest's physical presence is important for

---

5. Hamilton, "Pope Francis Grants Plenary."

sacramental care. Thus, I —a Catholic priest—sometimes became a teacher to persuade others of the efficacy of the plenary indulgence. In observance of the plenary indulgence, I was able to modify care practices to provide emotional and spiritual support when the situation left the patient or family unable to absorb the Church teaching. The plenary indulgence should have allowed me to refer some requests for sacraments to my non-Catholic spiritual care colleagues. Instead, I still visited many patients in person, not only to save time, but to manage the litany of questions from families.

Some dying patients and their families requested their last wish to be the physical touch of the priest. Because of COVID-19 safety measures, I used pastoral discretion in physically anointing the patient with the consecrated oil only when the medical team assessed imminent death of the patient. For these people I used the personal protective equipment—gloves, gown, face/eye masks—to anoint them and provide the sacramental care they needed before the transition. Sometimes the family watched on video. Such moments also increased my risk of exposure. I exercised pastoral discretion based upon the philosophy that informs our Spiritual Care Service's program that no one who wants company should die alone, even if they are COVID-19 positive.

One patient, who could not talk, wrote on a board that he needed a Catholic priest for confession before he died. Attempts to explain the plenary indulgence to him and his daughter failed. This dramatic situation affected the doctors and social workers. I entered the room while the family watched via video. I conducted a penitential rite with general absolution and administered the sacrament of the sick. I prayed with the family. This brought a calming, soothing presence to the family.

When another family requested a pastoral visit by the priest, my assessment revealed that the family wanted anointing— sacrament of the sick—for their dying COVID-19-positive loved one. The medical team insisted on reducing risk, saying only the nurse could touch the patient. I said prayers to accompany the sacrament through a glass window in the ante room. I soaked the oil in cotton, gave it to the nurse through the partially opened door, and asked the nurse to make the sign of the cross on the patient's forehead while the family watched via video. I then recited the final prayers. The COVID-19 pandemic has underscored the importance of the Roman Catholic priest's physical presence and touch as a way of providing comfort and care for Catholic patients.

Sarah

My care-work with bereaved families were severely altered due to COVID-19. My work was moved to phone calls devoid of non-verbal communication cues, moderation of physical proximity, and healing touch. End-of-life visits were restricted. Once the decedent had been moved to the hospital cold room, hospital viewings of decedents were no longer possible. In-person funerals/memorials were suspended or severely truncated, and gatherings to comfort and support bereaved loved ones were prohibited, due to the fear of health and safety of the living. The pain of death is already challenging, but these additional losses multiplied the layers of traumatic grief.

I started calling all bereaved loved ones a couple of days following the decedent's death to check in on them. Call after call was marked by expressions of shock, sadness, anger, and/or powerlessness. It is devastating for an elderly wife who cannot see the full face of her husband the last few months of his life. The family that would have held a modest service with extended loved ones now surrendered to holding an in-home service with a mere trickle of folks gathered safely around a kitchen table to share stories in remembrance. The adult child—who would have flown over immediately to see their dying loved one—declined the invitation to ride in the helicopter, not knowing that would be his last chance to say, "I love you." The family member— already on the margins economically—was now disproportionally impacted by the pandemic and unable to scrape enough money together to pay the rent, let alone cover bare cremation expenses. There were many such stories of pain and complicated suffering, resulting from the public health safety measures to which we had to adhere during the COVID-19 year.

For those who were facing injustices and understandably angry, I also listened for ways I could support and advocate for them. Acknowledging my professional place of privilege and relative power, my listening was informed by wisdom first gleaned from John M. Perkins and his work to mend broken relationships and build more just communities. For example, with the support of my boss and department, we created a special fund to help families cover cremation expenses. At times, I also allowed myself to be a safe container for their venting and anger, empathetically listening to those in denial or angry that their loved one died of COVID-19 and "was now a statistic." Saturated feelings of isolation, anger, and regret reverberated in virtual grief group sessions, where participants expressed gratitude for "[Stanford] not abandoning us."

In addition to the 'usual' chaplain presence, and reflecting on trauma theory, it became important to create as many options/choice-opportunities as possible, even waiting for *them* to hang up the phone as one, small, subconscious act of agency. Rather than rushing in to respond or fix their wounds, I invited their reflections/resources for strength and courage to meet the days to come. Additional, elevated actions to support their grief processing included soliciting storytelling, holding the silence, sitting with the unknowing — all usually with eyes closed to honor the sacred space, actively and non-judgmentally listening, and asking gentle questions as their sharing unfolded: "What are you missing most about <decedent's name>?" "What do you wish you could have said?" "What do you think your <relation> would have said in return?"

Grappling with Racial Injustice and Structural Racism

Lori

Our spiritual care team has grown increasingly diverse in recent years along intersecting axes of "race,"[6] ethnicity, gender, sexual orientation, and religion. Before this year, we spoke frequently about how to be religiously inclusive and act as cultural brokers when white, European, Christian, heteronormative, male, cisgender norms created suffering. However, we rarely spoke of white supremacy, racist violence, and racial injustice.

The long-overdue reckoning with the murders of unarmed Black men and women, the gut-churning stories of child migrants and asylum seekers from Latin America placed in cages by our government, the disproportionately high number of Black and Latinx people sickened or dying from COVID-19—all these injustices pushed us to do more as chaplains. Our CPE faculty has been implementing strategies to dismantle unconscious white supremacy in their educational methods. As a team, we attended the Stanford Medicine Community's March for Racial Justice in June 2020 to commemorate all the murders of Black people that had burst into public view. Stanford Medicine as an institution has

---

6. Menakem states that "[R]ace is a myth with teeth and claws." Menakem, *My Grandmother's Hands*.

taken a more assertive stance by doing the following: it has encouraged everyone to intervene when we witness overt racism, and it has created a Commission on Justice and Equity to create an action plan to make Stanford Medicine more inclusive for employees. The Commission has enabled the organization to better address health conditions arising from the consequences of racial inequity.

Our first team-wide discussions felt well-intended yet awkward. Each of us, regardless of our racial background, came with our own ideas about how to proceed. Some team members of color wanted to share their experiences—even educate—others not speaking at all. Some white team members eager to engage, others wanted to make space for our colleagues of color, while some team members of color wanted to hear the ways in which white colleagues shared their anguish and moral outrage. We shared as a whole group and in smaller affinity groups. I have engaged— and noticed other team members do similarly—in deeper one-on-one conversations, sharing our individual, sometimes painful life histories, dreams, anger, disappointments, and hopes.

Kafunyi

I immigrated to the United States in the 1990s from the Democratic Republic of Congo, a country colonized by Belgium from 1908 to 1960. The United States has had a reputation as the most free country, with its American Dream rooted in the Declaration of Independence, proclaiming that "all men" (and women) are created equal with the right to life, liberty, and the pursuit of happiness.

COVID-19 and the death of innocent black people (such as George Floyd, Breonna Taylor, and countless others) from police brutality and excessive force have visibly exposed what has been going on in the country for 400 years. Only recently have such racial injustices received the visible social media exposure and publicity we see today. How can we rise to this moment to disrupt the cycle of systemic racism and biases that devastate communities of marginalized people of color, LGBTQ+, Muslim, and Jewish communities? As a Black person with Black children, I thought that I had come to the "land of the free" where the ideals of liberty, equality, and justice could be achieved through hard work regardless of where you come from, what you believe, and whom you love. Instead, we now live in a state of constant fear of racial injustice and discrimination. Due to a long history of social injustices in our country, many African

Americans live in a state of a pandemic with high unemployment, limited access to healthcare, education, housing, and basic needs of life.[7]

As a spiritual care provider in a health care system, I encounter people from different spiritual, religious, cultural, gender, class, and sexual orientation backgrounds representing sometimes marginalized communities. They need a listening ear, companionship, encouragement, and comfort in a sacred and safe space where healing occurs with empathy and compassion for our collective humanity. This aspiration meets challenges for healthcare staff to understand other cultures and traditions, creating barriers to providing patients with appropriate care. It is our role as chaplains to advocate for them during their stay. COVID-19 and racial injustices are opportunities to stand up against discrimination, prejudice, stereotypes, inequalities, and health disparities in the healthcare system. We also need to make changes in the recruitment, hiring, and professional development of health care workers.

There is no easy walk to freedom anywhere, and many of us will have to pass through the valley of the shadow of death again and again before we reach the mountaintops of our desires.[8] We need to work tirelessly, just as Nelson Mandela did for decades in South Africa. We need freedom, justice, and equality by any means necessary.[9]

Sarah

This strange yet important time—woven with disappointments and failures—has demanded our best efforts and invited us to examine individually and collectively our values, implicit biases, and responsibilities to self and others. Our emotions of pain, anger, regret, fear, loneliness seemed magnified within and outside the hospital. This was true in my own immediate family, where three of four of us are first-generation immigrants and two have come to this country as Unaccompanied Refugee Minors. The daily prayer-mantra that emerged for me was the familiar, "What is mine to do?" in my interactions with bereaved loved ones, colleagues, and collaborating agencies and organizations. How may I best support groundedness, resilience, and wholeness? For one, I began checking in more intentionally with colleagues of color, as an invitation—not expectation—to welcome their story-telling. By humbly listening to their

7. Zahnd, "The COVID-19 Pandemic."

8. Mandela, *No Easy Walk.*

9. Malcolm X., *By Any Means Necessary.*

stories, I can continue to examine my own implicit biases and consider how I keep growing and become a more supportive ally.

Resilience in the Midst of Shared Trauma

Samuel

I hold the image of the crab walking on the seashore. The crab knows the sea will make noise. The waves and storms of the sea will roll onto the bank and hit it. And yet, the crab continues toward its destination. All that the crab needs is groundedness—firmly grounding its claws in the sand and keeping the focus in view—while knowing it can do nothing to change the direction, pace, movement of the sea waves. Groundedness is what enables the crab to *respond* to the dictates of the sea rather than *react* to the actions of the sea.

The pandemic challenged me to differentiate between *responding* to situations rather than *reacting*. I took this lesson from the experience of the crab. Like the stormy nature of the sea, the pandemic invited me to reflect on my groundedness and also rethink my responses. I only have so much ability and time. This brought me to an awareness that responsibility = response + ability of the team = the concept I need to explore to make the necessary adjustments needed to attend to my pastoral duties during this unusual time.

Anna

"These are unprecedented times…" I heard this phrase in different contexts so often in 2020. I found this to ring true. People from all over the world were challenged to find strength, meaning, inner reserves, and community resources to deal with uncertainty, fear, anxiety, and grief. The most difficult for me was uncertainty. How long will pandemic last and will it end at all?

Stay-at-home orders, restrictions on activities and travel, online schooling, even the loss or transformation of jobs provided an unexpected opportunity for many of us to "slow down" and to pause. It also allowed people to attend to spiritual questions often forgotten in "normal times" such as the following: what kind of meaning and joy does work give me? What relationships are life-giving? What does true friendship mean to me? What matters the most?

The loss of routine, order of life, and uncertainty recalled my experience of living through the collapse of the Soviet Union in the 1990s. The emotional state of living through such a historical event felt familiar to what I experienced during the pandemic. It comforted me now that I survived those challenging times and even thrived later in life. Many people in the Russian-speaking community found common themes between the pandemic and the collapse of the Soviet Union. As I dealt with challenges at work and home, I also felt deep connectedness with others, knowing that I am not struggling alone. It would not be an exaggeration to say that "the whole world" was under the stress of adjusting to meta-changes such as working from home, supporting kids' online learning, traveling less, and spending more time with loved ones.

This awareness of shared struggles lightened the burden. I found great comfort in my belief that human beings are resilient. Historically each generation may have at least one big challenge that we endure. Ours is to live through the pandemic with hope—to become wiser, and more compassionate—and emerge as better versions of ourselves individually as well as communally.

Sarah

Many of my colleagues seemed to be grieving their inadequacies. They were traumatized by their own perceived failures of being forgetful, confused, or over-functioning. I began to ponder what we needed to continue the important work ahead of us. Again, I reflected on my daily prayer-mantra, "what was mine to do?" Drawing from my spiritual tradition as an Episcopal Priest where loving others correlates to how well one loves themselves (e.g., Christian Bible Mark 12.31, drawing on the Hebrew Pentateuch) and where sources of joy are believed to offer strength to endure, I began looking for ways to build up colleagues' sources of joy and gratitude. I offered a hospital-wide "laughter" meditation, posted puns in my office ("What did the fast tomato say to the slow tomato? Catch up!"), and practiced concrete expressions of gratitude. I tried to practice curiosity and non-judgmental listening, offer specific words of affirmation, extend grace, and practice forgiveness with colleagues. In very stressful situations where miscommunication and frustration can emerge, I thought about types of compassion narratives I could imagine surrounding each colleague with whom I came into contact. How could I ask clarifying questions or clarify shared expectations instead of assuming? Echoing Maya Angelou's "Do the best you can until you know better.

Then when you know better, do better"; [10] what would it sound like to affirm our collective "good enough" and growth-mindset?

Kafunyi

In discussing resilience, I provide an excerpt from one of the daily prayers I offered for the Stanford Health Care community in April of 2020: "source of joy and beauty, help us to find joy, beauty, goodness, meaning, and purpose during this pandemic. Open our eyes to experience the beauty that surrounds us this day in every person that we meet and in every creation that we see. As we endure this new reality in our lives, we pray for all people who have entered the doors of this hospital— the patients and all the employees who go unnoticed and unrecognized for the good work they do, for the compassionate care they offer, and the healing they provide, whether physical, spiritual, emotional, or psychosocial . . . .. We pray that their cups be refilled every day with joy and satisfaction as they return home to be with their families and loved ones. So, let it be!"

Lori

Fall 2019 through winter 2020 brought intense work to open and adjust to the new hospital. In spring 2020, the pandemic and witnessing racial violence upended everyone's lives and focused our response-ability. Our first COVID-19 surge, wildfires, threatened evacuations, days of choking smoke marked our summer. Fall through winter 2020 brought an even bigger surge in COVID-19 cases, crises in our democracy, and the vaccine. Through it all, I have tried to stay in balance by walking, singing, praying, studying sacred text, cherishing my wife, family, friends, and treasuring our spiritual care team.

"We shall be known by the company we keep.... In this Great Turning we shall learn to lead in love." [11] Holding my team members in *chesed*, Hebrew for loving kindness, has always been a source of resilience for me. It has never been as meaningful as it has this year, when each of my team embodied courage, calling, determination, *chesed*, ingenuity, and action despite fear. I feel grateful to engage in meaningful work alongside compassionate, creative colleagues.

10. Angelou, "Do the Best."
11. Longaker, "We Shall Be Known."

Coda

This is from our team's blessing for the new hospital in 2019:
Blessed be the hands that will reach out to others with compassion.
Blessed be the hands that cleanse rooms, beds, and bodies.
Blessed be the hands that will hold a scalpel to begin a surgery.
Blessed be the hands that fix a patient's bedside call button.
Blessed be the hands that will comfort the dying.
Blessed be the hands that turn us toward gratitude, well-being, and peace.

vernal pool
this communal lease
on life
        —Tom Painting

PART THREE

Fugitivity & Escape in Our Heterotopic World

8

Creative Escapes

Peace within the Grounding Rhythms of Life

JILLIAN EUGENE

As A YOUNG GIRL, I remember existing in a world of pure freedom—playing outside all day long, climbing trees, engaging in imaginative play, and doing all sorts of arts and crafts to my heart's content. Of course, what an innocent freedom it was, unaware of the world at large—and the limits of freedom for people of color. My peaceful and happy spirit was nurtured by a feeling of safety, freedom to be myself, and the ability to explore where my heart took me. And now, what an unattainable vision—for myself and I believe many others—to always feel safe, feel free to express oneself, and be bold enough to both physically and emotionally go where our heart desires.

Humanity Denied

As an African American, I realized the limits to such a vision of liberation. During this year of 2020 alone, we have witnessed countless acts of police brutality against Black people, violence against transgender people of color, COVID-19 vulnerabilities that disproportionately affect people of color, and the profiling of Black people for simply spending time outdoors to enjoy nature. Such forms of violence and limits to our liberty are exacerbated by a president who does not condemn white supremacy, belittles women, and is unwilling to address the structural inequalities and violence that plague this country. These have been the dehumanizing realities that have weighed heavily on my heart this year.

Oftentimes, just "being" is exhausting. I generally like to be well-informed of current events, but this year I stopped following the news as closely as before for the sake of my mental health. It seemed that at least once a week there was another Black person senselessly murdered, with the white killer walking free or without appropriate reprimand for taking a life. What is equally troubling is seeing the on-line comments made by so many hateful people, justifying the murders due to the alleged mild imperfections of the victims. Even so, trying to avoid the news altogether was a futile endeavor as hashtags, photos, and video clips soared all over social media, dictating the conversations around various communities.

What has been difficult for me with all of this is the nonchalant way that Black and brown deaths are depicted. Such media portrayals of the violence have raised my level of anxiety. I find myself hoping and praying that my loved ones do not become a hashtag. I think especially of my brother, with his bold, brave, and fiery personality. He never hesitates to express his true feelings—they are never hidden from his face nor his tongue. What a gift, in the right situation, to be true to oneself and un-afraid to speak one's mind. Yet, what an obstruction to one's life, to be a Black man with a quick, unrestrained tongue.

I also wonder if this recent surge of interest in protecting and providing justice for people of color may just be a phase. In this year of COVID-19, we have seen people checking in on their friends and colleagues of color, supporting the Black Lives Matter movement, marching for justice, sharing resources, incorporating regular racial equity discussions and plans in the workplace, and finding ways to support and uplift Black and brown voices (within and beyond their communities). I have been thrilled to see and experience this, though it does make me wonder where all these supporting voices were before 2020. Are these uplifting voices and systems of support here to stay, or will they be pushed to the sidelines once something else catches our national attention?

I do not have an answer to this. Only time will tell if racial justice and healing stay on the forefront of our national agenda, or if this year of collective outrage was just a fleeting moment prompted by successive acts of racial violence. What I can confidently state is that racism is the backbone of the United States that has fueled this society for the past four hundred years, when the first slaves were shipped to British colonies in Virginia in 1619.[1] We have seen so much historical and cultural change in the past four hundred years, and still Black people are oppressed. While it is no longer acceptable to be outwardly racist and use race specifically for exclusionary purposes, our country has time and time again found ways to keep Black Americans from advancing in society.[2] This system of oppression has come in many forms from slavery, Jim Crow segregation laws, the War on Drugs, housing and employment discrimination, voter suppression, the era of colorblindness, and the current criminal justice system that thrives on mass incarceration of brown and Black people.[3] With this knowledge of the fluidity and veiling of racism and oppression within our contemporary society, it is important to remember that even when life seems to go back to normal and there are not as many headlines about Black deaths, there will always be so much more work to do in combating racism. Racism keeps adapting and changing throughout time in the attempts to oppress Black people and maintain white supremacy.

It certainly seems that things have been exceptionally bad this year in terms of police brutality and Black fatalities. Yet I would argue that these brutalities, while in varying shapes and forms, have been happening since the creation of the United States, and that what has changed is the recording of these numerous injustices in action. Violence against Black and brown people is nothing new, nor has the violence increased. It is certainly more *visible* because of social media. With this visibility, we have the opportunity to amend some wrongs, uplift families who have lost loved ones to racial violence, demand justice, hold racial violence perpetrators accountable, and start working towards reconciliation.

Hopefully, we will continue to go deeper and find ways to support each other and actively work on uplifting people within and beyond our communities. While tackling issues as large and complex as racism and systemic poverty can seem completely overwhelming for an individual, it is important to remember that even small practices of care are important and impactful. Practices of care could include supporting businesses operated by people of color. We can actively seek out supporting them by eating local, donating one's time or money to organizations that empower and uplift people of color, reading books to elevate and evolve one's own

1. Shaw and Adolphe, "400 Years."

2. Alexander, *The New Jim Crow*, 2.

3. Alexander, *The New Jim Crow*, 2–12.

understanding of the complexities of racism within the United States, and using our own voice to speak up and advocate when needed.

Humanity Upheld

I am very grateful for the attention the Black Lives Matter movement has gotten this past year. At the same time, I am disheartened by the fact that it takes a whole movement, rapidly recurring murders, and an ongoing struggle for a Black person to simply say, "my life matters." It has been energizing to see so many people sharing resources on how to support Black lives, disseminating information on black-owned and indigenous businesses to hold each other up during these trying times, getting the word out about the numerous injustices against Black and brown people, educating each other, participating in protests, and having difficult conversations with friends and family members. Change will not happen if we are compliant with the current system that actively oppresses people of color, and as long as we ignore the social problems that indirectly and directly affect *all of* us.

This year of 2020 has honestly been a wakeup call that we as individual people and as a community must be a part of this change. It took a global pandemic, mass layoffs, an insurmountable amount of severe illness and deaths affecting predominantly people of color, murders of innocent and unarmed Black and brown people, and wildfires raging in the western United States, for us to finally decelerate from our hectic lives and reevaluate the state of our country and of our lives. While 2020 has been both literally and figuratively up in flames, people have gathered in marches and protests, demanding unadulterated justice. Many people have realized that change is very slow at the higher up governmental levels and are turning to grassroots movements to promote quotidian, small-scale (yet equally important) changes. Most importantly, people acted upon their civic duty and voted for changes that would protect and uplift people from all backgrounds.

Care as Liberation

While an overall devastating year, there have been some positive repercussions from 2020. People are checking in on each other more often. I have noticed this at least amongst my community of friends and family.

Conversations have progressed beyond the typical "how's it going," thus allowing for deeper connections and more authentic discussions. I have started having regular Zoom calls with my extended family as well, which has been a great way to stay connected since we cannot physically see each other. I have experienced that even among strangers I encounter while walking or hiking outside, there is less of a sense of the usual rush and more of a peaceful and friendly openness.

Not only are people taking the time to check in with one another; they are also taking the time to slow down, stay in-tune with themselves, and delight in nature. Working at an environmental nonprofit that has five community garden spaces in Atlanta and Decatur, I have seen these effects up close and personal. Each year at my job, we have a fall and spring plant sale. In a regular year, I would be busy leading environmental science field trips, teaching farm-to school lessons, as well as leading after-school gardening and cooking clubs. However, when the pandemic hit and schools went online, we shifted gears and had all hands-on deck in the hopes of making our spring plant sale a success. We had both a socially distanced in-person plant sale and an online sale, and with this, we more than doubled our sales of the previous year. Many people came by our garden spaces, happy to have a safe outdoor space to enjoy, and a place where they could get a wide variety of plants to grow in their own gardens. Being outside, working with your hands, and growing some of your own foods are extremely beneficial for both physical and mental health. I am very happy that many people had the opportunity to take some time and decompress while working in the dirt. Ideally, more people from diverse backgrounds would have the freedom and feeling of security to enjoy the benefits that nature has to offer.

Taking time for myself during this tumultuous time has been very important. Some activities that bring me peace are gardening, painting, hiking with my dog, doing yoga, journaling, and delving into a good book. Gardening is especially therapeutic as it gives me time to be outdoors, dig in the dirt, slow my thoughts, and grow my own vegetables. It gives me a sense of purpose and is a wonderful way to decompress and become in-tune with the rhythms of nature. Painting is a way to convey my feelings onto paper, stroke by stroke, releasing my stress and turning it into an artistic creation. Hiking and yoga are great for both my physical and mental health. When I am hiking outdoors, I can take in the fresh air and sunshine, and simply enjoy the beauty of nature. When I practice yoga I focus inwards, calming my thoughts and finding my inner balance.

Reading a good book is a great temporary escape into a different time and place, while journaling helps me to practice interiority and engage in self-reflection, meditating on my experiences and problem-solving. Not every day is perfect, but all these activities help me stay uplifted, healthy, and able to put my best foot forward.

Beyond the pandemic, I find liberation when I step onto new soil with a task of getting to know a new place and culture. Some of my major trips thus far have been studying in Spain for a year, doing ethnographic research in Mexico for a summer, and teaching English to energetic students in Thailand directly out of college for a year and a half. During these journeys and experiences and all the smaller trips in-between, I have found myself getting to know elders in small Maya villages, working on organic farms in northern Thailand, testing my physical and mental stamina while trekking through Nepal, getting completely lost in new territories, and having to rely on the kindness of strangers to get me back on track. I had these amazing life experiences, while maintaining a genuine smile on my face.

During my travels, I have had the opportunity to meet people from all walks of life. While oftentimes our cultures, languages, and experiences have differed greatly; I have found ways to connect and engage with various people, a simple testament to having an open mind and open heart when meeting someone new. Many times, I have been warmly welcomed to share a conversation or a meal with a newfound friend, giving me a chance to learn something about the people in their own spaces. Likewise, it gives them an opportunity to learn a little bit about myself and what led me to my destination. I believe that everyone who has the means to do so should take a trip somewhere new and outside of their regular comfort zone. I encourage this not only to see the top destinations; I believe it is a way to learn, to grow, and to expand one's mindset and compassion. Through traveling, one gets to experience the world from a new perspective and see how there are so many ways to live life, to practice religion, to socialize, and to care for one another. This openness to learning and having new experiences is not only useful while traveling; it also is the key to being open to each other when meeting new people from different backgrounds within the United States. It is easy to quickly judge and have assumptions about people, though a great part of our nationwide healing could consist of simply giving people the time and space to show who they truly are as a person, instead of letting other people define, curb, and categorize people based on their limited preconceived notions.

Reconciliation and Healing

Upon reflection on everything that has happened this year, it would be a shame if we learned nothing and just went back to how life was beforehand. What should we take away from this year of 2020? Spending time outside is wonderful and so beneficial to one's overall health. Supporting local businesses builds community. Everyone needs time to rest and decompress. If you are sick, you should not be expected to come into work. Everyone should have access to quality healthcare. Our essential workers—including teachers, caregivers, grocery clerks, farmers, doctors, and public transport workers—are all so valuable, and should always be fairly compensated for the work they do. Being Black, brown, poor, LGBTQ+, and not speaking English fluently are all too often considered a crime in the United States, and it takes everyone—especially those with privilege—to advocate and promote a more equitable society.

We all play a part in healing our broken nation. Take care of yourself, your family, your neighbors, your community. Learn from one another and engage with people from different backgrounds or cultures. Have difficult conversations, and talk with family or friends who may have harmful beliefs and opinions. Read, learn, and listen. Be open to unlearning and relearning. Continue to advocate for Black lives even when it is not trending anymore. Donate your time, your energy or your money to organizations working to promote a more equitable society. And always, remember that a little bit of empathy goes a long way.

9

Patriotic Drag and Performance in the Time of COVID-19

Yukiko Takeuchi

As an Asian American raised in predominantly white environments, the issue of performance has always been intricately woven into my life. Born in the 1970s, the American immigration narrative of my childhood was all about assimilation. When it came to my racial identity, I was focused on "fitting in" and was conditioned to believe that the goal of race relations was to have people forget my race. Although I was never ashamed of being Asian American and was proud of many aspects of my Japanese heritage, I found myself automatically adapting to the needs and expectations of whomever I interacted with to mitigate any burden that my distinctiveness might present. As I matured and my worldview broadened, I gained and embraced a more nuanced understanding of race. During this time of growth, there was a period in which I felt shame for what I perceived as my complicity in the racism that I experienced growing up, such as laughing it off or repeatedly turning the other cheek. In time, I came to forgive myself. I recognized that I was young and learning to navigate a world that did not necessarily have a place for my difference, but in which I still needed to figure out how to live. As an adult, I moved forward, embraced my racial identity, and consciously worked on reversing my old practices of prioritizing other people's comfort or acceptance of me over who I am as a person of color.

Given this history, with both the pandemic and the racial violence/ Black Lives Matter (BLM) movement that has defined 2020 and beyond, my greatest internal conflict has often hinged on the issue of performance. Whether in response to the anti-Asian American sentiment that was exacerbated due to COVID-19, the protests and other actions in support of the BLM movement, or the decision-making around returning (or not returning) our kids to school safely; I had conflicted emotions about what I should or could feel comfortable doing to care for myself and my family while still adhering to (or failing to adhere to) my principles or ideas of authenticity. Suddenly, an act as simple as grocery shopping became anxiety-inducing, loaded with consequences for me and others. The same was true of countless choices throughout this time. Trying to perfectly balance safety, mental health, ethical priorities, and sensitivity to external perception became an impossible practice. Ultimately, I had to find the same forgiveness for my imperfections now that I found for my youthful self.

From the start, the COVID-19 outbreak struck at the heart of the feeling of "otherness" thrust upon Asian Americans in this country. For many of us, being made fun of or made to feel abnormal due to the look, smell, or contents of our food is a formative experience. When the virus started spreading in China, the identification of the Huanan Seafood Wholesale Market as the possible source of the virus dovetailed nicely with the American predisposition to be suspicious of Asian food. Subsequent studies indicate that the market was more likely the site of a super spreader event and not the source of the virus at all, but the narrative of COVID-19 starting because Chinese people ate bats persisted.[1] In Atlanta, where I live, plaques depicting Winnie the Pooh eating a bat adorned with the phrase "Wuhan Plague" popped up around the city, including on my local neighborhood market.[2] The early proliferation of this kind of bias made me feel vulnerable in a way I had not experienced in a long time.

In the late seventies/early eighties, I was aware of a growing anti-Asian and, more particularly, anti-Japanese movement. There was a very specific kind of patriotism that was demonstrated by rejecting Japanese cars and only driving American models. I was not sensitive to the economic power dynamics between the two nations, but I knew that people

1. Woodward, "Chinese CDC."
2. Habersham, "Wuhan Plague."

did not like the Japanese and thought they were hurting the country. As a young adult, I learned of the murder of Vincent Chin by two white men in Detroit in 1982, attributed, at least in part, to the perception that Mr. Chin was Japanese American.[3] I internalized his fate as the resulting danger of this kind of racial animosity. So, when reports of anti-Asian American attacks started making the news in conjunction with the rise of COVID-19, my protective instincts went on high alert. I fell back into the patterns of my childhood where I proactively tried to disarm prejudice by fitting in and seeming as innocuous as I could.

In the early days of the virus, before the quarantine, I would feel conspicuous in public. If I were checking out at a store for instance, I would speak loudly to the cashier in my unaccented English to demonstrate that I was from "here." If I were unlucky enough to have a tickle in my throat, I would suppress the cough as aggressively as possible so as not to be seen as a disease carrier. An Asian American friend commiserated at the time saying, "In public, Asians are holding in coughs like they're big, juicy farts." Once we went into lockdown, the environment became even more fraught. When they traced the first cases in Atlanta to the outbreak in Italy, my friend and I were so relieved. They could not blame it on us even though she is Korean American, I am Japanese American, and neither of us had traveled recently. Unfortunately, the span between identifying these first cases and going into full lockdown was incredibly short.

Quarantine and the virtual schooling that attended it were stressful for almost all the families that experienced it. It was certainly the case in my home. My son was completing seventh grade and adapted to the change as well as could be expected. My daughter, who was finishing third grade, however, had a very different experience. Both children attend Atlanta Public Schools (APS). I give credit to APS for being as responsive and moving as quickly as they did when we shifted to a full virtual model. They faced this sea change with a nimbleness and dedication to serving our students that was impressive, but it would have been impossible for them to replicate an in-school environment over the course of a weekend. My daughter's academic needs are much more extensive than my son's, particularly in math where she had an identified deficit. Spring virtual schooling left her in a position where she would have to learn the bulk of the curriculum independently. This was simply not going to happen so I, in essence, became her third-grade teacher. I have many strengths and a

3. Wang, "Vincent Chin."

variety of skills; but teaching third grade standards to a recalcitrant and somewhat traumatized nine-year-old is not among them. Our mother/daughter dynamic did not lend itself well to this new relationship. Where my daughter would defer to the expertise and authority of her teachers, she felt no such compulsion with me. Rightfully so, to be fair, as I was not equipped to perform as a third-grade teacher. The stress of virtual school, coupled with the stress of quarantine, the fear of the virus, and worries about my husband's Broadway-Theater-dependent job, created a whirlwind of anxiety from which we all needed some form of escape.

Again, like legions around the world, the greatest solace I could find was spending time outdoors. The natural world was one of the only places that seemed to benefit from the global pandemic. In those early days, even the heart of the city got a little bit wilder. There were fox, coyote, deer, and otter sightings in town. My kids and I started taking our dog on long daily walks. We explored our neighborhood more thoroughly than we ever had before, miles at a time. The streets were empty. The city was quiet, and the air itself felt fresher. We were also blessed with a long, beautiful spring in Atlanta that made those times outdoors even more of a salve. When our schedule allowed it, we would venture even further afield to go hiking.

My spiritual practice is in communion with nature. I was not raised with any specific "religious beliefs," but my mother particularly had a profound respect for the natural world, likely born of the traditions of the Shinto tradition with which she grew up in Japan. In that vein, engendering a love—or at least an appreciation—of the outdoors has been a big part of my parenting approach. Before I had children, being atheist was not a prominent part of my life. Spending a significant portion of my upbringing in the South, I accepted Judeo/Christian traditions as the norm for America and my lack of religion as an outlier. It was another thing that made me feel less "American." Though I did not hide my atheism, I also did not assert or proclaim it. When I began raising children in the South, this ambivalence was no longer possible. If we did not share the foundations of our belief system with our children, they were similarly in danger of thinking of the Abrahamic religions as the default and themselves as outsiders.

We explained to our children that while we respected other people's faiths, we did not share those beliefs. We emphasized that, from a scientific perspective, we believed we were profoundly lucky to be able to experience life on this earth, and, because we do not believe in an afterlife, the time we have here is precious. We also taught them that because all people are limited to such a short time, we have an obligation to treat others the way we wish to be treated and to preserve our community and our environment so that our fellow humans and future generations might have an opportunity to enjoy the time they get to spend here. It is when I am in nature that I most feel the interconnectedness of humanity's fate and the enduring quality of the earth's beauty and power to sustain.

There is a Japanese phrase called "forest bathing" that is meant to reflect the restorative effects of engaging with the natural world. The phrase artfully captures the feeling of renewal that washes over me when I am hiking. Retreating to the mountains gave us respite from the overwhelming shadow of the virus and quarantine. We were active hikers prior to quarantine, but during quarantine we became obsessive hikers. My son loves hiking nearly as much as I do. After relentless exposure, my daughter begrudgingly admits that she "got used to it." Before heading out, I would let the kids choose what "kind" of hike they wanted to do (e.g., a waterfall to play in, a forest trail, a hilly climb with a view), and then I would try to find somewhere new that fit the bill. These trips were therapeutic in a very real sense. Having something to do and the benefits of being outdoors—looking forward to a new experience, getting exercise, escaping the house and the neighborhood—were vital to my mental health. There was very little joy to be had in the beginning of the pandemic but sliding down a smooth rock face into a pool of cold water on a hot summer day still had the power to delight. Working hard to climb some elevation and being rewarded with miles of views and a breeze on my face made my heart soar. We swam in lakes, snuck up on deer, fished rivers (unsuccessfully), skipped stones, played in cascades, took pictures of every kind of mushroom we could find, ate wild berries, and basically did anything else we could think to do outdoors. So much of this COVID-19 year was portrayed as a time of loss, restrictions, and pleasures foregone; but for me, these outdoor moments proved they were still attainable.

As a parent, I also hoped to achieve a minor miracle with these trips. My kids lost so much with the lockdown. Their education, friendships, social life, extracurricular activities, summer plans, opportunity to travel; all were devastated by having to quarantine. I feared they would look back on this time only through a lens of trauma and loss. Although I know these hikes could not erase the darkness of this period, I hoped they would serve as a silver lining. My son hiked over 200 miles with me in 2020 and my daughter was along for most of it. Maybe when they look back on the year, the memories made on those miles and miles of trails will soften the dark memories of the time. In essence, I did not want the pandemic to steal a year of their childhoods, and these adventures were my attempt to defy the suffocation of lockdown.

That said, even though I felt the benefits of breaking free from our home and the city, each foray was also tinged with the concern that I would be exposing myself and my kids to the risk of encountering some-body who would be hostile to us because of our race. Our hunt for new and interesting hikes meant we were checking out trails near and far, some almost two hours away from Atlanta. Despite the "Wuhan Plague" plaque incident, our home neighborhood is generally progressive and an environment in which I feel safe and accepted. Nevertheless, throughout the pandemic, my kids and I have always taken the added precaution of scuttling out of the way of any other pedestrian we might see on the sidewalk or the street. My reasoning is that if we take the initiative to create the six feet or more of distance to keep people safe, there will be less grounds for suspicion or animosity that might be aroused by our appearance.

When we would leave the confines or our neighborhood, my strat-egy became even more proactive. The farther away we got from the center of Atlanta, the greater my fear was of running into racial hostility. On those hikes, I would dress in what I called "Patriotic Drag" to project my American-ness as loudly as possible. I would wear my red, white, and blue hat from Crater Lake National Park and choose from a couple t-shirts from Atlanta's annual Fourth of July Peachtree Road Race that depict American flags. I wanted to telegraph that I was not a foreigner and not a threat. When the importance of masks became clear, we would wear buffs around our necks and every time we passed anybody on the trail, we would pull them up over our faces. Early on, I did not think this precaution was necessary from an epidemiological perspective since we were distancing and outdoors, but I did it anyway to perform my conscientiousness, just as my outfits performed my "fitting-in" and harmlessness.

As a practical reality, I did not want to be attacked so these steps I took were out of self-preservation; nevertheless, I felt weak for playing into the racism that prompted the charade and uncomfortable implicat-ing my children in this performance. I often struggle with the dichotomy of surviving the world as it is, while at the same time feeling that I am thereby undermining progress in working towards an anti-racist world. It felt like warning my kids of the danger and telling them we were behaving in this way as necessary preparation in navigating our society as people of color. I worried, however, that it was also teaching them to accommodate this type of bias and, perhaps, reinforcing it by normalizing it. Maybe if I were alone, I could be more cavalier, but with my children's safety at stake practicality won out over principle.

This same tension between performance and principle also played out in connection with my feelings toward my community's response and my own response to the BLM movement. When Atlanta took to the streets in protest of George Floyd's murder by the Minneapolis police, the movement spread beyond big protests downtown to smaller demonstrations in neighborhoods throughout the city, including my own. While I believe in the power of protest, it has never been my natural form of activism. When struggling with injustice or inequality, I find the most comfort in volunteer work. For example, after Trump's election made me fearful for the vulnerable populations his administration targeted, I began volunteering regularly at an organization that aids unaccompanied migrant children. I knew I could not combat all the harm his presidency inflicted but doing a small part against some of the damage provided relief from the negativity I felt during his presidency. Unfortunately, the pandemic effectively cut off this avenue of expression as lockdown and my kids' virtual schooling needs made continuing my volunteer work impracticable.

When the BLM protest movement gained traction in my community, I felt conspicuous in my non-participation. I also struggled with some uncharitable thoughts about whether some of the people I saw publicizing their activities on social media were merely performative in their support of the BLM movement. I experienced a complicated push/pull in feeling like I might be judged for not joining even though it did not feel authentic to me while also judging others for taking actions that might be superficial or potentially short-lived. I could not resolve the space where performance and protest co-exist. I asked myself whether protest, in its simplest form, is a performative act. If so, does it matter whether the participants are "pure" in their motivation? Can the act of protest be sufficient on its own without examining or expecting other actions in the space of racial justice? In the moment, I could not get beyond the feeling that if I participated in my neighborhood or social media demonstrations, I would be doing it for the wrong reasons or in the wrong way. In retrospect, I believe my focus on motivation undervalued the good that could be done through action with "imperfect" motivation.

This dance around my feelings of hypocrisy didn't end with the BLM protests. They reared up again as we faced the realities of another round of pandemic schooling. Many private institutions and some public schools outside the city were planning an in-person return in the fall of 2020. However, when summertime COVID-19 case numbers in Atlanta began to surge, APS said that it would assess the possibility of a hybrid in-person return (limited students and/or days per week) only after a nine-week 100% virtual start. This approach immediately kicked up a storm of controversy, particularly among parents seeking an option to return on a full week, face to face basis. Though members of this group made arguments that included equity considerations and seeking to support the most vulnerable, it was perceived by many as being comprised of rich powerful parents who wanted to get their kids back in school in defiance of public health guidance and the well-being of teachers and the community. Further President Trump's insistence that schools reopen with seeming disregard for public health data politicized the issue for many. Some began to see the position of seeking to reopen schools as a Republican position and the desire to stay virtual as a Democratic one. The question of whether kids should return to in-person schooling ceased to be about getting the kids with the highest need reintroduced in the safest way, and, rather, became a divisive topic that had people taking all-or-nothing positions that in a less politicized climate they may not have embraced. It was difficult to find the boundaries of decision making based on science vs. self-interest vs. political alignment vs. virtue signaling, etc.

I was torn. I really felt that my kids would benefit greatly from attending school in-person. I worried about my youngest because she was already behind in math, and I feared virtual schooling was only exacerbating her deficits. Both my kids were also experiencing feelings of isolation and social disconnect. Based on the science I had been reading from schools that had opened both here and abroad, I believed face-to-face schooling could be done safely. However, I was reluctant to express this opinion publicly. Even though I felt my position was well-reasoned and defensible, I worried that I would be perceived as selfish, or anti-science or somehow aligned with President Trump (whom, if it has not already been made clear, I find repugnant). So here I was again, struggling with authenticity and perception.

Ultimately, after repeated delays, APS invited all students back to face-to-face learning in a phased approach starting at the end of January 2021. There was still a good bit of controversy because the public health data was much worse than when they originally rejected the possibility of in-person learning, but evolving science on the dangers posed to and by children attending school and the implementation of more aggressive mitigation strategies shifted APS's opening strategy. When the opportunity was given, I chose to send both my children back to school. I was trepidatious about the decision for both practical and social reasons, but, given the needs and desires of my family and the relative risks to ourselves and our community, I felt it was the right choice. I'll admit, though, I didn't broadcast it; no back-to-school pictures on FaceBook. I was not ashamed of my choice, but I was wary of community judgment and censure.

In this way, so many aspects of daily life had become a minefield. Almost every decision about how we navigated the world became vulnerable to the harsh judgment of others. Shopping, schooling, exercising, socializing, nothing was simple anymore. Depending on where you found yourself in Georgia you were as likely to be found suspect for wearing a mask as you would be for not wearing one someplace else. In addition, all of these things were happening in the shadow of the presidential election. Though 2020 was an incredibly trying year, for many of us it was merely the pinnacle of four demoralizing years under the Trump administration. With or without the pandemic, I would have been very focused on seeing Trump voted out of the presidency. With the trauma of this year in particular; however, getting Trump out of the White House seemed vital to navigating our way out of our country's current nightmare. All the performative side-taking that came from the politicization of masks, policing, schooling, and generally living life under the shadow of COVID-19 became explicit, Trump vs. Biden. It was refreshing to have a simple overt political fight to focus on.

I am writing this chapter in the beginning months of Biden's administration. For the first time since 1992 (the first election for which I was old enough to vote), Georgia voted for the Democratic candidate for president. In a year where it was hard for me to find reasons to be optimistic, this outcome provided some of the most unmitigated joy and celebration that I have experienced in a long time. Realistically, the virus is not going anywhere nor is entrenched systemic racism, but I now have *more faith* that we, as a country, can find a rational path forward.

All these conflicting drives to perform—escape performance or move (or fail to move) beyond performance whether in connection with my efforts to care for and educate my children during the pandemic, the racial unrest, or simply surviving the pandemic—have been mentally taxing. I recognize for these to be the issues that I expend my mental energy on, in and of itself, makes me luckier than vast swathes of the world who are dealing with much greater hardship. I know this to be true. Just as I know that I am making imperfect choices and that being aware of my hypocrisy does not relieve me of the stain of that hypocrisy. Ultimately, I've decided that I need to make hard choices and take actions that are aligned with my values, but I also need to offer myself and others clemency when we invariably flounder. None of us is perfect no matter what we might pretend to be.

predawn rain
a change in plans
by the sound of it
  —Tom Painting

10

Root Systems

Community and Gratitude as Self-Care

Miranda Dillard

When I am among the trees,
especially the willows and the honey locust,
equally the beech, the oaks and the pines,
they give off such hints of gladness.
I would almost say that they save me, and daily.
—Mary Oliver.[1]

Introduction

A drone flying above the forest captures images of the tree canopy. As it descends, the view changes to show branches, then the trunk, and finally the base of the tree. Our drone must stop at dirt level, but the tree continues below ground as its network of roots spreads to both support and nourish. The forest is not one, but a community of trees forming a protective environment that enables the collective to weather storms and defend against predators far better than individual trees could. Scientific

---

1. Oliver, *Thirst Poems*, 4.

evidence suggests a tree can signal danger to its neighbors for threats such as disease, insects, and weather.[2]

Just as trees need the support of the forest community, we need community to help us weather our "human" storms. I grew like a tree with roots that stretched towards neighboring trees for knowledge and support. The pandemic and the heightened awareness of racial trauma made it clear we would have to find new ways to reach out beyond ourselves. My story begins with the root system. It then travels upwards to the central core— or trunk—of community and rituals of gratitude. It spreads out amidst its branches representing the practice of mindfulness, my passions, and my profession as a music teacher.

From Roots to Branches

Where the roots provide stability, they also send nourishment to the trunk, communicate with other trees, and become a storage container for life experiences. Every year adds a ring of strength and adds to the ability of the tree to reach out with its branches. Groups of trees form forests which, in exchange for additional collective needs, create a protective environment. Roots and branches reach towards others to provide and gain support, communicate danger signals, and even exchange nutrients.[3]

In the same way weather systems and environmental changes affect trees, the pandemic and the unjust murders of unarmed Black people threatened our human life systems and prompted us to redefine our lives in a framework of self-care, reflection, and restoration. George Floyd's death was a lightning bolt, igniting practices of protest and counter-protest that exposed the wounds and scars created by generations of racism. For many of us, the seclusion and fear of the pandemic permitted us space to reflect on how we are all harmed by racism; in that regard, positive changes occurred.

Finding Community During a Pandemic

March 13th, 2020 was the last time I taught my students in person. After class that day, I scoured my classroom hoping to choose all the things I might need to teach from home and loaded them into my car. Trying

2. Wohlleben, *Hidden Life of Trees.*
3. Jabr, "Social Life of Forests," 34.

to quiet the sense of heaviness descending on me, I decided that stay-ing connected with my students would become as important as teaching the music lessons. I embraced distance learning and put my energy into making the experience as fulfilling as possible. At first, I found it difficult to engage effectively with my online classes, so I became a student of this new technology. Turning to webinars and online classes, I found teachers from all over the world freely sharing ideas, materials, and lessons. With this new way of learning and sharing, my peers and I built a new video-conferencing community to serve the learning needs of our students.

My daily existence changed overnight. What was a school campus and my classroom became faces inside squares on my computer. My physical community was reduced in size to the walkable space in my tiny neighborhood. Relying on the strength of my trunk and branches, I con-structed a new sense of community by practicing gratitude and mindful-ness. Nourishing my soul with music, I fed my body from the goods of the Earth and strengthened it with exercise.

The garden in my front yard is my happy place; and as my neighbors strolled by, we would talk about the flowers, the weather, or just enjoy much needed conversation. In-between my virtual music classes, I would dash outside to gulp the air and feel the warmth of the sun. Ultimately, I got to know my community better than before COVID-19. We humans need contact with other humans, and fleeting as these outdoor encoun-ters were, they helped sustain and reinforce a much-needed sense of togetherness. If we cannot have our "normal" community, we can create one with what we have on hand... each other.

Gratitude

I live with a brain condition called Chiari malformation. In the simplest of terms, this means that my skull is too small for my brain. The pressure this exerts on my spinal cord causes chronic pain along with other unpre-dictable symptoms. Chiari is incurable, but there is a surgery that makes it more livable for most. It involves removal of a piece of the skull— just above the neck—filing down some of the bone matter in the first ver-tebrae of the spine, and cauterization of the part of the brain that has herniated into the opening of the spinal canal. The brain is encased in a protective sac called the dura. When the dura is opened exposing brain tissue, unexplainable things can happen to patients' cognitive abilities. I was no exception. Walking to school along tree-lined streets was a new and wonderful experience after decompression and laminectomy surgery. It was as though the thick and gnarled old oak trees had come to life and were sharing their energy and spirit with me. I have always loved being in nature amongst the trees, and its importance increased tremendously following my surgery. Tree bathing was a large part of my self-care rituals.[4]

Though not all my symptoms were abated by the surgery, I am grateful to be alive, thankful for all the abilities I have regained and appreciative of the new ones bestowed on me. Although it took two years after surgery to return to a mostly normal existence, it became clear to me that my experiences with Chiari malformation gave me the gift of waking up each morning thankful to be alive. No longer did I take things for granted, and in those times when the painful symptoms of Chiari were difficult to endure, I would temper them with thoughts of the times when I was symptom-free. This provided a well of emotional strength that I called upon to survive 2020.

My pre-Covid practice of placing glass jars with my garden flowers on my fence along with a note that said, "Take me with you," became even more important. I expanded this by driving around Atlanta dropping bouquets on the porches of friends who I knew were struggling. Neighbors both lost their jobs due to the pandemic and needed to proceed with their wedding plans without spending any money. White hydrangeas from my front yard were just what they needed. When the grocery shelves started to empty, I shared whatever surplus I had with neighbors. It was important to find a farm that was part of a local farmers' market and pre-purchase food from them. Buying more than I needed made it possible to give to those in need, and supporting a local farm became part of my practice of gratitude.

Since my fifth-grade membership in the Chicago Children's Choir, singing has been a very important part of my life. The intentional diversity and emphasis on equity in all parts of that choir are the main reason I am a music educator and social justice activist today. While attending a world drumming course in Washington several years ago, I learned of the existence of a choir created to sing at the bedside of people in hospice. Inspired by my discovery, I sought out and joined the "Voices of Love," a Threshold Choir in Atlanta, eventually becoming the director.[5] I find

4. Bobby Jones Chiari and Syringomyelia Foundation.

5. Threshold Choir uses song to bring comfort to people at the end of life. See https://thresholdchoir.org/Voices_of_Love.

great joy in helping bring grace and beauty to the end-of-life experience. Our acapella trio brings solace and ease of pain during the last steps of life's journey.

The virus made it impossible to go to the bedside when we were most needed, so we relied on technology to make recordings for hospice workers to share with patients. Our group adapted to the challenges of videoconferencing to create more effective rehearsal techniques. Viewing social distancing as an opportunity, our Threshold Choir used the time to learn new songs, get help with learning Spanish lyrics, and study the death and dying process. We focused on the book *Final Gifts* by Maggie Callanan and Patricia Kelley, as well as videos covering the five stages of grief.[6] Using the lyrics from our songs, we sent cards to our hospice organization to let our patients know they are not alone.

Branches

My profession, passions, and practice of mindfulness are the three branches of my life force. Leaves and branches lean and rest on each other, as do these aspects of my life. My branches became an even greater source of my self-care and resilience in 2020 with the onslaught of CO-VID-19 and the struggles of confronting racism. In 1996, I left public school teaching to work at a private independent K-12 school in Atlanta. My new school's diversity committee provided me an outlet for my passion for activism and Cecelia, the group leader, inspired me to be a better person and teacher. Listening to parents and students helped me move beyond meetings and reading books. This led me to understand that the impact of my actions was more important than my intent. This revelation was the first piece that propelled me into deeper work examining my personal biases and privileges associated with whiteness.

President Trump's inauguration was the second piece that shook my core and told me I needed to be even more actively involved in fighting against racism. As I walked through a mall to renew my driver's license, a jewelry store owner called me over to get me to shop at his kiosk. "I voted for Trump," he said. "Come see my store," as if this were a secret code. The old "me" would have silently walked away, but now I was compelled to let him know exactly how I felt.

6. Callanan, *Final Gifts*.

This event and other experiences would prove to be the catalyst for beginning work with various anti-racist organizations such as AWARE-LA, Coming to the Table, the Racial Equity Institute, the Privilege Institute and attending the White Privilege Conference.

Prior to 2020, I struggled to find white people who were willing to discuss issues of race and social justice. Affinity groups are part of the White Privilege Conference, and with the help of a colleague, we started a white affinity group at our school. Nine white educators met in February 2020 to examine the Building Anti-Racist White Educators (BARWE) inquiry series. Unfortunately, the pandemic would stall our work. We devoted our energy to virtual teaching, and BARWE was temporarily put on hold. As classes ended in early June in 2020, the elementary faculty realized we could no longer put off our anti-racist work. During our summer break, our BARWE group met six times to read and discuss issues such as the culture of white supremacy and the Black Lives Matter movement. This work has not stopped. Our elementary faculty and staff continue to meet twice a month, following the BARWE inquiry series.

The origin of my interest in mindfulness began many years ago when on a flight I experienced a frightening landing during a thunderstorm. Flying became a traumatic experience, causing me to change travel plans and not attend conferences to which I could not drive. The only way I could visit my brother in Germany was to get on an airplane, so I had to find a way to manage my fear of flying. Cognitively Based Compassion Training (CBCT) courses and Mindfulness Based Stress Reduction (MBSR) classes were the tools I needed, and I learned to employ them as part of my daily routine. My enriched daily practice was key to the self-care I relied upon to get me through the year 2020.

Following the refinement of my own practice, I incorporated mindfulness into my music lessons. Virtual teaching challenges —along with student anxiety and the stress of the pandemic— created a need for mindfulness in every lesson. While hiking in the summer of 2020, I took videos of streams and lakes to share with classes as a centering exercise. When a student asked for more of my water videos to help him get ready for class, I knew this was a valuable tool. I also incorporated yoga-based movements with music, mindful breathing, and mindful moment exercises to help my students achieve a calmer and more present state of mind.

Teaching and mindfulness branches could not exist without my passions. Singing was restricted by COVID-19, which meant I had to find new ways to use my voice. In Zoom classes, at-home students and I can safely sing, and all students share their voices through recordings on an online app called Seesaw. Though the patients needed our presence more than ever, Threshold bedside singing had to be done with recordings. Despite these challenges, I remained focused on what could be done and kept moving forward. We never gave up. My roots, trunk, and branches have sustained my source of nourishment and support. Self-care relies on my passions, teaching, and mindfulness practice. When my trunk wavers, I reach out to my roots, branches, and community for support.

Weather Forecast

My hope is that living through the pandemic has renewed our commitment to the goodness of life. Through gratitude rituals, understanding the importance and beauty of nature, and redefining our sense of community, we can discover new ways to care for ourselves and each other. Educators can learn from the failures and successes of virtual teaching. Changes in our teaching methods forced us to reconsider our curriculum, teaching style, and traditions. Being physically apart from our communities gave us time to reflect on what is most essential for life. With continued work on anti-racism and the dismantling of the white supremacist structure of our country, we will create a new form of "normal," one that emphasizes the importance of an intentional life strengthened by gratitude and the value of community. May the trees in the forests, and the people in our communities reach out to sustain each other so that our planet can be its best.

the cat sees the moon
on water
she tries to lick it
      —Madeleine Moon-Chun

11

What's Cooking

Food, Love, and Community during a Pandemic

Namju Cho

Coming Home

WHEN I RETURNED TO Korea in early 2019 after having lived in the United States for twenty years, I never thought the move would be one of the most unwittingly prescient—and revelatory—decisions I'd ever made. My father passed away unexpectedly in 2017 and my family—especially my mother—was still reeling from the shock, guilt, and overwhelming sense of loss. I had long felt out of place in the United States, despite having lived there the longest period of my life. I had returned to Korea to take better care of myself and my family. COVID-19 struck on my one-year anniversary return to Korea.

Going through COVID-19 with my mother and sisters brought me closer to them than I could have ever imagined. Shortly before CO-VID-19, my eldest sister fell and broke her leg in a freak bus accident. Deep into the pandemic, my mother fell on a moving escalator and broke her hip. Meanwhile, I grappled with the prospect of removing my thyroid that doctors told me wasn't functioning properly. While far from over, my family and I helped each other endure the pandemic through our love of and appreciation for food, cooking, and each other. Staying connected to my community of friends in the United States and worldwide also helped me feel less isolated, where every text or video call boosted my mental and emotional well-being.

The racial justice movement in the United States and beyond, as well as the historic US presidential elections and the Capitol attack that followed on Jan. 6, 2021, made me feel—perhaps for the first time in my life—oddly "American." That's saying a lot for me, given that questions and the complexities of identity have been a lifelong journey. I never felt like I fit in and certainly never felt very American since naturalizing in 2015. I remember impatiently wanting to return to work during the swearing-in ceremony, while other families cried and hugged, overcome with emotion. Being the sole American among my family in Korea (an American sister lives in San Francisco), I longed for camaraderie to celebrate victories and vent over outrageous events unfolding stateside. Seeing "diversity, equity, and inclusion" become buzzwords made me wish they weren't just a passing fad. While long overdue, I was encouraged by the faces and shapes seen, as well as voices heard in the mainstream. Still, the recent wave of hate crimes against Asian Americans seemed like a culmination—or continuum—of the age-old racism we face in America.

As someone raised in different countries with diverse identities, I've developed my own definition of care. Care includes love of food and cooking for family at the individual level. It also includes bridging communities and crystallizing my own ever-evolving identity—just as America comes to terms with its own. Finally, care means trying to apply the ideals of diversity, equity, and inclusion to my family, my community of friends and associates, and to Korean society at-large.

Mothers & Sisters

Before COVID-19, my family—and especially my mother's unconditional love and support—helped me cope with work-related stress and re-adjust to life in Korea. I cherished every moment spent with her, even as she chided me to keep my less-than-demure laugh down for the neighbors ("we have thin walls!") or balked every time I salted my hard-boiled egg ("it's bad for your health!"). This dedicated time with family often felt like a dream—precious but ethereal. My mother and sisters helped me through my formative years when we were uprooted and moved to a new country and school every few years, following my father who was a Korean diplomat.

I also happened to be in Korea, a country that avoided a full lockdown thanks to its quick response to the pandemic early on. Koreans experienced COVID-19 a bit differently than most people around the world. My friends in Italy for a time were fined or arrested if they ventured outside without a permit showing they were on essential duty, such as buying food or on assignment. My friend in Chile hadn't seen her parents in person in over six months and her daughter was finding it difficult to focus on online schooling.

Not being on full lockdown meant that I commuted daily to one of the most densely populated areas in Seoul. We were surrounded by office buildings. I rode a packed bus for three hours round trip—daily. While I was fortunate to have a job during the pandemic, I lived in constant fear that I may infect my elderly mother with whom I lived.

Fortunately, the Korean government made COVID-19 testing widely available, and the country was one of the pioneers of drive-in testing.[1] Parks, museums, and businesses such as theaters and gyms were shuttered or mandated to close early. Some analysts pointed to the small size of the country, Korea's collectivist nature, and the contact tracing system for positive COVID-19 cases as reasons for the country's early success. I believe Koreans understand science and did what they needed to do to contain a virus. A few rogue ones certainly went to church, saunas, *kimchi*-making gatherings, or night clubs against health warnings. By and large, however, many Koreans stayed home and when they went out, they wore masks.

The sudden surge of demand for masks hit Korea too and Koreans hoarded masks. The government started rationing masks and for a time, it was a cat and mouse game of 'find a pharmacy with masks,' using homegrown apps. Every week, the app directed me to a pharmacy where I stood in line to buy my two masks. We sent extra masks to my sister in San Francisco. When she got them, my twelve-year-old niece marveled at the quality of the masks. It was baffling to learn that the richest country in the world couldn't provide better quality masks to its people. Korea stopped rationing masks on July 11, 2020.

I quit my job in July 2020 to take care of my health. Korea was seeing fewer new cases during the summer of 2020. In retrospect, I got

1. Watson and Jeong, "South Korea Pioneers."

complacent and callously hopped around town to see friends, albeit fully masked and while taking other precautions. I also reconnected with friends near and far in New York, Los Angeles, Seattle, Atlanta, Little Rock, Rome, Bologna, Santiago, and Tokyo.

I followed with dismay the coverage on COVID-19 deniers who refused to wear masks in the United States, Spaniards rioting against the lockdown, and the heart-wrenching death tolls and bodies being buried across the globe. It didn't dawn on me that something as innocuous and critical as wearing a mask could become politicized. Getting vaccinated was equally polarizing, although plenty of right-wing politicians —including the former US president—got their shot and did so behind closed doors so as not to upset their base.

Korea's track record with COVID-19 vaccinations is less illustrious. As of July 23, 2021, about one-third of South Korea's fifty-two million people had gotten at least one dose of the vaccine or full doses, placing it 34th among the Organization for Economic Cooperation and Development's thirty-eight member states and lower than Czechia, Latvia, and Costa Rica, respectively.[2]

Did Koreans give up a level of privacy unthinkable in the United States and elsewhere? Maybe. As of July 23, 2021, Korea recorded 185,733 infected persons and 2,066 deaths from COVID-19, far lower than several other industrialized countries.[3]

Food in the Time of Corona

I'm beyond grateful I didn't have to be on lockdown by myself in Los Angeles where I had lived up until early 2019. Growing up, family was the one constant in my life when other aspects of my life were not. I was born in Australia and raised in the Netherlands, Ivory Coast, France, Korea, Chile, and Venezuela. Moving frequently to different countries and schools brought our family closer. My sisters and I understood each other even though we didn't always agree on everything. COVID-19 made it difficult to see my sisters—let alone friends—or travel. My love of cooking for—and sharing food with—loved ones was now a health hazard. My mother is a terrific cook and I learned to cook Korean food by looking over her shoulder and helping her in the kitchen throughout the years.

2. Our World in Data, "Share of People Vaccinated."
3. Worldometer, "Reported Cases and Deaths."

Eating, cooking, thinking about what to cook or eat, and watching others enjoy my food is a favorite pastime and personal passion. I've often found cooking therapeutic, and sharing my food has brought me closer to my community. Cooking during the pandemic made the connection more pronounced.

After quitting my job and suddenly finding myself with ample time on my hands, I immersed myself in cookbook after cookbook, recipe after recipe. I wasn't sure when I would try out all of the recipes I was saving but it sure felt good accumulating them. It turned out I had the perfect place to unleash my inner "Iron Chef"—a little country house in the city of PyeongChang,[4] the site of the 2018 Winter Olympics located two hours East of Seoul. The state-of-the-art kitchen came complete with a gorgeous island and plenty of counter space to chop, mix, and lay out ingredients for our epic meals. A panoramic view of the mountains took it over the top. My sister and her partner own the house. She is an avid cook herself, and we often tried to outdo each other with absurdly elaborate meals. We logged boxes and bags filled with meats, seafood, breads, rice, wines, and cheeses for our feasts. Something about the house inspired us to go all out.

One time, I made Chilean *empanadas de "pino"*[5] from scratch simply because I craved them and couldn't find them in Korea. These savory pastries are filled with minced beef, onions, raisins, olives, and hard-boiled eggs and seasoned with cumin and other spices. The dough alone took hours. I kneaded, folded, mixed, and baked while eighties hits by Falco, Queen, and David Bowie played in the background and took us back to our time in Chile. Cooking in "PC," as we've dubbed the venerable city of PyeongChang, is undoubtedly a blessing and privilege. The place has become our new cooking laboratory, fun house, and pandemic getaway. As Koreans like to say, a place for "healing." PC also gave us fertile land to grow corn, radishes, potatoes, herbs, chili peppers, and beans. We made *kimchi* with *artali*[6] radishes. We shucked, dried, and roasted corn for tea. We made potatoes every possible way. We now have a newfound appreciation for farming. Sharing the bounty with friends and family only added to the experience.

4. I have used the Revised Romanization of Korean words based on the National Institute of Korean Language guidelines. All other non-English words are spelled in their native form or spelled using US transliteration.

5. Classic filling of minced beef and onion.

6. Korean for small, thumb-sized radishes. Also known as *chong-gak* radishes.

Just as I had introduced Korean food to non-Koreans in the United States (I wrote about Korean food, gave cooking classes, led food tours of Koreatown in Los Angeles, and hosted monumental dinner parties for friends), I brought global cuisine to my family. I served *falafel* with *hummus*, chicken *enchiladas*, and beef *rendang*, Malaysia's delectable slow-cooked national dish that was voted the world's best food by *CNN* in 2017.[7] I also learned to make classic Korean dishes from my mother, including a cold broth *kimchi* with radishes, cucumbers, and napa cabbage often eaten in the summer.

Our cooking bonanza was suddenly cut short by an unexpected accident. In October 2020, my mother fell from an escalator and broke her hip. She had surgery and couldn't walk for months. My sisters and I were still traumatized by our father's sudden passing in 2017 after he injured his spinal cord in a freak accident. We felt we should have been more aggressive in ensuring he received the best care. We surmised we were probably blindsided by his relatively good health. We vowed not to let our guard down with my mother and were on extra-high alert throughout. I was my mother's caretaker. While part of me had always prepared for this role that I knew would eventually come, I didn't expect it to come so soon, albeit temporarily.

Being a caretaker was both rewarding and challenging. I am heartened I was there for her when she needed me the most. However, being on-call around the clock was taxing. I was constantly on-edge for fear she may fall again. After all, she had fallen once at home after recovering from surgery. I heard a thud and rushed over, only to find her on the floor next to her wheelchair. She fractured her rib. From that point on, any sound resembling a thud would trigger panic. I cherished spending more time with her and consoled her when she blamed herself for the accidents. Still, a lack of sleep, being on standby 24/7, and making sure she was eating well soon took a toll on my physical and emotional health.

I'm grateful that my sisters checked in on me regularly, which helped immensely. My oldest sister always called my mother at least twice a day. She is like a second Mom—always there for me—who is ready to provide any support I may need. My third sister often called us from her commute home after work and we'd chat for nearly an hour—about Mom's recovery, food, Saturday Night Live skits, and Netflix shows. It was therapeutic for both of us. She has a demanding job and manages to simultaneously raise

7. Cheung, "Your Pick."

two boys, be a caring daughter, and be a supportive sister. I marveled at how she juggles everything. Yet, she does it all with grace, warmth, and a great sense of humor. At times, she tended to deprioritize her own well-being and I reminded her to take care of herself.

For a time during my mother's recovery, my two sisters paid us a visit almost every Sunday and we soon created a new tradition of Sunday Supper. These quickly replaced our PC culinary adventures since we couldn't travel to the fun house for some time. One Sunday, I cooked the classic Persian dish, chicken *fesenjan* with *tah dig*, the wonderfully crusty part of basmati rice at the bottom of a pot. *Fesenjan* is a slow-cooked stew flavored with pomegranate paste, walnuts, and spices, sprinkled with pomegranate seeds. On another Sunday, my third sister's family stopped by to see my mother for the first time since her surgery. I made three kinds of dumplings including pork and *kimchi*, shrimp and garlic chives, and vegetarian with shitake mushrooms and tofu. I made two additional Korean Chinese dishes, *nanjawanseu,* beef and pork patties smothered in a luscious vegetable sauce and *kkanpunggi,* deep fried chicken morsels in a sweet and spicy sauce. They were a hit.

Then there's the wrap-up. My sisters and I are self-proclaimed Bag Ladies because we often come and leave with food for each other in bags large and small. I would give one sister my superfood granola containing more than seventeen ingredients such as grain and bean powder, almonds, and home-dried persimmons. My oldest sister would bring me my favorite tangy, spicy, and sweet cucumber side dish that is her specialty. My third sister would bring me bright red pickled beets and cabbage, the creamiest pumpkin soup, and a box of giant homemade chocolate chip cookies inspired by the famed Levain Bakery in New York City. I would deliver my mother's exceptional beef bone broth to my sisters with a few more dishes I made like savory candied dried baby anchovies or homemade pork *tamales*. In other words, we reliantly fed off of each other.

I love traditions and creating new ones that recharge us. Sunday Suppers are now a special gathering where my sisters, mother and I eat, laugh, cry, and support each other as we weigh in on our daily lives. Thankfully, my mother resumed walking normally within a few months following surgery.

Another food tradition that brought us closer during the pandemic was *jesa*.[8] In our family, food has always been a big part of *jesa*—a memorial ceremony honoring our ancestors. We celebrate my father's life and honor him through *jesa* three times a year—on Lunar New Year, on the anniversary of his passing in March, and on the Harvest Moon Holiday named *Chuseok* (the equivalent to Thanksgiving). Ostensibly, *jesa* is about paying respects to one's ancestors. In practice, it is sexist. I have conflicting memories of *jesa* I attended when I was younger. I liked honoring deceased grandparents and catching up with my uncles and cousins at the gatherings, but I didn't like seeing the men eating and drinking in a separate room after the ceremony while women slaved away in the kitchen.

Jesa was a rare occasion to have some of my favorite foods, such as *sanjeok*— savory pancakes skewered with neatly arranged carrots, beef strips, green onions, and mushrooms, dusted in flour, dipped in egg batter, and pan-fried. Once the *jesa* was over and the men were served food and drinks, it was our turn to eat. My female cousin would grab a giant bowl, throw in some rice and *namul*,[9] add a dollop of red pepper paste and sesame oil and mix thoroughly. While the aunts ate a proper meal with individual rice and soup bowls, a group of us would hover over the bowl and dig in with our spoons, family-style. I can still smell the intense aroma of sesame oil emanating from that communal bowl of *bibimbap*[10] to this day.

My mother was determined to prepare the very best *jesa* for my father. The problem: she had never done one by herself, and some rules were archaic and arbitrary. Which dishes should go on the offering table and how should they be placed? Garlic and scallions were off-limits. No red *kimchi*, Korea's national dish of fiery fermented cabbage, but white cold broth kimchi was okay. Fish with no scales: not okay—including, sadly, my father's favorite, *galchi*.[11] Food should be stacked in odd numbers, never even. Our offerings included a mix of dried and fresh fish, fruit, rice cakes, raw chestnuts, dried jujubes, savory pancakes, different kinds of *namul*, white rice (he disliked other grains), and soup.

8. This is an account of my personal *jesa* experience, which may be different from those of others. The tradition has evolved over the years and this account is not meant to be a representation or historical description of *jesa*.

9. Korean for seasoned vegetables and roots often eaten as side dishes in a meal.

10. Korean for rice bowl mixed with vegetables.

11. Korean for the fish called hair tail.

The *pièce de résistance* was *dongpayuk*, a braised pork belly chunk smothered in a rich salty and sweet sauce that was one of my father's favorites. Alongside these delicacies were two decidedly non-traditional additions: Paper-thin slices of *Jamón Ibérico*12 *de Bellota* and a glass of full-bodied Chilean Carménère, as an homage to my father who loved both (Chile was his first post as Ambassador and Spain was his last before he retired).

After preparing the feast for weeks, we laid out a table packed with offerings. We paid our respects by bowing twice and offering a glass of wine (we leave the door to our home ajar for his spirit to enter). Once it was over, we cleared the offerings and enjoyed the feast together. We then packed multiple bags with copious amounts of leftovers—savory pancakes, *namul,* and beef bone soup (with all the trimmings including slow-cooked meat, radishes, and green onions).

Cooking at the PC house, Sunday Suppers, and *jesa* helped me and my family through the pandemic. In an odd turn of events, my mother and I traded places. Just as she recovered from her hip surgery in early 2021, I developed a severe case of frozen shoulder on my left and De Quervain tenosynovitis (an inflammation of tendons) on my right thumb and wrist. I was unable to do what I love—cook—or much of anything else. My mother now took care of me, doing all the cooking.

Korean and American

During the pandemic, the shootings of Black men ignited mainstream America to rise against police brutality and racial injustice. I watched story after story of innocent Black men and women being choked by the knee or shot by police officers. I was outraged, and then inspired by the movement. Most of all, I was proud. I was also puzzled. I had always felt out of place in the United States even after I naturalized in 2015. What I was feeling now felt like patriotism, but the feeling was so novel that I couldn't help but doubt myself. After all, I wasn't even sure I *felt* American. How could someone unsure of their American-ness be proud of America? Then again, I never felt very Korean either—even when my diplomat father instilled in me and my three sisters a distinct pride in being Korean nationals. One thing that became abundantly clear while living in America is that the conversation around race often focused on

12. A variety of Spanish ham.

relations between whites and Blacks, with Hispanics included sometimes. Rarely were Asians part of the conversation even though Asian
Americans are the fastest growing segment of the US population. The
recent wave of Asian American hate crimes momentarily prompted a
more inclusive discussion on race in the mainstream, but we can—and
should—do better.

Becoming a Hybrid Identity

COVID-19 heightened the role of care at a personal, communal, and
global level. My family's pre-existing bond and love of food and cooking
kept us close during the pandemic. Our well-being, in turn, fed into the
well-being of our local community and further into our greater global
community. Just as I got closer to my family while growing up in seven
countries and in times of adversity, so did my relationship with the United States as I watched it being battered and bruised with the pandemic,
political turmoil, and racial strife.

The racial justice protests, the nerve-wracking presidential elections, the storming of the Capitol followed by the inauguration, and wave
of hate crimes against Asian Americans all contributed to my identity. I
surprised myself at how emotional I got watching President Biden get
elected. I was proud that I had played a small role in it—by texting two-
hundred voters in swing states. The buildup to the victory speeches was
long and anxiety filled. The wave of emotions cascaded during a climactic
inauguration. Perhaps it was a cathartic response to four years of oppression and calamity. I listened to a simple speech by a President who spoke
of unity and reconciliation, and a moving poem recited by 22-year-old
African American woman, Amanda Gorman. Biden was inclusive and
thanked others. He was empathetic, compassionate, and firm. He was
presidential. Hearing his words, words we longed to hear from a president for so long, got me choked up. This is the America I want to be a part
of. This is the America I *am* a part of.

Growing up as a foreigner in various countries, I held onto my Korean identity for dear life—until I landed in Korea and experienced a
different reality. Years later, being away from the United States and seeing it under siege made me feel more American than ever. I'm not quite
done being Korean either, however. I am committed to bridging cultures
because that is where I find fulfillment and purpose.

Our most important relationships and efforts of care sustained us during a trying time in more ways than one. In fact, it made us stronger and more hopeful than ever. This optimism directly fed into my sense of identity. My identity doesn't belong to any one country or another. Just like America, my identity is evolving every day, influenced by people and communities that uphold the same values that matter most to me.

I go back to my sister's thesis about Korean identity (but could be applied to any nationality-based identity).[13] She questions the premise of Korea as a homogenous society. She calls for diversity and to reexamine the social norm of wanting to absorb, ignore, or discriminate against those who have gone through a different experience. We need to redefine what is considered "we," just as we understand an individual's identity is constantly evolving. I believe the same should be true for how we define American identity or any identity, for that matter. This also aligns with current dialogue about diversity, equity, and inclusion worldwide.

Identity is based on one's own understanding and derived from a society that one believes represents oneself.[14] However, this society has usually been defined by country borders, aka. Nationality. Furthermore, as international movement across borders increases, the concept of nationality as an identity for many doesn't always match its cultural and social identity. This is especially true in the United States where people come from all over the world. There are plenty of examples where one is born into a certain nationality but as the background of where the person was raised changes, the meaning of nationality evolves. As such, identity is constructed through culture. It is constructed through people, communities, relationships, and movements.

Perhaps a hybrid identity most closely describes where I currently stand. A hybrid identity is about belonging here, everywhere, or nowhere.[15] Most importantly, those with a so-called hybrid identity are the very entity that can execute translation between cultures and bridge communities. Many of my friends who are Indian American, Mexican American, or "Third Culture Kids" who have lived in different countries say they can relate. One of my Mexican American friends uses the expression, *"ni aquí ni allá,"*—which translates to "neither here nor there," to describe her sense of dislocation. I have pieces of all the countries in

13. Cho, "Crossing Borderlines."
14. Cho, "Crossing Borderlines."
15. Cho, "Crossing Borderlines."

which I have lived, including Australia, Holland, Ivory Coast, France, Korea, Chile, Venezuela, and the United States—regardless of what my passport says, what I look like, where I was born, or where my parents came from.

"Where is home for you?" I get asked a lot. Home is where my family, friends, and community are. I miss Korea when I'm in the United States and miss the United States when in Korea. When I hear Chilean slang (even in a film), I light up. When I hear an old *chanson* (song) circa 1978 from France, I reminisce about how we used to listen to cassette tapes in the car during our many road trips with four rowdy girls cooped up in the backseat of a tiny sedan.

All my life, I was happiest when I was harnessing my multicultural background for a purpose. Specifically, I want to help foster deeper understanding between people in different generations and cultures. Amplify our voices as Asian Americans. Call out racism and sexism in Korea. That is what care looks like to me. I've always tried to achieve this throughout my life and would like to think I have made a small dent thus far.

The Front Yard

Jackie Weltman

Gardening

It was March of 2020. Pandemic shelter-in-place orders had been issued, and we needed to lay in provisions. I stood in the produce aisle of our little local grocery market, mouth agape. The wooden pedestals of the produce bins were naked, their rich covering rainbow of produce had entirely vanished. It looked like the house lights had gone up on a theatre set, leaving a few dull, undersized winter squash lined up against the shop window. Dismayed, I grabbed two and flung them into my handbasket.

In touch with some vague new famine-fear, I began to zoom around the aisles, cutting a wide berth around others and grabbing what useful goods I could find. Long forgotten parental warnings about the privations of undernourished countries-other-than-ours bobbed in the haze of my mind. What *was* this?! Almost no packaged foods were left on the bare shelving, no household goods, and no (do I need even to say it?) toilet paper. I nabbed a few lonely, misunderstood cans of jackfruit-in-water, and then I left.

In late autumn of 2019, I had told my wife Peggy that I wanted to scale back the garden come spring. There was far too much work planting, spraying, prepping, and harvesting, followed by cooking, drying, and freezing the harvest. I wanted to return to the weekend hiking we used to love, to go on more day trips, and take more short vacations. "Let's be more like 'normal people' and do leisure activities," we had agreed enthusiastically. In an afternoon— nay, in an hour and a half—that idea was out the window. "I think we are going to need a bigger garden this year," I explained soberly when I got home.

My wife and I are used to whirling about the world, commuting to and from work, going to restaurants, visiting places, *doing things*. Almost overnight there were no places to go and no "things to do." This did not rattle me much. I am a former professional baker and a passionate amateur of the distaff arts. I am very frequently by myself in the garden, cooking, or noodling around with a recipe; baking, canning, or fermenting one thing or another. Pandemic America, throwing up its hands, apparently soon joined me, because the nation seemed to have cleaned out every speck of bread flour in a zeal to learn to bake sourdough bread, and people bought up the entire stock of every seed catalog known to human while trying their hands at their first gardens.

I've been gardening since I was nine. My urban father learned to Victory garden during World War II in Brooklyn. He taught my sister and me old-school row-style gardening, aided by liberal applications of (very bad) chemicals. I was the one who took to growing things, however, and by the time I was in junior high school, I had a subscription to Rodale's *Organic Gardening* magazine. I would bet anyone that I was also the only fifteen-year-old around with a subscription to *Mother Earth News*.

Anywhere I have ever lived, if there was an opportunity to plant, I planted. A yard, a patio, a driveway strip, a well-lit sunroom, all could host vegetables and herbs in the ground or pots. In my favorite Haight-Ashbury flat, bereft of a usable yard, I spent six years tending thirteen square feet of hydroponic units, growing all our salad greens and basil, and balancing on a wooden stool while tying monster tomato vines up on string as they reached to the sky then crawled further and further across the tiny kitchen ceiling. So, as the pandemic darkness of unknowing descended upon our little neighborhood, I planted. I didn't know what would happen; I still have no idea what will happen, but I am certain that if I plant a garden, some of it will grow.

In the winter, before the pandemic, we had started our garden project for the year. We put a hügelkultur bed in our front lawn. Hügelkultur is a labor intensive, permacultural method of building an organic raised bed atop piled up logs, branches, and mulch. As the wood breaks down, it becomes a home for fungi and invertebrate critters of all kinds, forming a long-term biotic community that plant roots love. Though sod-whacking, digging the thick local clay, and rototilling flared my old back and arm injuries into terrible pain, we parlayed last year's Yule tree and a mound of collected branches and twigs into a very nice six-by-six bed in the best southwestern exposure on our small lot. I could not wait to plant!

Who needs a lawn anyway, right?

The new bed debuted just in time for the pandemic garden. I jettisoned plans for another even larger hügelkultur bed, worrying that it might put me in the hospital. Instead, I ordered some wooden raised bed kits, wrestled them into completion and plopped them in the front yard. Suddenly, the front yard *was where it was at.*

"Nice looking beds you have there." I was so busy that I did not realize neighbors were noticing.

I've usually worked weekends on the raised beds in our private back yard and the small forest of fifteen-gallon black plastic pots on my side patio, which is partly exposed to passersby. Every so often, someone walking with a kid or a dog would see me behind the tall picket fence and approach to ask a question or compliment the vegetables. I would hang my palms and elbows on the fence, conversing with them as if I were in prison. But now I was in the front yard a lot, directly exposed in the middle of my village, an outdoor pandemic pod of gardeners and curious neighbors.

A lot of the World War II cottages in our neighborhood have small gardens of flowers, vegetables, shrubs, fruit trees, or a mix of all these. Neighbors, I am curious about your plants as I walk by. I watch how your plants change as the seasons change; I note if you are preparing, cleaning up, or trying something new. I wonder about you by what you grow, but I cannot truly have a relationship with you unless I see you there in your front yard. I have great affection for my plants as clearly you do for yours. I raise mine from seed and their seasonal needs must take precedence in my weekend plans. Last year they told me they wished to grow in the strong southwestern sunlight on the front lawn. They lead me out towards you. I love them and now you love them too. I can tell this by the way you stop and marvel. I watch out the window as some of you take pictures of the plants you like. I slide open the window and chat with you. Even behind a window, I am only about twelve feet from you. But I want you to know I see you and that it is okay, it is good, for you to be curious about the garden. I want to relate to you. By both of us loving the plants, you and I triangulate a relationship in these confusing and difficult times.

Yes, I really want to travel out of my neighborhood. I want to take the subway or bus somewhere; I want to venture into my beloved San Francisco from my suburban home; I want to see a dear friend I miss. I ache to go see the live music I love, to visit an art museum or a restaurant, to take a walk somewhere I love. I want to do all kinds of things I cannot or should not do, but in the immortal words of Stephen Stills, *"there's a rose in the fisted glove,"*

> And the eagle flies with the dove
> And if you can't be with the one you love, honey,
> Love the one you're with, love the one you're with.

Zucchini Love

Let's talk zucchini. We live on one cool side of the Golden Gate. It is temperate in the daytime, chilly at night. I am used to growing things that thrive in a marine-influenced, short-season climate. Greens, for example, do well. Zucchini were the toe-in-the-water for whether a true fruiting crop was going to work in my new front yard bed, so I planted several. I started the seeds in my greenhouse window above the kitchen sink. The babies were happy there and grew into tweendom, so I moved them outside into a greenhouse rack to become teenagers and get used to the weather. Finally, I brought them out to the hügelkultur bed and tamped the soil around their roots. They flourished.

They were a southern Italian heirloom called San Pasquale. The seed catalog described lovely alternating dark and light green stripes with interesting ridges and a galaxy of tiny dots. When I got my first small fruits, I was stoked. I knew zucchini had a reputation for plentitude, even excess, but I still managed to be surprised when four small plants got huge; I mean really huge. They covered the bed. I remained surprised when the squash seemed to grow overnight from ordinary supermarket-sized zucchini to oddly tender monsters. In half a week, they seemed to add four or six inches. Some were almost two feet long when picked. But I did not want to pick them too soon because they had gained a fan club. Neighbors I had never seen before were swinging by the front yard, clocking the growth of these rock stars. Moms were using the zucchini as lesson plans for their preschoolers.

"Mom! Mom! It's bigger today!"
"Show me how much more it grew, sweetie!"

My neighbor Julia is Italian American and in her late seventies. We dawdle in the front yard, at a 10-foot distance in our pandemic masks, and she tells me about her childhood, about her dad's garden, about how he grew zucchini. She tells me I should trellis the vines. "They don't vine," I quibble. "Oh yes they do; my Italian dad knew all about it." "Okay," I say. "If you turn out to be right, I will owe you five bucks for a latte." "You're on," she says.

I used to show you my love by inviting you into my house, by cooking a beautiful meal, by feeding you, body, and spirit, with food pleasing to both eye and palate. Now I must love you by listening to your stories from six or eight or twelve feet away, standing on the front lawn or sitting in the sun on my haunches in the driveway. I will also love you by giving you some zucchini.

People did not want to ask but I could see it in their eyes: "I'd really like to have one of those mondo zucchini." First, the young marrieds across the street, Perez and Yinny, got one. We discussed possible recipes. Then Viktor and Meg had one delivered to the mail basket on their porch. Shelly got one. And Bee got one. Bee is a retired biochemist in her eighties and lives alone. She, having survived lung cancer, was wary of getting too near anyone during the pandemic. I called on her, carefully placed the zucchini at the top of her porch stairs, then skipped back down as she came forward to take them. We sat in the sun for a good, long time with our masks on, she at the top of the stairs, I on a walkway at the bottom. We talked about how she'd gotten into her profession, her health, her nephews. She had never actually cooked a zucchini, she told me. What do you do with it? I told her exactly how to make a simple sauté, and that very night she cooked it just so, then texted me to tell me she really enjoyed it.

I did not realize Bee had a plum tree in her yard, but she texted me shortly after that to ask whether I wanted some of the many plums that were falling to the ground and going to waste. "Bee has plums," I told Peggy. "They need a home." Peggy knows what happens in situations like this. "Don't take them if you are going to complain that you are too busy for anything else because you are trapped in the kitchen all the time," she warned.

I dithered. "You're right. I probably shouldn't."

Bee left them for me on her stairs in a paper grocery bag. Unable to let there be orphaned plums, I made plum jam with fresh ginger and sour oranges from my tree. The jam was a jewel-toned deep purple with chunks of plum and ginger. I labeled the jars, then promptly brought a few back to Bee, who exulted! She polished them off quickly with her daily toast.

Meanwhile it turned out that I did not have to trellis the zucchini after all. Julia was abashed. "Forget the five bucks and the latte," I said. "Take some zucchini!" Masked appropriately, I laid a big, beautiful, bi-colored squash on her porch and greeted her though the door. Later, when I asked her how she'd liked it, she told me it was far too big for her alone and she'd given half to Marni across the street. And in this way, zucchini as love was spreading through the neighborhood.

Orville

I still do not know much about gardening. I often fail with a crop. I work a lot, so I am not as attentive and methodical as I should be. And gardening encourages beginner's mind, the Zen Buddhist term for a fresh, enthusiastic mind not frozen in place by its own self-congratulating expertise. In gardening, there are endless things to not-know.

Down the street was my neighbor Orville, who served in World War II and returned to a long career as a supermarket butcher. He'd grown up on a farm in Kentucky, and knew how to hunt, fish, and plant. He'd cared lovingly for his small house for over fifty years, building a custom marine-varnished gate with a little boat bell on top, and constructing impeccable stone beds to replace the front lawn. He buried his fish guts therein, so that by the time I met him, he was ninety and the beds were unbelievably fertile.

It seemed like Orville could grow anything —fat green and red cabbages, cages bursting with tomatoes, frilly lettuce in tight rows, tall trellises covered with beans, fencing entwined with squash. And how did nothing get eaten by critters?!

Orville thought organic gardening was expensive nonsense but did not use a lot of chemicals, unless you count Miracle-Gro, of which he was fond. Every week, there was some flawless atomic vegetable ready for harvest in one of his front yard beds. He was my inspiration, and I adopted a new practice: Whatever Orville is doing…just do that.

Before I met him, I was afraid to talk with him because neighborhood lore had it that he was mean and gruff and once had shot a guy for stealing food out of his garden. It's like he was the real-life equivalent of the mythic kid-chasing old-guy-with-a-rifle. "Is that really true?" I asked Perez.

"That's what he told me."
"What happened to the guy he shot?"
"I guess he didn't make it."

I was aghast. Still, I longed to talk to him about his garden, determined to be unfailingly polite in order to prolong my life. When I did finally approach gingerly on the sidewalk to gush about his produce, he was a charming flirt with endless tales of gardening and cooking. Out on the sidewalk, he'd detail in exacting color what he prepared for all three meals and how. Much of his diet consisted of what he grew himself paired with the meat and fish his younger hunting and fishing buddies would bring him. He was especially enamored of red onions - "hamburger onions" he called them - and planted at least two beds full of red and Vidalia onions, as well as plastic tubs full of onions in his alleyway. "I'm an onion freak," he said.

He urged me to grow red onions and offered to gift me his favorite seed. I failed miserably at growing them, but I will try again to spread red onion love and honor Orville, who we lost at ninety-two after a neighborly, green, generous life. He had outlived his whole family and left his house to the neighbors across the street who had co-gardened with him in his old age.

Coming Full Circle

Returning the favor to the universe, I wrap tomato seeds in waxed paper parcels for Fred, who asked me for seed from the heirloom tomato that got the most attention this year. "Chestnut Chocolate" turned out to be a deep black tomato with a hidden blush of red on its derrière. It was so black that it looked like a midnight metallic hotrod paint job. Passersby were stopping cold, with wide smiles of surprise, to snap tomato selfies. Larry and Sue from the next block, whose acquaintance I'd recently made, stopped by in their Mighty Mouse masks when I was watering and reminded me that I'd promised to let them taste one when they got ripe.

I made a little pile of tomatoes on the walkway and moved back to give them space as they stepped up to take their adoptees home.

Fred is eighty and late in life completed the rigorous program to become a University of California Extension Master Gardener. He has long white hair and a long white beard, which he braids. Fred is an artist. He dresses like an artist. Fred is, basically, a hippie. We started off on the wrong foot. I had never even seen him before and was offended when a few years ago he asked if he could just walk up and pick some of our apricots while we were in the process of planting the bare root apricot tree, then little more than a stick.

"It will be a few years before this tree has any fruit," I objected. "It's… it's just a stick. If it fruits, and you are hungry, you can knock on my door to ask for some."

Damn entitled hippie, I muttered to myself when he walked away.

It's been three or four years and still no apricots. Now I fold fermented, dried tomato seed into little packets for Fred, with hot pepper seed, and dill seed besides, and label it with painter's tape. I look around to see what other seed I could give him. It seems I've forgiven Fred. Talking about vegetables will do that to an initially distrustful neighbor. Right now, we all need each other, and besides, you do get to know someone better talking at a safe distance from across the wide street, talking ten feet away while right out front, unhidden, exposed, on the front lawn.

Isn't it what we all want – to be truly seen?

13

Things Seen and Unseen

Anne Gardner

So we do not lose heart. Even though our outer nature is wasting away, our inner nature is being renewed day by day. For this slight momentary affliction is preparing us for an eternal weight of glory beyond all measure, because we look not at what can be seen but at what cannot be seen; for what can be seen is temporary, but what cannot be seen is eternal.
—2 Corinthians 4:16—18

March 10th. That was the day COVID-19 brought my world to a screeching halt. For a few months prior, a growing sense of unease had been building. In early January a handful of reports emerged regarding a strange new virus in the Wuhan province of China. By the end of the month, the Centers for Disease Control and Prevention had confirmed the virus had reached the United States. The onset of February brought air travel restrictions, the beginning of quarantine protocols, and rising concerns about infection rates. And finally, on March 11, the World Health Organization officially declared COVID-19 a global pandemic, one day after I canceled my JetBlue flight to Los Angeles. Call it intuition. Call it luck. But deep down in my bones, I knew not to get on that plane. It just didn't feel . . . right.

My trip to southern California was a house-hunting mission. Just prior to the start of the 2019-20 academic year I was offered the opportunity to lead the chaplaincy program at Harvard-Westlake, a private secondary school in Los Angeles. Enamored by thoughts of palm trees and swimming pools, it seemed like the perfect capstone to my ministerial career. On the cusp of turning sixty, I had assumed my professional journey would come to a quiet and predictable end, including retiring from my then position at Phillips Andover, an elite boarding school located roughly twenty-five miles northwest of Boston. But life, I discovered, does not always go as planned.

Reinvigorated by the thought of a new start, I gratefully accepted the position. My call would begin the following August, giving me plenty of time to prepare for the upcoming transition. First on my checklist was to find housing. Given Los Angeles's reputation for steep rents and burdensome commutes, it made sense to begin the housing search early. After months of scouring the possibilities online, my wife and I decided it was time to get a feel for the neighborhoods firsthand. With spring break just around the corner, we booked two airline tickets to Los Angeles for March 10th.

By that time, news of my upcoming departure was well-known. Nonetheless, many of my Andover colleagues remained surprised and confused by my decision to leave. After all, the Andover brand was known worldwide and ranked at the very top of programs of its kind. The cache was undeniable. The resources were plentiful. The opportunities incalculable. Unbeknownst to them, my colleagues weren't the only ones second-guessing my decision. As my start date grew closer, the thought of changing jobs became a source of simmering angst. Moving across the country and away from a support system I had carefully nurtured suddenly unnerved me. Leaving the comfortable routine of a job I knew inside and out was daunting. And after twelve years of living in a dormitory, surrounded by the constant hum of thirty-seven teenage girls whom I adored, I was already grieving their soon-to-be absence from my life.

Leave-taking is a complicated and tricky business, particularly for those of us in ministry. This is, in part, because in my business the messenger is far too often mistaken for the message.

This conflation of *who we are* with *what we do* can lead to a host of problems. To combat any potential missteps, the rules ministers must follow when leaving their congregations are well-documented and substantial. A clean break is required, for the sake of the new minister as well as the former. These protocols weren't designed to make departures more painful, but rather to underscore the importance of *the work* and not the person charged with doing it.

The rigidity of these boundaries makes perfect sense theoretically. But the heart wants what the heart wants. And leaving, particularly when the end grows near, is emotionally daunting. Never had I felt the burden of these strictures more than when leaving Andover. In the preceding dozen years my family circle had grown to include the girls in my dorm, my colleagues, and my congregants. Severing those ties would be no easy task.

I came to school chaplaincy in rather circuitous fashion. I knew from the start that this kind of work offered the best vocational fit. An earlier stint in parish ministry proved this initial hunch was spot-on. Although my time working in a traditional church setting gave me satisfaction, the day-to-day routine left me feeling lonely. I longed to be surrounded by the wisdom and companionship of a bevy of colleagues. But nearly all parishes exist on a shoestring budget, rendering them unable to support more than a handful of staff. In addition, ministers follow a schedule that runs contrary to the standard work week. Evenings and weekends are filled with obligations, a cycle that left me feeling out of step with the tempo of my family and friends.

In stark contrast, the school calendar is the metronome by which life in America runs. Indeed, if COVID-19 has taught us nothing else, it has demonstrated the central role schools play in maintaining the well-being of our families, our economy, and our communal mental health. Without a reliable school system on which to depend, our societal security blanket quickly begins to unravel. Working as a school chaplain meant I was now in sync with this driving force, happily marking each September as the start of a new year. Even more importantly, I was part of a fulsome team of colleagues. Together we ran dorms, coached teams, sat on committees, and taught our students both inside and outside the classroom. School was where I fit. Always was. Still is.

The fact that I became a school "lifer" did not come as a surprise to anyone. The academic year had always been the axis on which my life had revolved. As a child, I looked forward to September, always preparing myself with a fistful of freshly sharpened pencils and a new lunch pail. As I grew older, the accoutrements changed but not the feeling. As summer pivots to fall, I figuratively and literally turn the page. Going to school is like breathing to me, both unconscious and life sustaining.

My professional alliance with schools began early on with a career in college admissions. My first position was at a Jesuit university, followed by a few years at a school for the performing arts, and finally, for more than a decade, at Harvard University. In my forties, rather unexpectantly, I began to seriously wrestle with a call to ordination. It was something I hadn't previously imagined given my Roman Catholic upbringing. But a change of jobs, landing me at the helm of Harvard Divinity School's admissions office, proved to be the petri dish in which my vocation would take root. Suddenly I was surrounded by people whose primary task was to interrogate religion; whether intellectually, spiritually, or both. Encouraged by their openness and fervor, I too began to rethink my relationship to Christianity, specifically, to the Roman Catholic tradition. I had stopped attending church years ago and now, surrounded by believers on all sides, came to realize just how much I'd missed it. But I was so blinded by an allegiance to the Church in which I was raised, I couldn't see another way. Until I did.

To familiarize myself with the various faith traditions many applicants were coming to study, I began to attend a panoply of worship services. Over the course of a few months, I spent time in synagogues, mosques, and assorted Protestant churches. One Sunday morning, I ducked into a pew in the back of an Episcopal church. The cadence, the liturgy, the sun streaming in through the stained-glass windows stirred in me a distant spark. It was all so very familiar. And yet I felt welcomed in a way I had not in the church of my youth. My gender, my sexual orientation, and my relentless questioning were embraced in this version of Christianity. I had stumbled upon my Cinderella slipper. Believe me when I say, no one was more surprised than I was.

It wasn't too long before my reinvigorated personal devotion began to transform into an interest in corporal leadership. Looking for a sign from above, I asked my then boss for a sabbatical to move to New York City, the site of the national headquarters of the Episcopal Church. I had been offered a three-month research position there, just enough time I thought to assure me the spiritual connection I felt was more than just an infatuation. By the end of the term, I was convinced it was time to take a leap of faith. I returned to Cambridge and announced I was going to apply to seminary.

The decision to leave my plum position at Harvard was met with a healthy dollop of skepticism. "And for what?" my colleagues posited. The slimmest of chances the Episcopal Diocese of Massachusetts would be interested in the vocational aspirations of a middle-aged, monolingual, white woman? I didn't disagree. It was more than a tad risky. But the heart wants what the heart wants. Off the cliff I leapt.

Grist for the Mill

One of the things the ordination process requires is a thorough excavation of the major influences that have shaped every prospective ordinand. In many ways, the emergence of COVID-19 forced me to do the same thing, sifting through each day's grain and chaff to discern what I needed most to sustain my emotional and spiritual stability.

In the end, it came down to two things. They were the same two things I had always counted on to give ballast to my life, passed down to me by my tempestuous and blazingly bright lodestar. My mother.

The first was her love of words. When I was a child, while other kids salivated over the thought of a shiny new bicycle or what the supple leather of a new catcher's mitt might feel like, I dreamt of books. I loved everything about them; how they fit in my hand, the smell of the pages, the anticipation of a new story waiting to be discovered. It was a love affair that needed to be curated of course. My mother championed that cause, luring me into the world of words in a most unusual way.

The child of a career military man, our house was one of order and discipline. My mother, perhaps sensing my irritation, announced one day my brother and I were going to be allowed to draw on the furniture. This was an unprecedented, and frankly unimaginable, breach of protocol. I was stunned by this act of parental surrender and thrilled at the thought I would be allowed to partake in such deviant behavior. Following her proclamation, she quickly proceeded to wrap the bottom half of our refrigerator in cheap butcher block paper. With a quick slice of a scissor blade, the paper was cut down the length of the door, ensuring continued access to a glass of milk or roast beef sandwich. When she finished, she turned to me and stated there was just one small caveat. I returned her gaze with a sudden suspicion. She ever so casually explained the refrigerator would be the only piece of "furniture" we would be allowed to draw on, oh and one more thing, we could only draw the magnets that were stuck to its side.

"That's it? Those are the only rules?" I queried. My mother nodded in agreement. I glanced at the side of the refrigerator and saw it was covered in brightly colored magnets, none of which I recognized. My mother quickly separated them into two groups, one she called "letters" and one she called "numbers." She promised me I could draw anything I wanted with my crayons while sitting at the kitchen table. But if I wanted to have the freedom, the thrill of drawing on the "furniture," I would have to stick to tracing the magnets. I smirked at my own cleverness, convinced I had outflanked her somehow in this strategic parent-child contest. What did it matter what I was drawing as long as I was allowed to draw?

From very early on, I was taught that reading and writing were privileges, acts that wielded enormous power. My mother dutifully replaced that butcher block paper every day. And while I continued to be attracted to my coloring books, they eventually lost their allure. Initially I was befuddled by the magnets. But it wasn't long before I recognized their mysterious coupling as a code. Suddenly I understood that *these* symbols were *everyone's* symbols. Within that clump of magnets lay a message, and I begged my mother to show me how it all worked. Outflanked indeed. Like most writers, I first fell in love with reading. I distinctly remember the day I got my first library card, my passport to a lifelong relationship with words. After pestering my mother for months, she finally agreed to drive me to our local library to inquire about getting a card. Standing on the opposite side of the checkout counter, a sturdy middle-aged woman watched as I carefully scrawled my name across the back of my newly-minted paper card. After examining my signature, the librarian slid it back across the smooth wooden surface. I was so awed by this new possession that I picked it up quite gingerly, carrying it in my hand the whole way home for fear it would become creased or damaged if placed in my pocket. After pulling into the driveway, I bounded up the stairs and raced down the hallway to my bedroom, extracting a cardboard box from underneath my bed. I placed my new treasure atop a pyramid of kite string, baseball cards, and bubble gum before gently closing the top. It was official. I was now part of the club.

Literacy, the reading and writing of those alluring symbols, proved to be the great equalizer for me. It allowed me to enter into the world of adults, regardless of my height or strength or age. And not surprisingly, writing became the mechanism through which I would later process my thoughts. Karen Armstrong, a former Roman Catholic nun-turned-writer, speaks to this same experience in her autobiography *The Spiral Staircase*. In it she recounts a comment made by a friend on the benefits of keeping a journal. "'I don't know how anybody manages without a diary,' she used to say. 'You should have kept one in the convent. I bet you would have got out sooner; you see things so much more clearly when you write them down.'"[1]

The serenity of a clean white page. The cathartic release of rapping the black squares of a keyboard. The way the whole world slows down as you sort through your emotional clutter; looking for one sentence of clarity, and then another, and then another.

Writing has long been my way of shedding light on the unseen. It made perfect sense to me to conscript my oldest ally, the written word, in my fight against the invisible virus. Today's journal entry is sure to become tomorrow's COVID-19 kryptonite. The virus never stood a chance.

Solvitur Ambulando (It Is Solved by Walking)

March in New England is not for the faint of heart.

As news of surging infection rates splashed across headlines worldwide, I hunkered down in my dorm apartment steadying myself for Armageddon. Occasionally I would dash through the aisles of my local grocery store, stockpiling toilet paper, disinfectant, and canned goods. But for the most part, I spent the month of March of 2020, isolated and inside.

Andover's students had gone on spring break just a week before announcements regarding COVID-19 became a regular part of our news cycle. But it soon became apparent they would not be able to return to campus. We all held out hope in the beginning. But as the death toll began to rise, the school reluctantly prepared for a virtual spring term. Zoom became part of my new lexicon, both as a noun and as a verb. Suddenly ministry felt like a technological feat instead of an embodied connection. It all left me feeling detached and disconnected. At first, I relied on my usual set of coping mechanisms; binging my favorite television shows, enjoying an afternoon snooze, and making sure a plethora of carbohydrates were at the ready. When it became apparent that we were all in this for the long haul, I knew I had to take it to the next level. I quickly rolled out my other emotional guidewire. If writing pulled my insides out, walking pushed the outside in.

---

1. Armstrong, *The Spiral Staircase*, 207.

As the child of two redheads, the beach was a place for walking, not sunbathing. In the autumn, as the air blew cool off the water, my mother would take me to the ocean. I would jump in tide pools and scramble over rocks. I would search for sea glass and skip shells across the waves. Seemingly unaware of my frenetic buzzing, my mother would just walk. She used to have these big round sunglasses, like the kind Jackie Onassis made popular in the 1960s. Shielded behind those dark lenses, I could never quite gauge her mood. I only knew that by the time we circled back to our gas-guzzling Oldsmobile, she somehow seemed lighter. Her mercurial Irish timbre was soothed by the walking, and the silence, and the sea. A trait she passed along to me.

When the virus began to paralyze our nation, I knew I too had to start walking. And not just a quick loop around the neighborhood either. I knew I needed to embark on a quest worthy of the pandemic-level malaise that was sloshing all around me. I scoured books and websites for a pilgrimage that fit the bill. And then I found it. A 225-mile ring around Boston called the Bay Circuit Trail. The path begins on the sand of Boston's North Shore, then makes a wide loop through the suburban and rural bedroom communities of the city, before landing back on the beaches of Kingston Bay. Just a few weeks into the quarantine I began my hike, encased in my warmest gear, waiting for the Atlantic gale-force winds to jumpstart my healing.

The first section of the trail followed the winding roads that made their way inland from the coast. Soon thereafter, I found myself deep in the woods, surrounded by the pungent pine and spruce groves for which Massachusetts is known. I walked in the shadow of giant eskers; granite boulders left in the wake of a long-ago passing glacier. I heard the rustle of deer in the distance. Red-tailed hawks sailed overhead as nervous chipmunks dove for cover. The sheer beauty and stillness of my winter surroundings calmed me, a familiar and comforting balm. It was as if the earth were murmuring to me, "let the sky and dirt and air work their magic."

As the weather grew warmer, the trail took on a different disposition. There was mud. Everywhere. Bogs swelled by spring rains brought frogs and snakes and mosquitos out of their hiding places. I found myself turning my face toward the sun during my strolls, eager to feel its growing intensity. I watched flowers begin to blossom and ducks return to ponds. It felt like the earth had begun to breathe again. Many months later, I reached the last segment of the trail. I noticed the terrain had changed once more. Swaths of forest gave way to cranberry bogs. I let my palms brush the tops of cattails. I could once again smell traces of the nearby ocean in the breeze.

What I didn't see on the route were people. I was completely alone for almost the entirety of my hike. I turned off my phone. I left my headphones at home. It was just me and the trail, pulling at each other like saltwater taffy. I have found that ambulation offers a strange cocktail of presence and detachment to its devotees. But it is this very combination that gives walking its ability to alleviate our anxieties. It offers us time to sort through the brambles that are choking off our thoughts and emotions. As our legs churn, the nervous energy we harbor begins to dissipate. Walking allows *us* to breathe again.

Saying Goodbye

At the end of July, my wife and I moved out of the dormitory. The residence hall had been dormant for months by that time, as students had been prohibited from returning to campus for the remainder of the school year. I felt their absence palpably. Every minute of every day. Living under one roof, hip to hip and day after day, builds an intense connection between those who share the collective space. And while I certainly played a parental role for the girls under my charge, I was not, in fact, *their* mother. Which left me free to engage them without the emotional baggage they often ascribed to their own parents.

Without fear of the usual array of petulant or acerbic outbursts, I was able to encourage them to get enough sleep, ply them with vitamin-rich fruit, and gently inquire about their latest boyfriend or girlfriend. I helped them with homework. I taught them how to do their laundry and how best to angle a snow shovel. And sometimes, after a particularly hard stretch, we just washed the day away with an ice cream cone. Was it taxing? Of course. But here's the thing about teenagers. All they really want is for you to love them. Their barometer for feigned interest is quite sensitive. They know, instinctually, if you *really* care about them. And even if your fatigue or lack of patience occasionally gets the best of you, they will forgive your shortcomings. Because they know when push comes to shove, you'll choose them.

While some of my colleagues were careful to remain at arms' length with the students who resided in their dorms, I chose a different path.

Without small children of my own, and with the support of an equally invested spouse, the dorm became my home, our home. Running the dorm was the most gratifying work I have ever done.

As spring turned to summer, the COVID-19 infection rates continued to rise. Without another option, I began to say my goodbyes virtually. Goodbye to Andover. Goodbye to my colleagues. Goodbye to the ministry I had built from scratch. Only by leaning on the two spiritual practices I learned at my mother's knee, writing and walking, have I fashioned an uneasy truce with this pandemic. And while COVID-19 has kept me in Boston thus far, relegated to working remotely, I am busy building a new ministry.

One step and one word at a time.

PART FOUR

Conversations, Reflections, & Poetry:
"Study" from the Community

14

Will They Know My Name?

A Tribute to Breonna Taylor

LAHRONDA WELCH LITTLE

Sleeping through unjustified, sanctioned violence
    and wanton endangerment -
Unknowingly, huddled under the covers of despair and reproach;
    Even in rest, I cannot rest.
    Even in dreams, I cannot dream.
Will they know my name?

Dangers seen and unseen converged
    To become my imminent reality.
Will they feel the intensity of my pain, the force of my anger,
    The coldness of my stare?
Will they know my name?

Silenced while awake
In the day-to-day doldrums,
Silenced while working and caring
For the uncared for;
Silenced while worshipping in the pews
With other defiled and traumatized saints;

Silenced yet asleep
    Wrapped in cotton
        Behind closed doors
            Unbothered and unnoticed
Will they know my name?

I loved to dance rapt in
    Waves of staccato beats
        and staggered cadences.
I craved soul food cooked in
    My Granny's kitchen.
Back in the day I ran across Muskegon Beach
    with my cousins.
I read books and played Life.
I rode motorcycles with my Mom.
I admired my own hair — the kink, bend, and curl,
        Pin-ups, pinned back, baby hairs in a twirl,
        Braided, straight, rolled and bumped.[1]
But will they know my name?
Will they know my name when my mother sheds spontaneous tears?
When my boyfriend looks over his shoulder in fear?
When my sister snaps back like last year?

Will they know my name
    As my soul cries
        from the depths of eternity,
        out of the blackness of night,
        from the heat of the sun?
Will they know my name
    When the wind blows through the weeping willow?
Will they hear my roar in the gales of spring?
Will they feel my death like sheets of ice on Lake Michigan?
Will they ever taste fear like salty blood from the inside of a bitten cheek?

Or will they continue to be sense-less, enter without knocking, and shoot
to kill?
Will they know my name?

1. The details of Breonna's life are gathered from an interview with her sister,
Ju'Niyah Palmer. See Grady and Palmer, "Breonna Taylor."

15

Fighting for Change and Inclusion in 2020

Tools for the New Generation

JETTA STRAYHORN, PHEBIAN GRAY, TAYLOR POWELL

Jetta

I was hot.
Inside and out.
There is no other way to put it.

The worst feeling, I've discovered, is when your blood is boiling in the middle of the summer. Sticky heat melts your legs to your seat as you try to position the fan towards your red, glowing face to feel a kind of calm, coolness on the outside because your insides are just as hot as your skin.

I was hot with sadness, hot with fear, hot with exhaustion, and, of course, hot with anger. I made that clear on my social media, which apparently was a surprise to some people because so many—too many—comments reminded me of how the anger I felt didn't mix well with the skin in which I stood. Funny, I always thought black and red looked great together.

One thing I always let myself do was get angry. Chant after chant, I reminded myself that my anger was necessary. "Your feelings are valid. You are angry for a reason. And if you need to cry, cry," I whispered to myself every now and then. I wondered if anti-maskers whispered the same things to themselves at night. Would they cry over a mask? Did warm, salty tears stream down their cheeks when they remembered that we were living through a pandemic and they needed to wear a mask, like how my warm, salty tears washed away my blush every time I remembered the phrase, "I can't breathe." I doubt it. Because they were allowed to protest in government facilities with guns, while we protested in the streets with signs. It's a privilege to get to scream and spit with weapons instead of cry and chant with posters.

My family only got to attend one protest, but that memory is welded to my brain. The Atlanta sun shone bright on the sea of sweaty college students and high schoolers. I like to think that even if the sun had not been out, the crowd would have been just as hot, with the coals of systemic racism and police brutality burning blue fires within us. We walked from the park in front of the Mercedes-Benz Stadium to the CNN Center. Everyone rested at the intersection between CNN and Centennial Park, but my mom made me and my siblings sit back, away from the crowd. She kept COVID-19 in mind during the entirety of the protest. Of course, me being my rebel, "stick it to the man," self, I was upset that I couldn't keep walking on with the rest of the independent Millennials and Gen-Z'ers screaming, "No justice, no peace, no racist-ass police," at the stone-faced men dressed in black and/or camouflage. We left the protest a little bit after arriving at the CNN Center because my mom didn't want us out there at dusk—that's when the protests got louder and more violent.

My legs were sore from walking across a highway, my arms ached from holding my sign above my head, my skin was flushed and damp, and my face had a prominent line that distinguished parts that were covered by a mask and parts that weren't. We were exhausted. But not just from the day itself. Sure, we were worn-out by the protest, but we were exhausted from having to explain ourselves. We were exhausted from having to protect and advocate for ourselves. We were exhausted from hearing people respond to our "we deserve" with "but…" and combating our "black" with "all." I was tired of thinking of the time back in 2019 when my mother, sister, and I were driving back home from the movie theatre and got pulled over by a cop. We all held our breath as the black boots stepped up to my mother's window. We were only stopped over an expired tag, but that was enough to make me cry with anxiety once the cop got back in his car. Once again, hot tears filled with animosity and memories of generations of brutality rushed down my cheeks. I was scared for my life. We were scared for our lives. We are exhausted from being scared for our lives.

I am hot. And I have come to the conclusion that I will always be hot.

Maybe that's why we tan instead of burn in the heat of a summer's sun. Burning isn't an option when being hot is your reality.

Fortunately, crisp, Autumn air and Winter's icy wind will surround me soon, so I won't burn as much on the outside.

May 25, 2020

Phebian Gray

One day and seventeen years belong to me.
I wake and revel in the rush of my heartbeat
The smoothness of my skin
The flesh in my face
I am grateful.
Too careful, I could never be.
These things never happen on accident
I take care to braid my hair with shea butter
And keep my thoughts between me and myself.
Trees are lush and alive in my backyard
Four days until I'm meant to move on
Four days until I'm free to use my time
Five years ago, I was told how wise I was
To braid my hair with shea butter
and keep my thoughts between me and myself
For the first time.
Six years later, I imagine I'll do the same.
I hope.
Eight minutes and forty-six seconds[1]
Was all it took to take away
Seven months and forty-six years.
At least seventeen years and one day belong to me.
That, I know.

---

1. 8:46 is the amount of time that the police officer had his knee pressed down on George Floyd's neck, killing him in broad daylight. 8:46 became a symbol of police brutality associated with the murder of George Floyd. That time was later determined to be 9:29 (nine minutes and twenty-nine seconds).

June 1, 2020

Phebian Gray

Don't

Waste.

Work your body into something new

Invent muscles and ligaments

If you're not in pain, you're not doing it right.

Stretch your mind to find new ways

To thank your skin and bones

Watch your fingers callous as you progress

Hear your voice quiver.

Do

More.

Have you no idea what you are?

You, resource.

You, commodity.

You.

Remove your clothes and show them your pain.

Then, they will understand.

Now, you haven't done enough.

Don't

Die.

Dress up to go nowhere.

Anywhere would be too painful, and you're not meant to feel pain for
yourself.

Drape yourself in fancy fabrics

Or polyester

and isolate yourself

How sad it would be to die for what you believe in

"Do be patient"

Why should I?

"Black Lives Matter"

Then show me

"Progress isn't linear"

Progress isn't real.

June 14, 2020
Phebian Gray

I love the look of light on leaves
As the sun rises on them in the mornings
And the birds and all the songs they sing
None are mine, but still all me.
The wisps of magnolia in the air
Tell me I've taken myself back

June 21, 2020
Phebian Gray

Anxious

> Black squares
> Infographics
> Random texts
> Emails
> postcards??
> "Tell me how I can be a better ally to you"
> First, stop.

Avoidant

These are some of my favorite things you say:

"Why does everything have to be about race?"

"Isn't this what you wanted"

"Just go to public school"

Secure

> I am not differentiated enough to know what this would look like.

July 4, 2020

Phebian Gray

I had a dream about a princess who saved herself.
Her skin has a blue tint in the moonlight.
More and more, you comment on it
And look to her, her gaul
More and more, she retreats
You speak plenty of the work
The trouble
The pain
The healing
I never reply
I had a dream about a princess who saved herself
With silver in her nose and red in her hair
Less and less, you ask about her
And lean on her, her strength
Less and less, she is available
You speak little of the who
The how
The when
The why
I never reply
The more you speak, the less I understand
You tell me about food for the soul
And following one's spirit
Allowing those who want to help you inside
Yet the pile of clothes in the corner of my room
grows and grows
I used to say things that made a difference

August 20, 2020
Phebian Gray

I know today is my last first
The day I mourn my heart coerced
For you, for them, for better or worse
The time I gave, results reversed
Do you remember your first last?
The sunken summers from your past
Running sour, moving fast
The ever-present house of glass
Each time feels like the first and still
Like every other time until
Emotions flooding, waters spill.
The things I'd give for you to feel
What it means to lose a friend
Again again again again.

Taylor

The creation of blackatpaideia initiated changes at Paideia that I had hoped for but never truly anticipated. It started out as a page made for the school's black student body so that they could have an outlet to air their grievances. For years, black students have felt ignored, disregarded, and unheard. We watched the impact that other schools had, and we wanted to do the same thing at Paideia. It took off in a way that I don't think any of us had prepared for. The submissions were overwhelming. It wasn't just current high school students that had stories but junior high students, alumni, parents, and even a few faculty members. While it felt good to be able to give a platform to the black people within the Paideia community, it was disheartening to see that almost everyone had a story. There was a sense of comfort in seeing that we weren't alone in what we were feeling, but there was also a clear sense of trauma.

Dear Breonna

Taylor Powell

There was a girl who had dreams and plans and
Yeah her mom was a single parent
But she grew up round a nice fam and
Aunts and uncles did the best they can
Yeah she went to school round the neighborhood
Kept her head down and knew what was good
Violence and drugs, nah she wasn't into that
She wanted to help people and give back
She grew up and she was doing well
She became an EMT by herself
She worked hard for the life she had
She even was a college grad
One night, she was fast asleep
She was peaceful and looked so sweet
Cops bust in and shot em both
Now she lives with us as a ghost
Her dreaming ended early that day
A couple months before May
She was sleep so she couldn't scream
And the cops, yeah they watched her bleed
So Dear Breonna, I apologize
Your story could've easily been mine
You deserve better than a couple mil
Your life had purpose and it always will

However, Black people are more than their trauma. We are more than our stories of microaggressions and violent attacks. We are more than tales of our single mothers or the poverty that we've experienced in our communities. We are a people that search for community in every place that we enter and nourish it. We are a people that laugh so boldly that the ground shakes because we've cried so many tears and need to replenish our bodies. We are a people that get continuously knocked down and help one another back up. We are resilient. We are kind. We are beautiful. We are worthy. We matter.

Dear Brown Skin Girls

Taylor Powell

You are enough.
Dear 4c's, you are enough.
Pigmentation poppin' like the clear lip gloss we stay rockin'.
Rooms stop when we walk in.
Jaws drop, you know we cause it.
Apologies for the distractions, but we can't help their attraction.
Honey spurs when we speak, plus our cocoa skin—nah they can't
    compete.
Chins up.
Edges laid.
Our melanin shines as we suit up for today's rampage.
Pace yourselves, ladies. It's gonna be a hard one.
You know they'll try to stop us, but our magic shall prevail.
Ignore the Instagram posts about "light skin baddies."
Do not give those rappers pleading for redbones the time of day.
Change the radio station if you must. Listen to Cole ask for that "real
    love."
That "dark-skinned and Aunt Viv love."
That broken skin girl love.
That big-lipped love.
That wide hip love.
That "girl, you know I ain't gettin' in the pool unless my hair is natural
    or in braids" love.
That black community love.
The kind of love that sustains the bounce in your curls and explains the
    extra swerve in your strut.
The kind of love that holds families together.
The kind of love that people would die for. You are that kind of love.
And brown skin girls, oh my fellow beautiful, brown skin girls,
I hope you know our stories don't always have to be sad.
Don't always have to end in tears over injustices or broken-hearted
    mamas reminiscing on that last kiss on the forehead from their black
    boys, no.
Our stories can end with in-sync wobbles at family cookouts
or out-of-tune renditions of "Before I Let Go" by Frankie Beverly and
    Maze.

Brown girls, I want you all to love yourselves like old black aunties love that song.

You deserve that type of unwavering love.

Brown skin girls, don't forget who you are.

Be a hot girl and stay in your bag.

You do not have to be what they say.

We do not have to be what they say.

Loud.

Angry.

Aggressive.

Ghetto.

Sidekick to the white main character.

Assistant, never CEO.

Don't you see, brown girls?

It is time for us to take our rightful place on the throne.

Rise like the queens we are—like the queens we have always been.

Brown skin girls, you deserve more than second place.

Plant your feet in first and immerse them deeply into the soil.

Allow the sun to kiss your beautiful brown skin and accept its compassion for you.

Dear Brown Skin Girls, Beyoncé said it best: "Brown skin girls / your skin just like pearls / the best thing in the world / never trade you for anybody else."

No, I'll never trade you for anybody else.

　　　　Love always,
　　　　　Your Fellow Brown Skin Girl

16

Caregiving and Contemplative Spiritual Care Practices in the Age of COVID-19

Leenah Safi

I POSITION MYSELF IN this conversation as a pastoral theologian and chaplain, interested in contemplative practices as a method for colonial resistance in the field of intercultural spiritual care. I describe my social location as Syrian and American, Muslim and woman—and from the paradoxical privilege of having been born in the United States to parents well acquainted with the refugee experience. My parents lived their lives far from their ancestral home, remaining largely without the support of family or the ability to belong to a congregational community for extended periods of time. As a nuclear family, we moved from state to state looking for viable work and school opportunities. We were always out of place in the neighborhoods in which we lived, our existential identity on shaky ground as the threat of "making it" in America meant loss of self and distance from those we needed most. And yet, the presence of Islam and Muslims in the United States—whether by migration, indigenous experiences, or a mixture of the two—offered a variety of generative faith communities that would inform my formation and vocational commitments.

In October of 2020 I took part in the preparatory washing for the burial of my mother after her extensive and trying journey with cancer. It was not my first time seeing a motionless body on a table; this time, however, I was charged with a different kind of spiritual care from that which I had been accustomed. What I imagined to be primarily a symbolic ritual turned out to be an involved and ultimately consequential undertaking. The ritual washing (*ghusl*) of a deceased Muslim requires warm water, washcloths, possibly a gentle soap, and the application of camphor oil on the temple and limbs that touched the ground in prayer (*salat*). After the washing, the body is wrapped in a simple white cloth (known as *kafan*) in which Muslims are uniformly dressed for burial. The physicality of this in combination with the familiarity of the body and the finality of the *kafan* elicited involuntary tears as my central nervous system understood what my mind had not yet grasped.

Caregiving during the pandemic meant leaving the hospital chaplaincy training program I was in for fear of transferring the virus to my mom as she underwent the tenuous experience of waning chemotherapy treatment. We began a new phase of agitated living together, peppered with reminders not to be in "too close" physical proximity with one other. I was both essential as a caregiver, and suddenly also possessing the ability to inadvertently infect her with a virus that would kill her faster than she was already dying. There was nowhere to run from this moral distress, so we coped the only way we knew how: morning, afternoon, and evening discussions, over coffee and hazelnut chocolate wafers. She was a newly graduated PhD in sociology, and I was making my way through the first year of PhD coursework, so talking about our intellectual ventures was a mutually meaningful reprieve.

During one of our nightly chats, I expressed taking issue with the continual use of the shepherding image for pastoral care from an Islamic perspective, for the ways I felt it limiting engagement with other images from the Prophet Muhammad's life, prayers of peace and blessings upon him. My mother was incensed (much like I am whenever I think about the remark to not get "too close" to my dying mother), with what she perceived as a slight toward the meaningfulness of prophetic formation. Now I understand her case for an underlying significance in the shepherding metaphor that I had not seen before. By drawing on the beauty and awe-inspiring experience of being alone in the desert—the clarity and expanse of the night sky granting an unmediated connection with creation and experience of Creator—she had effectively drawn the metaphor away from that of one man with a flock and toward a practice of fostering connectedness, transcending space and time. In this way, she could lean on defining moments and practices in her life that inspired awe and meet the Prophet Muhammad in the solitude of his defining moments. This expression caused her eyes to well with tears as we sat in our dimly lit living room, lingering and slowly confronting the reality that as each night passed, so did our days together.

Emmanuel Lartey's and Hellena Moon's anthology, *Postcolonial Images of Spiritual Care* took great strides in complicating the Christocentric history of the field of pastoral care and engaging with images that might be more pertinent than Hiltner's shepherding image as a standard model for practice.[1] Lartey defines spiritual as that which enables connection,[2] underpinning the important move from *pastoral care* to *spiritual care*. The spiritual care experience that *ghusl* offered me was one of the hardest moments of my caregiving journey, and at the same time it felt like resistance in the face of the severe disconnection that both caregiving and dying yield. *Ghusl* is a right that every Muslim has; the entire community is responsible to make sure the deceased is given their due of *ghusl* and burial. And so, by virtue of this collective understanding, I was not alone in the washing. I felt cared for by this intimate group of women who were present that day to orchestrate and bear witness. After months of solitude and concern about keeping six feet distance from loved ones and strangers alike, we rolled up our sleeves and got to work together.

In her distinguished book, *Joy Unspeakable*, Barbara Holmes draws on contemplative practices of the Black church and speaks to the ways in which they are generative of social justice movements.[3] She mentions El Hajj Malik El Shabbaz, more widely known as Malcolm X, as having undergone the Hajj as one such contemplative practice that changed not only his life, but arguably American intellectual and spiritual history.[4] I better understand my own religious tradition via the paradigm proposed by Holmes, as already possessing meaningfully generative practices if they were to be engaged as such. Putting her work in conversation with spiritual care is to think of the community's ability to hold and experience time of distress *with* one another and sometimes beyond words, like taking part in the *ghusl* was for me. She notes the importance of this engagement and calls attention to what aversion to engagement may be communicating, "*Engagement* refers to the willingness to involve body

1. See Lartey and Moon, *Postcolonial Images*.
2. Lartey, "Be-ing In Relation," 21.
3. Holmes, *Joy Unspeakable*, 140.
4. Holmes, *Joy Unspeakable*, 167.

and spirit in the encounter with the Holy. It is upon this ground of cov-
enantal reciprocity that relationship becomes paramount…However, engagement also evokes trepidation and avoidance".[5] Before caregivers and
care providers can talk about connecting meaningfully with one another
and within our congregational communities, we must recognize the ways
we are experiencing and reinforcing systems of significant disconnection.

I find the Qur'anic image of "steep road" as more central to Islamic
tradition and more capable of generating social justice movements than
that of shepherding. The steep road draws on everyday opportunities and
relationships as contemplative spiritual care practices. Individuals caring
for their flocks alone is not a practice that many will experience, but images of people within a community that can meaningfully care for one
another through the very disconnections of life's circumstances is ubiq-
uitous and necessary work. Furthermore, if pastoral theologians were to
accept such an image, it would require a reorienting around professional
identity and seeing spiritual care as present in meaningful relationships,
preemptively working against systems of isolation. Whether the salience
is in our identities as children, parents, siblings, academics, scholars,
chaplains, community members or simply as human beings, the journey
can be difficult. I provide a brief excerpt from the Qur'anic metaphor
below found in chapter ninety, "*The City*":

> *And do you realize what is the steep road?*
> *It is freeing of a human being*
> *From bondage,*
> *Or offering food*
> *On a day of hunger*
> *To an orphan*
> *Who is a relative,*
> *Or to a person*
> *Who is down in the dust-*
> *All the while,*
> *Being of those who believe-*
> *And who encourage one another*
> *To [persevere in faith with] patience,*
> *And who encourage one another*
> *To mercifulness.*[6]

---

5. Holmes, *Joy Unspeakable*, 30.

6. Hammad, *The Gracious Qur'an*, 1072.

The power in the Prophet Muhammad reciting these verses, is the way we can see him standing amid them as a young child. Orphaned by the age of six, his life was based on mutual caregiving and a sense of belonging to extended family and community, even before prophecy. His attention to people and encouragements to offer a smile, share in food, and speak kindly point to spiritual care as connection through such impactful practices that make a difference and help people to flourish.

In the aftermath of the significant losses that the pandemic has wrought, those of us who remain embark on the difficult journeys of imagining and creating new ways to survive and thrive. As pastoral theologians survey the needs of individuals and communities in this phase of coming together again, there may be remnants of interpersonal accountability and responsibility evoked that will need to be addressed. We must fan those flames and engage with them in written form, conversation, and creative expression as contemplative spiritual care practices. Through these intentional practices, we powerfully resist the tendency to relegate connections to a life-review of the dying, and instead courageously confront them as the necessary and shared work of the living.

17

"STOP AAPI HATE"

A Practice of Restorative Justice

Conversation with Russell Jeung
(Transcribed by Hellena Moon)

The following is a "conversation" that the Paideia high school students from the Asian American Alliance student club had with Dr. Russell Jeung, Professor of Asian American Studies and co-founder of the "Stop AAPI Hate" movement. Jeung co-founded "Stop AAPI Hate" in March of 2020 when the pandemic exposed the racial violence against Asian bodies. The organization tracks and monitors incidents of hate, shunning, violence, and bullying (see website: https://stopaapihate.org). He discusses the goals for "Stop AAPI Hate" and the impact that the movement has had on our community.

In desiring to find solutions to the racial animosity towards Asian Americans during COVID-19, the Paideia high school students wanted to hear Dr. Jeung's thoughts on his work to eliminate violence against Asians. Jeung reflects on the long-term racial trauma from this COVID-19 year, his visions for youth who are striving for racial justice, and his own ongoing work of care and healing in the midst of such difficult racial justice work. The goal of "Stop AAPI Hate" desires restorative justice, a practice of indigenous and African communities that seeks to repair harm to the victim and to lift up—and highlight—their stories so that the healing process can begin for them. Dr. Jeung and I (Hellena) had a phone conversation structured around the questions posed by the high school students. We then had a follow-up phone conversation one month later.

Phone Call with Russell Jeung (June 16, 2021)[1]

High school students: What everyday activity could we do to help raise awareness and fight AAPI hate?

Russell Jeung: Please interrupt, intervene, and attend to targeted victims when you see any hate incidents. Showing support is important. It is important that we are reporting the hate incidents. Holding people in power accountable is also important.

High school students: How has hatred or racism towards the AAPI community affected you personally? Was there a specific event that you recall vividly (it can be an event that has happened years ago)? How has it shaped your own work on racism?

Russell Jeung: Yes, my family and I have personally been impacted by the racial violence during COVID-19. My wife was out running and someone blocked her path, deliberately coughing in her face. Also, my son and I were out in a store, and people were purposely moving away from us—more than the six feet social distancing guidelines, shunning us. This is juxtaposed with an ammunition store nearby where we see people buying weapons and arming themselves (with a one-hour wait time). It is interesting that people see us as threats and the image of seeing people arming themselves is interesting. My mom is 94 years-old and she told me that she only stays in safe neighborhoods in the Chinese community. This is not okay. It limits our freedom of movement. It is a form of segregation.

High school students: How can people of other ethnicities help contribute to the "Stop AAPI Hate" movement?

Russell Jeung: People need to intervene and report the hate incidents or crimes. As the #BlackLivesMatter emphasized how we need to continue

---

1. I would like to thank Dr. Russell Jeung for our phone call on June 16, 2021, as well as our subsequent follow-up conversation on July 21, 2021.

to support Black-owned businesses, similarly, we need to continue to support Asian American businesses and groups. Their businesses are hurting.

High school students: What is something you think everyone should know about the movement?

Russell Jeung: AAPI hate is more than about daily hate crimes (Jeung's group has documented 6, 600 anti-AAPI hate crimes since March of 2020 to March 31, 2021). Instead, we are experiencing verbal harassment, emotional and physical abuse, shunning, and forms of hatred. We have seen negative graffiti, inscribing the hatred. Racism has many forms. Focusing on just the hate crimes is not enough. It is not just individual racism. Racism is institutionalized. The policy makers have suspended visas (migration and refugee visas), etc. We are perceived as outsiders.

High school students: Do you have a long-term plan (i.e., or for the next five years) in terms of the work of "Stop AAPI Hate?"

Russell Jeung: Thank you for asking this. Our plan is to tackle the roots of racism, not just when it has reached downstream in the form of hate crimes. We need to address it upstream and support the ability to humanize and empathize with Asian Americans by doing the following:

1. support curriculum studies revisions in schools that incorporate learning more about stories and histories of people of color. The more compassion we hope to build in others, the less animosity is built towards us/them.

2. expand civil rights protections. There is a denial of public accommodations for Asian Americans.

3. promote restorative justice, teach empathy, and hold people accountable.

High school students: What problem do you think goes most overlooked in Asian Americans and Pacific Islanders?

Russell Jeung: Stereotypes of the model minority are what people know. What often gets overlooked is the stereotype of the perpetual foreigner. We are always seen as not belonging in this country—many in our population are non-native speakers of English, recent immigrants, and refugees. We are all being treated as perpetual foreigners. Even if one is a foreigner, one should not be treated with such hostility.

What I see as a powerful method is a restorative justice model, which I feel this data model is a part of by focusing on the harm inflicted on the person and seeing how we can restore healing of the harm in the person and in society. It means seeing both sides of the situation (seeing the Other as human is one of the most powerful tools of developing empathy). A redemptive approach that focuses on healing: healed people can heal others. Holding people accountable and helping to repair the damage is key.

Follow-up Phone Call with Russell Jeung and Hellena Moon (July 21, 2021)[2]

To continue the conversation on the data-collecting project as a work of restorative justice, Moon and Jeung had a follow-up conversation.

Hellena Moon: The "STOP AAPI Hate movement" [that Jeung and others have started] has really provided visibility for—as well as exposure of—the violence against Asian Americans (at the same time further highlighting forms of gender-based violence). I see how your work is an adaptation of the restorative justice model that is being used by Fania Davis in schools. Davis discusses how restorative justice is—and was—an indigenous practice of repairing harm within precolonial communities. I would love to hear you discuss how you see the work you are doing as part of the restorative justice work within communities of color.

Russell Jeung: Yes... well let me briefly describe my understanding of restorative justice and then show how our work is an adapted process of it. Restorative justice seeks to restore individuals to their broader communities by doing the following:

1. holding people accountable

2. seeking amends

3. helps victims if they are given a voice to dissolve their anger.

4. Develop empathy and care

---

2. Hellena Moon and Russell Jeung had a follow-up conversation on July 21, 2021.

Broadly speaking, many Asians might become racist or perpetuate racist stereotypes of those who harmed them because they're angered by the harm they have experienced. Hurt people hurt others. There is a tendency for us to perpetuate the harms they/we have experienced.

There is a fight or flight mode associated with racial violence. We see Asians arming themselves. Or, they put their "head in the sand" and ignore the violence, worrying they'll get harmed if they do anything. We can be complicit in the system and also be part of the cycle of violence. Unless we heal, we will continue to perpetuate the cycle of violence. The "Stop AAPI hate" project demonstrates how we can become healers and then also work to heal the racial wounds in society.

Hellena Moon: Dr. Richard Mollica [Harvard medical school professor and expert in trauma-informed care] discusses the importance—which often is elided or ignored in Western medicine—of the agency of the victim and the role of self-healing in addressing trauma.[3] We don't give enough credit for people doing the work of self-healing. Mollica has demonstrated the power of self-healing as an important part of the recovery of trauma that our society tends to downplay. I do believe that self-care—and the potentiality for self-healing—is sort of built into the data reporting process. Story-telling is an integral part of healing, especially self-healing. Data reporting and reporting the hate crimes is a form of story-telling. I think the practices of self-healing care are a component of the steps involved in "Stop AAPI hate." Especially as a digital project, it shows how the power of community *can be* online spaces.

Russell Jeung: Yes, this is surprisingly one of the greatest aspects of this project is the self-healing that has occurred for many. One out of five people who have reported hate has experienced ongoing trauma. Reporting the trauma—even though it is on-line—seems to be healing for many. The story-telling aspect of it opens up space for people to talk about the harms with others in their community. The on-line reporting platform helps to articulate and externalize the story. Victims are able to share it with others and gain emotional support. By reporting such stories, they are developing a collective voice. People have developed a stronger sense of community through this project.

Hellena Moon: It, therefore, is more than an individual redress. As you have said, it has given agency, courage, and strength to the Asian American community as a collective voice. There have been fissures in

3. Mollica, *Healing Invisible Wounds*.

other Asian American community projects in the past, so this project seems to be a wonderful platform of collectively addressing the social, communal, politico-economic needs of the community that's actually a spiritual practice of restorative justice.

Russell Jeung: Yes, not only are we addressing the racial harms, and healing is occurring on the individual and societal level; we are also strengthening our community with the needed political and economic support. The data-collecting has helped make real concrete changes. President Biden recently signed a Hate Crimes law to address attacks on Asian Americans.[4] And just this month [July 2021], Governor Newsom [California] signed an Asian and Pacific Islander equity budget, which also included $10 million donation to our nonprofit. We have demonstrated the need to address AAPI hate via our data collecting, and law makers are responding.[5] And Illinois just passed a law mandating the teaching of Asian American history.[6] We—our community—are enacting concrete changes. This is positive news for all of us.

4. Sprunt, "Here's What the New Hate Crimes."
5. Bravo, "$10 million from California Budget."
6. Shivaram, "Illinois Has Become First State."

1 8

Poetry during COVID-19

Sᴏᴘʜɪᴀ Hᴜʏɴʜ,
Mᴀᴅᴇʟᴇɪɴᴇ ᴀɴᴅ Bᴇɴᴊᴀᴍɪɴ Mᴏᴏɴ-Cʜᴜɴ

Spotlight
Sophia Huynh

For so long,
Isolation became my friend.
A similar face only reflected across the mirror.
Never noticed, never covered
Never the spotlight.
Invisibility became our best superpower
As our history was erased from textbooks,
Our atrocities against us never displayed,
And ourselves hidden in the background of the media.
Yet now,
Even invisibility has been taken away from me,
The spotlight of every room,
My isolation that I was so used to
Evolved into something more.
As I step forward,
Others step back
The country is suddenly aware of our existence.

Instead of newfound curiosity,
Interest in learning the unknown,
They scorn and demean us,
Throw epithets and rhetoric.
And our government,
Instead of focusing on the weight of this unprecedented outbreak,
On the deaths of thousands,
And empty chairs at the dinner tables,
They reflect the blame on us,
Us who were unknown to others,
Overshadowed during events and news.
Although my power of invisibility has been stripped away,
My infamous spotlight has broken through,
Allowed me to voice my opinions
With experiences no longer cased in glass
And stories amplified by our pain.
The spotlight we never wanted can be our asset,
Changing the tide of history
And projecting our stories
One at a time.

Ode to Water[1]

Madeleine Moon-Chun

I love the thunderous sound
of rushing waterfalls or rivers,
the quieter bubbling of streams or creeks,
and the foamy, crashing ocean waves.
I love watching waterfalls pummel
the rocks below,
or the clear water of streams
winding around smooth stones,
and the last rays of light
behind the "endless" ocean.
Every form of water expresses a feeling:
the anger of lashing rain
or the serenity of a motionless
lake or pond.
The continuous pounding
of water
gives me a feeling of life,
tangible but as slippery
as the water itself.

1. This poem was originally featured in the "River of Words" poetry contest as a "Winner in Poetry," sponsored by the Georgia Environmental Protection Division. Madeleine and Hellena would like to thank Monica Kilpatrick (email correspondence on May 3, 2021) for featuring Madeleine's poem in the *Georgia River of Words Poetry Journal 2021*. Hellena also wants to thank Tom Painting, Madeleine's seventh grade humanities teacher, for guiding and mentoring the students in the writing of this poem, its submission for the "River of Words" poetry contest, as well as the other poems in this section.

Joy

Madeleine Moon-Chun

Joy lives at the seashore
in South Carolina.
It warms
my feet
with the granular sand,
and whispers
into my ear
with the slight breeze.
Joy is like the rays of
blinding, yellow sunlight,
like the blanket of sea foam,
resting motionless
on the shore,
like the bubbles underneath the waves,
doggedly rising
toward the surface.
Joy glides
on the graceful wings
of a gull,
rides on the endless stretches
of salty waves,
and sways on the tall, leaning grasses
in the dunes—
the images of peaceful solitude
before sunrise.
Joy has the voice
of pulsing energy
in the crashing waves,
kids playing near the shore,
or the high-pitched call
of a tern.
The voice of pure joy
is a firm guidance,
like a foghorn heard
through the storm.
Joy says

that life is short,
just a split second
in time.
So go out,
and experience all that life
has to offer.
For the most tangible joy
will only reveal itself to us
when we willingly
let it in.

Superpowers During COVID-19

Benjamin Moon-Chun

COVID-19
was actually not so bad because
I learned about myself.[2]
If not for COVID-19,
I would not have found one of my favorite passions.
That passion is birding.
In the first days of summer vacation, we went to the beach.
My mother had signed us up for zoom birding summer camp at our
school. At first, I was confused. I thought that it would be really hard
to do summer camp during COVID-19. But my mom said it would be
Zoom camp. I wasn't so enthusiastic on that. On Zoom doing stuff wasn't
so fun. But I was partly wrong, because bird camp was awesome.
Since we were at the beach, we saw even more birds than at home. On the
Zoom, our teacher Tom, would show us lots of cool stuff. So it made time
go by quickly!
Tom posts something called
"backyard bird of the day."
It is an email thing where he posts a photo and it has someone's name
[the person who sent it to him] on it.
It is really fun.
It is the first thing I look forward to seeing when I wake up.
I check my email to see who got backyard bird of the day.
Since my mom and dad had recently gotten me an email address,
I sent in hundreds of photos.
I think I like taking pictures of birds
almost as much as the birding.
Another hobby that I found in COVID-19 was biking.
My family and I did lots of biking during the school year.
We would go almost every day after we finished our work. We also biked
a lot in the summer. We biked and birded at the same time.
Once my mom and I were biking and a cooper's hawk flew right in front of me.
We went extreme on the biking.
The hobby that I didn't find during COVID-19 but I used a lot is reading.
I did a lot of reading.
I think I read over fifty books in 2020.
That is an estimate.
I also loved that I saw my aunt and grandmother
almost every day because they were stuck with us.
My aunt's dog Fernando got to live with us.

2. Benjamin Moon-Chun's diary entry on December 3, 2020.

Epilogue

Reflections on Irony and Eschatological Hope

Pamela Cooper-White

In June, 2007, the Society for Pastoral Theology held its annual Study Conference in San Juan, Puerto Rico on the theme of postcolonialism and the ways in which the complex history of colonization might inform our work as pastoral theologians. As plenary speaker Dr. Luis Rivera-Pagán noted at the time, "I find it highly ironic to converse about postcolonial perspectives in, of all places, Puerto Rico, a Caribbean island that has been aptly described by one of our foremost juridical scholars as 'the oldest colony of the world.'"[1] A still predominantly white, Protestant guild of professors, scholars, and practitioners of pastoral care at that time, we listened earnestly to Rivera-Pagán and our other speakers, with much nodding of heads and good intentions. We agreed about the urgency of the project to interrogate how colonialism and imperialism had shaped theology in general, and how slow we had been to recognize this in our own field of pastoral theology. To quote Edward Said, "We are at a point in our work when we can no longer ignore empires and the imperial context in our studies."[2]

Nearly fifteen years have passed since that conference, and this passage of time begs the question: How well did we pay attention? How much

---

1. Rivera-Pagán, "Doing Pastoral Theology," 1.
2. Said, *Culture and Imperialism*, 5.

did our good intentions actually transform our work and our field as we returned to our classrooms, our own scholarship, our clinical practices?

For three among us—Emmanuel Lartey, co-editor of this volume, Melinda McGarrah Sharp, and Phillis Sheppard—quite a lot![3] Lartey published his landmark book *In Living Color: An Intercultural Approach to Pastoral Care and Counseling* in 1997. His writings, those of Melinda McGarrah Sharp, and Phillis Sheppard have been field-defining. [4] And there has been important interdisciplinary work as well at the crossroads of theology, postcolonialism, postmodernism, critical race theory, eco-justice, and eco-theology. In addition, there has been foundational work by Latin American, Black, Womanist and other liberation theologians, and more recently from within our field, a strong critique of neoliberalism and its consequences for the well-being of people, communities, and the planet itself as a focus of care.[5]

But as I write this Epilogue, I still feel keenly the sense of *irony* that Dr. Rivera-Pagán set out as the opening of his address to us. Irony, or paradox, cognitive dissonance, or something even approaching surrealism (readers may want to supply their own noun, their own perception or sensation here) continues to haunt "postcolonialism" even in the term itself. To speak of "*post*-colonialism" in a still rabidly colonial and colonized world is to speak aspirationally, eschatologically. There is not as yet a worldwide postcolonial way of living, either as people or as nations. Despite numerous revolutions and the building of new nations, colonies still exist around the globe, while all too many modern revolutions have devolved into dictatorships. Here in the United States, we still have colonies, not only in the Caribbean islands and the Pacific,[6] but in the Apartheid conditions of the Native American reservations and redlined ghettos assigned to people of color. The "*post*" in postcolonial is as

---

3. Lartey, *In Living Color.*

4 Lartey's *In Living Color* was preceded in 1987 by the publication of his dissertation, *Pastoral Counseling in Inter-cultural Perspective,* and followed again by, e.g., *Pastoral Theology in an Intercultural World,* and *Postcolonializing God* in 2013. Melinda McGarrah Sharp published *Misunderstanding Stories* in 2013, followed most recently by *Creating Resistances* in 2019. Sheppard has (in a series of lectures and published articles) been confronting the field of pastoral and practical theology with its need to decolonialize as a field and to center Black bodies/Black women's bodies/Black LGTBQ bodies in our work. See Sheppard, "Hegemonic Imagination."

5. Notable among these many works directly addressing postcolonialism are Kwok, *Postcolonial Imagination* and Kwok and Burns, eds., *Postcolonial Practices.*

6. Diamond, "Telling the History." See also Immerwahr, *How to Hide an Empire.*

yet a dreamed-of possibility, a horizon we have only just now come to glimpse through the effort of colonized peoples worldwide to overcome their colonization. The "subaltern" is now speaking,[7] shining a light on the mystification, invisibilization, and brainwashing that keeps white supremacy thrumming through institutions and structures and infecting the reflexive thought processes of all of us in the so-called "developed" world.

While there are many forms of domination worldwide, as a US citizen by birth, I will focus my reflections on how colonialism, like an inherited multi-generational trauma, has saturated North American white culture from its beginnings—and how this impulse, this set of assumptions, has therefore saturated our institutions of learning, including our theologies and theological education, and our pastoral and therapeutic practices.

The original European "settlers" of North America were subjugated "colonists" themselves at the outset of the enterprise, some under the patronage but all under the thumb of the English monarchy.[8] The colonists who by the late 18th century revolted again British tyranny and dubbed themselves "patriots" managed to win the War of Independence from Great Britain, in part, by adopting tactics unknown to the strict marching lines of the Redcoat military machine (learned from skilled Native American warriors who had bested them in their own lethal clashes over territory in the densely forested landscape). As a daughter of New England, I was raised to take unquestioned pride in the American Revolution and my ancestors' role in it. When my stepsons were little, we once took them on the obligatory historic walking tour of Boston's "Freedom Trail." When we got back to my parents' home, the younger boy asked, "What happened at Bunker Hill where we saw that big monument?" Without a moment's pause, my mother growled as if reliving the moment herself, "WE LOST!" After moving to Texas in her early teens, my mother often recalled how annoyed she was at having to "study American history all

---

7. A reference to Gayatri Spivak's landmark 1988 essay, "Can the Subaltern Speak?"

8. A somewhat different story initially than that of the Conquistadors and their missionary counterparts who came to Latin America as men of privilege and military might, to conquer, to plunder, to forcibly convert to Christianity, and to claim for Spain and Portugal (See Rivera-Pagán, *A Violent Evangelism*), although the end result of cultural and literal genocide in North America was not so different. Pamela Couture further reflects on the need to consider multiple "colonialisms," e.g., in Africa, where both military conquest and religious conversion were tools of conquest. See Couture, "Reading Adam."

over again," because in her view, to know the history of the Massachusetts Bay Colony was to know American history in its totality, or at least as a synecdoche for all that was worth knowing.

To be fair, my mother was at times quite open to diversity, especially for her generation. Her high school years in Texas were perhaps her happiest, as she took pride in learning Spanish, and her best friend Yolanda—a fellow all-A student—was a Mexican American girl with whom my mother stayed in touch her entire life. When I was three years old and asked on a ride home from Sunday School why my best church friend Vicky, an African American girl my age, was "so dark," my mother replied, "Because don't you think God would have been bored making everyone look alike?" It was my first lesson on diversity, and in spite of my lily-white upbringing, one that at least planted a seed of subversion in me as a child against the unquestioned and unspoken racist status quo of our suburban context.

But the more powerfully socialized story of righteous American patriotism and family pride in military service, traceable back to the American Revolution, saturated our American Legion home, with little mention and no remorse about the genocide of Native Americans that preceded the United States becoming a nation. Like most old working-class New England families, mine thought of Native Americans generally in one of two ways: "Indians" were sometimes romanticized figures like the "ghost of the Indian" who my mother said roamed our hill and occasionally creaked our upstairs floorboards. I spent hours as a child playing that I was "Karana," the gutsy girl who survived alone on an ocean island with a wild dog she befriended, as told in my favorite book, *The Island of the Blue Dolphins*.[9] The real "Karana's" life story is actually yet another tale of Christian conversion and colonization.[10] More often, we unquestioningly regarded "Indians" as a group of dangerous, marauding savages who murdered and scalped the "innocent" white settlers. The history textbooks of my 1950s–60s childhood did not provide any alternative

9. O'Dell, *The Island of the Blue Dolphins*. The 1960 book was subsequently made into a movie in 1964. Island of the Blue Dolphins (1964) - IMDb.

10. The real woman on whom the children's book was based is described at Lone Woman of San Nicolas Island - Island of the Blue Dolphins (U.S. National Park Service) (nps.gov) accessed May 19, 2021. Born c. 1800, she lived eighteen years alone, left behind on one of the Channel Islands when her fellow tribespeople migrated to the California mainland. She was moved to Santa Barbara where she died in 1853, having been "conditionally" baptized with the Spanish name Juana María. She was buried at the Santa Barbara Mission. Her original name was never recorded.

view. The "Indians" were "primitives"[11] to be tamed, "civilized," converted to Christianity, or killed if they resisted, all for the sake of a divinely sanctioned "manifest destiny" to conquer the west. "Pioneers," like "patriots," were to be celebrated, and the true story of genocide, forced relocation, exploitative and broken treaties, and disease-infected blankets was never discussed. My mother and grandmother proudly told the story of Hannah Emerson Duston, a distant ancestor in our family tree, who scalped her Indian captors in their sleep (!?) and thus escaped. The prominent Puritan minister and judge Cotton Mather (of witch-hanging fame) hailed her for her heroism—comparing her to the biblical figure Jael.[12]

We never talked about African Americans or anti-Black racism in my family (with the rose-colored exception of that ride home from Sunday School). Hannah Duston's story was told aloud, but I had to discover the story of our closer Emerson forebears who were abolitionists much later on my own, although my grandmother did express what I now recognize as Transcendentalist and humanist beliefs that went beyond the teachings of the Episcopal and Methodist churches of my childhood. These views did not prevent her from also expressing clear racist attitudes: there was only one Black family in our town (maybe)—if they were mentioned at all it was to debate whether my kindergarten classmate from that family was "Negro" or just "dirty" because "his mother apparently never washed his neck" (it stings to remember this and to write it).

Nor, as I came into my teen years, did we discuss the Civil Rights movement, Dr. King, or the politics of the Vietnam War. I learned about these things as I grew up from my much more politically astute classmates. My first explicit awakening to the horrors of discrimination came—as a teenager—from the great majority of my friends who were Jewish. I learned about the Holocaust, and their beloved bubbies who had numbers tattooed on their arms, and why one of my friends refused to study German "classical"[13] music—not to mention the reality of antisemitism

11. Celia Brickman describes how the trope of "primitivity" seeped into psychoanalytic theory from its beginnings, especially in object relations theory, and with its views of adult rationality over both children and immature adults, as a parallel to nineteenth century anthropology's assumption of white European superiority to other races and continents. See Brickman, *Race and Psychoanalysis.*

12. For a more factual and de-romanticized retelling of the Hannah Duston story, see The Gruesome Story of Hannah Duston, Whose Slaying of Indians Made Her an American Folk "Hero" | History | Smithsonian Magazine. Accessed 5/19/2021.

13. The term "classical music" reflects, of course, another assumption of superiority of white European music, referring to compositions roughly from the

in our quaint coastal town (and sometimes in my own home). No one in my insular growing up years, at least to my recollection, whether teachers or peers, ever made the analogy between the persecution of Jews by the Nazis in Germany, and the horrors of chattel slavery in America. United States, good; enemies on other continents, bad.

It is no surprise, then, to speak in psychological terms, that such us-them, good-evil splitting, which is almost always a sign of an earlier buried trauma, trickled down through the centuries of American history, echoed in George W. Bush's speech after the World Trade Center attacks on 9/11/2001, in which he declared, "Just three days removed from these events, Americans do not yet have the distance of history. But our responsibility to history is already clear: to answer these attacks and *rid the world of evil*."[14] On the one-month anniversary of the attacks, he proclaimed the United States' unstained virtue (ignoring the harms caused by US covert military operations, assassinations, and support for coups and *escuadrones de muerte* in the Two-Thirds world):

> Americans are asking, why do they hate us? They hate what we see right here in this chamber—a democratically elected government. Their leaders are self-appointed. They hate our freedoms—our freedom of religion, our freedom of speech, our freedom to vote and assemble and disagree with each other.[15]

Later, addressing West Point graduates after the start of the war in Afghanistan, he drilled down on his assertion of pure American righteousness, stating:

> There can be no neutrality between justice and cruelty, between the innocent and the guilty. We are in a conflict between good and evil, and America will call evil by its name. By confronting evil and lawless regimes, we do not create a problem, we reveal a problem. And we will lead the world in opposing it.[16]

Nor has such one-sided patriotic pride been restricted to conservative politicians. It is a political requisite on national holidays. On Memorial Day 2021, President Joe Biden stated (with at least some minimal qualification), "This nation was built on an idea. We were built on an idea,

---

seventeenth–nineteenth centuries.

14. Bush, "Speech at National Day of Prayer," *Selected Speeches*, 59.

15. Bush, "Address to the Joint Session," *Selected Speeches*, 68.

16. Bush, "Speech at West Point Commencement," *Selected Speeches*.

the idea of liberty and opportunity for all. We've never fully realized that aspiration of our founders, but every generation has opened the door a little wider."[17]

In the United States, such patriotic pride has always been silently but firmly interlaced with white supremacy. As Nikole Hannah-Smith wrote in "The 1619 Project," "Our democracy's founding ideals were false when they were written. Black Americans have fought to make them true."[18] So it comes as no surprise that, as the 2020 presidential election came and went, Donald Trump's die-hard, delusional, white-supremacist loyalists claim the title of "patriots" while perpetuating the lie that the election was stolen by a cabal of left-wing "deep state" elites. During the Civil War, Confederates wrapped themselves in the mantle of "the patriots of old," a direct reference to their heroes of the Revolutionary War.[19] One state senator[20] present at the Capitol on Jan. 6, who sycophantishly has parroted Trump's every word, even went so far as to post photos of himself in Revolutionary war dress, mounted on a horse in a pose imitating George Washington.[21]

The rhetoric of the "lost cause" of the South did not fade away after the Civil War, in spite of Abraham Lincoln's exhortations "to bind up the nation's wounds, to care for him who shall have borne the battle and for his widow and his orphan ~ to do all which may achieve and cherish a just and lasting peace among ourselves and with all nations." The all-too-brief fresh air of reconstruction was again suffocated by the enactment of Jim Crow laws in the South.[22] To this day, a rallying cry of anti-racist

17. Biden, "Memorial Day Speech."

18. Hannah-Smith, "The 1619 Project."

19. In the lyrics to a popular Confederate rallying song, "The Bonnie Blue Flag," the final stanza (in one of many variant versions) reads: "Then here's to our Confederacy, strong we are and brave | Like patriots of old we'll fight, our heritage to save; and rather than submit to shame, to die we would prefer, so cheer for the Bonnie Blue Flag that bears a single star."

20. For more on this politician, PA state senator Doug Mastriano, see Griswold's illuminating article, "A Pennsylvania Lawmaker." Notably, Mastriano in one of his online "fireside chats" with his right-wing followers threatened Griswold using a practice known as "doxing"—reposting online information about an opponent which often leads to harassment, even death threats. *Pennsylvania Spotlight*, May 9, 2021. Mastriano was present at the Jan. 6 attack on the US Capitol, and as of this writing continues to passionately argue for the lie that the election of Joe Biden to the presidency was stolen by means of election fraud from Donald Trump.

21. Griswold, "A Pennsylvania Lawmaker."

22. For a detailed history of reconstruction and Jim Crow, see Gates, *Stony the*

protesters in the United States continues to be "I can't breathe."[23] As Michelle Alexander[24] and others have pointed out, in spite of the Civil Rights movement of the 1960s, mass incarceration and police impunity for shooting unarmed Black men, have simply morphed southern Jim Crow laws into an ongoing succession of violent racism attacks by both civilians and police, often under protection of legislation such as state "stand your ground" laws[25] and "qualified immunity" for police.[26]

Many among the unholy coalition of Christian nationalists,[27] Q-anon conspiracy theorists, and white supremacists who assaulted the U.S. Capitol on January 6, 2021, call themselves patriots. Many carried Confederate flags, with one even paraded into the Capitol itself. Many southerners—not only Proud Boys and violent skinheads—still subscribe to the myth of the "Lost Cause" of the South, that the Civil War was "all about states' rights."[28] This was a conversation I witnessed firsthand between a tourist mom and her young son near a Confederate monument on the Gettysburg Battlefield. This of course begs the question—"states' rights to do what"—to *own other human beings* as slaves, using, abusing, and killing them with impunity?

I still believe in the democratic ideal of equality, particularly in its most social-democratic forms. But the means for achieving such ideals are elusive, easily undermined from within by populist and nationalist movements that turn toward authoritarian rule (witness the Trump presidency in the U.S. and many other similar elections of authoritarian "strongmen"[29] from Bolsonaro in Brazil to Modi in India to Orbán in Hungary). And all too often industrial globalization and unfettered capitalist greed are exported in the name of "defending democracy," if not

---

Road.

23. A protest cry adopted first after the chokehold death of Eric Garner by NYPD, and again after the widely televised video of the murder of George Floyd by Minneapolis Police Officer Derek Chauvin, bearing down with his knee on Floyd's neck for 9 minutes and 29 seconds.

24. Alexander, *The New Jim Crow.*

25. E.g., see Douglas, *Stand Your Ground.*

26. Tucker, "States Tackling."

27. For more on this movement, see Cooper-White, *The Psychology of Christian Nationalism.*

28. Civil war historians concur, based on primary source evidence, that protecting the institution of slavery was the underlying cause of southern secession. Summarized in James, "Slavery, Not States' Rights."

29. Ben-Ghiat, *Strongmen.*

by diplomacy, then by military force (witness the war in Iraq, cloaked as a post-9/11 battle between innocent goodness and evil terrorists, but in reality a not-so-covert war over oil reserves that shook the fragile Middle Eastern equilibrium for decades to come). American exceptionalism and self-righteousness are baked into our American self-image. Isolationism and interventionism oscillate over the decades of U.S. history, but both are justified by an unshakeable belief in America's superiority.

So, returning to my opening statement about irony/paradox/surrealism: how do those of us who are white North Americans even *begin* to engage in a serious movement toward postcolonialism in our own work, our scholarship, and our pastoral and clinical practices—given that we live in a nation whose history is founded in twin genocides of indigenous peoples and kidnapped African slaves? A nation that, like its former imperial colonizers, broke free only to colonize other (i.e., Black and Brown) people – notably in Puerto Rico and the other US territories, but also in the death marches of Native Americans and forced relocation into increasingly small geographical areas, often beset today by poverty, addiction, and violence.

Given the pervasive death and destruction of peoples and lands, the freedom movements beginning in the 1960's (and foreshadowed by abolitionists in the 19th century) are miracles – signs of the unconquerable power of new life, even of resurrection power. Yet white supremacy continues virulently in our midst - and unlike COVID, there is no vaccine. What we do have, however, is the miracle of continuing conscientization and a commitment to resistance – which, like the vaccine, requires something like "herd immunity," a critical mass not just of white activists, but white scholars, teachers, counselors and caregivers, and ordinary citizens who commit themselves to the daily work of anti-racism.[30] Particularly as a profession that is dedicated to the study of theology and care, this must become a part of our practice, a sacred, intentional habitus.

As Ibrahim Kendi has written,[31] all of us are socialized from birth into racist attitudes and beliefs about white supremacy. People of color need safe spaces to undo the internalization of these damaging beliefs about themselves. White people—every last one of us!—need to stop protesting personally that "I'm not a racist," accept that we have all imbibed

---

30. Kendi makes the distinction between disavowing being a racist and making the lifelong commitment to being an antiracist, with detailed analysis and recommendations in *How To Be an Antiracist*.

31. Ibid.

white supremacy with our mother's milk, and know that we need to hold ourselves accountable for the larger ingrained social, political, and institutional bias that has saturated our North American "way of life" – the same "way of life" politicians speak of so reverently as a virtue to protect at all costs, even militarily – including a growing militarization of local police.[32]

As a field that integrates both theology and the social sciences, we also have some distinctive tools to bring to an analysis of the question: why is white supremacy, and the accompanying drive to imperialism and colonialization, so relentless and omnipresent throughout all of American history? Much ink has been spilled, especially over the last few decades, to try to explain the phenomenon of Othering and white (male) supremacy.[33]

I propose that one answer to the question of *why* American white supremacy is so virulent and tenacious is that, as noted above, the earliest history of the United States is mired in a multiple and complex series of traumatic events experienced by the white settlers/invaders. First, in Jamestown, Virginia, settled in 1607 (after a few failed attempts to establish settlements in the late16th century), white settlers violently forced the Native Americans off their lands, involving gruesome bloodshed on both sides – which created a feeling of terror and victimization among the whites, but perhaps also, more deeply repressed, what we now would term "moral injury." Only the objectification and dehumanization of the systematic massacre of the "savages" could allow a repression of their genocidal trespass and bad faith when treaties actually were negotiated. And it cannot be denied that, indoctrinated as they were with a belief in the righteousness of their cause, the early settlers were in turn terrified by Native Americans' (understandable) resistance and attacks on their families and villages - another example of oppression begetting trauma that in turn begets trauma, in repeating cycles of mutual objectification, resistance and retaliation.

Another brutal factor in this cycle of dehumanization was the importation in 1619 of the first African slaves. In the words of Nikole Hannah-Jones, developer of the Pulitzer prize-winning "1619 Project" of the *New York Times*...

32. Balko, *The Rise of the Warrior Cop.*

33. Jaco Hamman reflects on his own experience of apartheid in South Africa and the ways in which patriarchy/misogyny, racism, and colonization are interdependent ideologies and structures of power. Hamman, "Reclaiming Caritas."

It is not a year that most Americans know as a notable date in our country's history. Those who do are at most a tiny fraction of those who can tell you that 1776 is the year of our nation's birth. What if, however, we were to tell you that this fact, which is taught in our schools and unanimously celebrated every Fourth of July, is wrong, and that the country's true birth date, the moment that its defining contradictions first came into the world, was in late August of 1619? Though the exact date has been lost to history (it has come to be observed on Aug. 20), that was when a ship arrived at Point Comfort in the British colony of Virginia, bearing a cargo of 20 to 30 enslaved Africans. Their arrival inaugurated a barbaric system of chattel slavery that would last for the next 250 years. This is sometimes referred to as the country's original sin, but it is more than that: It is the country's very origin. Out of slavery — and the anti-black racism it required — grew nearly everything that has truly made America exceptional: its economic might, its industrial power, its electoral system, diet and popular music, the inequities of its public health and education, its astonishing penchant for violence, its income inequality, the example it sets for the world as a land of freedom and equality, its slang, its legal system and the endemic racial fears and hatreds that continue to plague it to this day. The seeds of all that were planted long before our official birth date, in 1776, when the men known as our founders formally declared independence from Britain.34

Meanwhile, in Massachusetts, Pilgrim settlers fled religious persecution, which in the early 1600s did not merely mean ecclesiastical or theological shunning or verbal vilification. Rebellion against the established church, whatever that might be across different regions of Europe, often meant death – even more so in the centuries preceding the Mayflower voyage in 1620.[35] While the oft-told story of the bravery of Pilgrims seeking a new land in which to practice their faith is well validated by contemporary documents, we might also consider that, especially following a dangerous sea voyage, the entire Pilgrim colony was suffering from a collective post-traumatic state.

34. Hannah-Jones, "1619 Project," Intro.

35. For a more nuanced account than the history books of my generation, see, e.g., Klein, "Why Did the Pilgrims Come to America? This view does not undermine the argument, however, that many of the early settlers/invaders to the North American continent had witnessed brutality, torture, and murder of their co-religionists, and believed strongly in their own narratives of the quest for religious freedom and the establishment of a Protestant theocracy–Cotton Mather's "city on a hill."

With the next wave of settlers in 1630 under Governor John Winthrop (several of my forebears among them), religious and economic aims subsumed the Pilgrims' project under a more vigorous and entrepreneurial theocracy, which spread from Massachusetts throughout most of New England. These early Euro-American "settlers"/invaders would in the next century seek freedom for themselves from British tyranny, but meanwhile perpetrated their own form of theocratic tyranny on the indigenous people whose land they arrogated to themselves as their own property (and not incidentally on other freedom-seeking pilgrims, Quakers, Lutherans, Baptists, Catholics, Jews, and Europeans of other sects whose religious beliefs and practices did not conform to their own strict Puritanism[36]). In New England, these were Congregationalists—Puritans —whose European Calvinist roots aligned with what Max Weber termed the "Protestant [work] ethic and the spirit of capitalism."[37]

In Salem Village, bloody warfare with Native Americans, terrible weather causing starvation, illness, and intermittent poverty, heresy trials against anyone who stepped out of line with strict Puritan beliefs and rules of contact (notably the "heretic" Quakers), and a mass hysteria resulting in the execution of 24 women and a few men accused of witchcraft, all fueled a paranoia and an enclave mentality held in place by continual fear. Living between the unpredictable sea and a dense forest wilderness, they believed themselves beset by two enemy Others, which were often conflated: Indians and the Devil.[38]

Finally came the trauma of the American Revolutionary war itself which was, in spite of the patriotic rhetoric that drew young men into battle after battle, a prolonged bloodbath, whose horrors were quickly

36. Elsewhere, Anglicanism was the established religion of the crown colonies (notably in New York and the South) and had strongholds elsewhere among British loyalists. Rhode Island and the Middle colonies—especially Pennsylvania (founded by the Quaker William Penn)—provided safe harbor for many non-Puritans fleeing religious persecution in the northeast. By 1702 every colony had some measure of state-supported Christianity, and a number of these established Christian denominations continued to receive state support until the 14th Amendment to the Constitution was passed in 1868. Britannica/ProCon, "Religion in the Original 13."

37. Weber, *The Protestant Ethic.*

38. Scheiding, "Native Letters and North-American Indian Wars," 137. E.g., Cotton Mather in his early history of New England, *Magnalia Christi Americana*, characterized the Native Americans as "devils in this wilderness." Quoted in ibid. Mather viewed the killing of Native Americans as a providential duty, paving the way for the later doctrine of Manifest Destiny. Griswold, op. cit., citing historian John Fea.

suppressed/repressed in the name of patriotism, independence, and even divine benediction.

As Judith Herman articulated so well in her classic book *Trauma and Recovery*, trauma is not only personal but social and political. And social and political trauma does not heal without conscious public acknowledgement, and communal support for truth-telling, redress, and change.[39] Without public efforts at truth-telling and healing, the trauma remains underground. But trauma does not remain silent. When repressed or suppressed, it continues to be re-enacted. The line between victims and perpetrators can wear very thin, as the formerly traumatized act out their traumas and in turn traumatize others while re-traumatizing themselves. As feminist psychoanalyst Jessica Benjamin has so clearly pointed out, a binary dynamic of "doer and done-to" can become a deadly unconscious cycle that may not be overcome without the intervention of some "third," some new awareness that arises like the *Aufhebung* of a Hegelian dialectic. And this is by no means guaranteed without some attempt to bring the unconscious "us-them" Othering to consciousness.

Trauma, as well known to pastoral theologians and psychotherapists—including social and political trauma, collective trauma – almost always begets psychological splitting, which, at least for a time, makes rational thought difficult if not impossible. The shock of trauma then may lead to a more permanent un-knowing, an unconscious and even neurological inability to know in an integrated way – mind, emotion, body, and spirit—what has been experienced. This splitting often results in the labeling of an Other (as in "us vs. them"). Claiming a victim stance of innocence and purity (which, paradoxically, is often the defensive strategy of narcissistic bullies, sexual abusers, white supremacists, and nationalists) projects badness onto the "not-me," the "not-us," the foreigner, the Jew, the Muslim, the black or brown or female or queer body, in order to retain a sense of superiority.

Unconsciously, however, this dynamic will backfire, because if all badness is outside of me, then the world is unsafe, and I can never stop being vigilant – in other words, I become paranoid. As the originator of "object relations theory," Melanie Klein, so vividly described,[40] such splitting – such lobbing of the hot potato of badness from inside myself to the other, to reclaim it again in order to preserve the safety of the outer world

39. Judith Herman, *Trauma and Recovery*, 7–9.
40. Klein, M. "Notes on Some Schizoid."

(all unconsciously of course) traps the individual in a repetitive cycle of "I am bad" vs. "you are bad," with no relief from shame vs. fear. Splitting is inherent in psychic life from infancy, one that often sets in in times of stress, but the capacity to hold good and bad together is a countermove that allows for mature relationships, and politics that are less polarized. Trauma, because it not only invokes but enacts the extremes of the bad other (who is truly bad) can ingrain the paranoid-schizoid psychic position as the default pattern—of a person, a family, a group, a nation.

Repression of trauma is often the only possible psychic defense against horror, especially during and immediately after a traumatic event, or more insidiously a repeated experience or "complex trauma," such as childhood sexual abuse. By not remembering or fully registering the overwhelming experience of terror and suffering—not even, in fact, "recording" it in the brain in the same way as a normal narrative event[41] —the trauma victim learns to survive. But repression is also dangerous —it can give un-metabolized terror and shame no other outlet than re-enactment through terrorizing a new Other. And unhealed trauma, like water, runs downhill through generations, long after the original terror is past, and the original story forgotten.[42] By oppressing the Other in the name of some ideal, some good, the experience of degradation and fear as a victim can be buried in the unconscious and replaced with a self-image of purity, goodness, and superiority. If the Other rises up in protest, a chain reaction of mutual traumatization and re-traumatization can ensue, as can be seen in toxic relationships, in local familial or tribal feuds, in civil wars, in surges of so-called "ethnic cleansing" and retaliation, and in centuries-old internecine, intra- and inter-national conflicts. It is no surprise, given these cascading enactments of unmetabolized trauma across generations, that Freud himself once declared that "man is wolf to man."[43]

If retaliatory cycles of traumatic reenactment seem inevitable in human nature, if Freud is correct that "man is wolf to man," and hatred

---

41. E.g., van der Kolk, *The Body Keeps the Score.*

42. Yehuda and Lehrner, "Intergenerational Transmission."

43. Freud, *Civilization and Its Discontents*, 111. Freud's increasing pessimism was not so unrealistic, considering that he lived through the brutality of WWI, the ensuing poverty, famine, and a pandemic (the 1918 Spanish flu of which we have all so recently been reminded) that took the lives of his beloved daughter Sophie and a favorite little grandson, and finally the Holocaust from which he barely escaped from Vienna to London, and in which four of his sisters were murdered in Nazi concentration camps.

based on skin color[44] and sexism/misogyny seem to be as ancient and persistent across the globe as humankind, where is the hope? And what role does pastoral theology have to play in living into this hope? I have just two reflections to add to the wealth of rich writings in this volume, where hope and care illuminate every page.

First, we need to recognize, and demonstrate in our living, that diversity is a gift rather than a threat. To embrace diversity is a beautifully wobbly, contingent, but sustaining and creative foundation for all our work as pastoral theologians and practitioners, and all our living. In Christian theology and practice in particular, one avenue could be to relax the traditional characterization of syncretism as heretical, as if Christianity itself did not spring from a particular time and context (Judaism in first-century Roman-occupied Palestine). As Christianity spread across the globe, it is well known to have incorporated and subsumed indigenous deities, beliefs and practices—often as an explicit strategy of Christian missionization. Neither evergreen trees nor bunnies toting colored eggs have anything to do with the birth of a Jewish baby in Nazareth or the Gospel resurrection narratives. Yet few North American Christians would feel that Christmas and Easter would be properly celebrated without these indigenous European fertility symbols!

All religious traditions are porous to different cultural contexts. So-called "folk religions" and attention to the sacred in ordinary daily life (Ada María Isasi-Díaz' "*lo cotidiano*")[45] are often more powerful in people's lived experience than any canonical or academic theologies and doctrines.[46] In particular, women's wisdom and rituals have often been suppressed but carry on richly underground as required by time and circumstance. Tara Hyun Kyung Chung argued in her groundbreaking 1990 book *Struggle to Be the Sun Again: Introducing Asian Women's Theology,* "My proposal for "survival-liberation-centered syncretism" as a new model for understanding Asian women's liberation theology may open the gate for the deeper understanding of God's activity in this pluralistic and divided world."[47]

Diversity of peoples, of cultures, of religious traditions *when respectfully engaged on their own terms* and not as a voyeur or a distanced

44. Lazaro, "How Colorism Haunts."
45. Isasi-Diaz, *Mujerista Theology.*
46. Carvalhaes, *Liturgies from Below.*
47. Chung, *Struggle to Be the Sun.*

observer impervious to influence—such engagement with and openness to diversity may even allow indigenous and non-western spiritual wisdom to re-animate moribund western theological pseudo-certainties (because what in the realm of faith is ever truly, monolithically certain?[48]) in order to re-value and restore the earth,[49] as it is imperiled by the current dominance of a hyper-capitalist and masculinist program of "extractivism" across the globe[50]—extracting by force the "resources" of the earth and exploiting the people on whose backs we live, and move, and have our consumerist being. Feminist psychoanalysts in the 1980's already pointed out that the earth, people of color, and women are unconsciously conflated in the masculinist psyche.[51] Patriarchy itself is a defensive product of the fear of what might be beyond control – so more dominating power must be exerted (including violence) to hold such imagined "wildness" down and in its place of servitude and material yield.[52]

Second, as a Christian theologian deeply impressed and formed early in my divinity training by the political theologians of the 20th century, I continue in this ironic present time of *still*-colonialism to embrace a theology of hope for a true *post*-colonial world in the future. I believe this can only be achieved by truth-telling, in the present, about the collective traumas of our racist, sexist past. My hope is not founded on a repristination of any mythical peaceful civilization in the ancient past (matriarchal or otherwise). As Homi Bhabha, one of the first postcolonial theorists wrote, we cannot recreate a pre-colonial past, some of which has been idealized through nostalgic remembrance of the good elements and a selective repression of the bad. But we must not reinscribe the imperialist forces that colonized others in the past—and the present. Bhabha's concept of "hybridity"[53] suggests a moving forward in which there is genuine engagement, honest dialogue about past hurts and fears,

---

48. Thatamanil, *Circling the Elephant*.

49. E.g., Gebara, *Longing for Running Water*.

50. The term "extractivism" itself has most often been used in relation to the industrial decimation of indigenous lands in Latin America, e.g., Gómez-Barris, *The Extractive Zone*, but it represents an attitude of entitlement toward "resources" that is common in the western exploitation of lands and labor throughout the two-thirds world, and, as well, in Native American lands within the U.S. See Willow, *ExtrACTIVISM*.

51. E.g, Merchant, *The Death of Nature*; Susan Griffin, *Pornography and Silence*; Dinnerstein, *The Mermaid*; and Ortner, "Is Female to Male as Nature Is to Culture?" Cited in Cooper-White, *The Cry of Tamar*, 67–68.

52. Cooper-White, *The Cry of Tamar*, 68.

53. Bhabha, *Location of Culture*, e.g., 159–66.

and perhaps eventually even an intercultural embrace, but in which, as Bhabha insists, each culture must retain its uniqueness. No "melting pot," no homogenization.

Post-colonialism as a yet-unfulfilled, eschatological hope cannot be lived into by repressing the horrors of the past, but by education and cultivation of consciousness of the split-off past that wants to remain repressed. Such hope is best achieved, I believe, by holding one another accountable to such consciousness in love and gentleness (which is far more effective than browbeating born of a defensive need to appear non-racist or a need to feel pure in oneself), and by being intentional about stretching our relational overtures to the "foreigner" and the stranger/the one who is strange or Other to us, and then listening—listening much more than we speak. I remain convinced that the first step toward lis-tening to the "foreigner," the Other, is to listen deeply to the multiple voices of the "foreigner," the Other *within* ourselves,[54] especially through meditation, therapy, spiritual direction—whatever it takes—to bring that internal Other we most fear to acknowledge into consciousness. And there are wonderful deep-probing theologians who will also help to get us there—many of whom are represented in this book and its predecessor volume[55]—as well as other prophetic voices, some now departed, whose words continue to inspire and incite us: Baldwin, Bhabha, Cone, Gutier-rez, Fanon, Spivak . . . It is precisely the Otherness that we most fear (or hate, which is an outgrowth of fear)—those strangers within and without —that may become the wisdom bearers we most need to allow humanity to retreat from our own violence and folly, and to save our imperiled planet.

54. Kristeva, *Strangers to Ourselves.* Cited in Cooper-White, "The 'Other' Within," 166, 169.

55. Lartey and Moon, *Postcolonial Images of Spiritual Care.*

Snow flurries
On the bowerbird's nest
She joins him
            —Hellena Moon and Tom Painting

Bibliography

Ahmed, Maha, and Pauly, Madison. "Wearing Masks at Protests Didn't Start with the Far Left." September 29, 2017. https://www.motherjones.com/politics/2017/09/masks-protests-antifa-black-bloc-explainer/.

Ahmed, Sara. *The Cultural Politics of Emotions*. 2nd ed. Edinburgh: Edinburgh University Press, 2014.

Alcoff, Linda Martín. *Visible Identities: Race, Gender, and the Self*. New York: Oxford University Press, 2006.

Alexander, Michelle. *The New Jim Crow: Mass Incarceration in the Age of Colorblindness*. New York: New Press, 2012.

Anderson, Meg. "Antifa Didn't Storm the Capitol. Just Ask the Protesters." March 2, 2021. https://www.npr.org/2021/03/02/972564176/antifa-didnt-storm-the-capitol-just-ask-the-rioters.

Angelou, Maya (@DrMayaAngelou). "Do the best you can until you know better. Then when you know better, do better." Twitter, August 12, 2018, 7:45 p.m. https://twitter.com/DrMayaAngelou/status/1028663286512930817.

Ani, Marimba. *Yurugu: An African Centered Critique of European Cultural Thought and Behavior*. New York: Africa World, 1994.

An-Na'im, Abdullahi Ahmed. *Islam and the Secular State: Negotiating the Future of Shari'a*. Cambridge, MA: Harvard University Press, 2007.

Anzaldúa, Gloria. *Borderlands/La Frontera: The New Mestiza*. 4th ed. San Francisco: Aunt Lute Books, 1987.

Arendt, Hannah. *The Human Condition*. 2nd ed. Chicago: University of Chicago Press, 1998.

Armstrong, Karen. *The Spiritual Staircase*. New York: Knopf. 2004.

Arora, Naveen Kumar, and Jitendra Mishra. "COVID-19 and Importance of Environmental Sustainability," *Environmental Sustainability* 3 (2020) 117–19. https://doi.org/10.1007/s42398-020-00107-z.

Arora, Rajesh, R. Chawla, Rohit Marwah, P. Arora, R. K. Sharma, Vinod Kaushik, R. Goel, et al. "Potential of Complementary and Alternative Medicine in Preventive Management of Novel H1N1 Flu (Swine Flu) Pandemic: Thwarting Potential Disasters in the Bud." *Evidence-Based Complementary and Alternative Medicine* 2011 (2011) 1–16. https://doi.org/10.1155/2011/586506.

Asad, Talal. *Genealogies of Religion: Discipline and Reasons of Power in Christianity and Islam*. Baltimore: Johns Hopkins University Press, 1993.

Astington, John H. "Pastoral Imagery in The Merchant of Venice" *Word and Image* 31, no. 1 (2015) 43–53.

Balko, Randy. *The Rise of the Warrior Cop: The Militarization of America's Police Forces.* New York: PublicAffairs/Perseus, 2013.

Barbash, Ilisa, Molly Rogers, and Deborah Willis, eds. *To Make Their Own Way in the World: The Enduring Legacy of the Zealy Daguerreotypes.* Cambridge, MA: Peabody Museum, 2020.

Beaulieu, John. "A Commentary on Cymatics." http://www.cymaticsource.com/articles/a2-article.html. Quoted in Hans Jenny. *Cymatics: A Study of Wave Phenomena and Vibration.* New Market, NH: Jeff Volk, 2001. https://monoskop.org/images/7/78/Jenny_Hans_Cymatics_A_Study_of_Wave_Phenomena_and_Vibration.pdf.

Ben-Ghiat, Ruth. *Strongmen: Mussolini to the Present.* New York: W.W. Norton, 2020.

Bennett, Jessica. "What if Instead of Calling People Out, We Called Them In?" November 19, 2020. https://www.nytimes.com/2020/11/19/style/loretta-ross-smith-college-cancel-culture.html.

Bhabha, Homi. *The Location of Culture.* London: Routledge, 1994.

Biden, Joseph. "Memorial Day Speech at Arlington National Cemetery." May 31, 2021. https://www.washingtonpost.com/politics/biden-offers-defense-of-democracy-in-memorial-day-remarks/2021/05/31/1fc623da-c21c-11eb-8c18-fd53a628b992_story.html.

Brahic, Catherine. "Parasitic Butterflies Fool Ants with Smell," January 3, 2008. https://www.newscientist.com/article/dn13139-parasitic-butterflies-fool-ants-with-smell/.

Bravo, Kent. "$10 Million from California Budget Goes to Stop AAPI HATE Co-founded by SF State Professor." *SF State News,* July 16, 2021. https://news.sfsu.edu/news-story/10-million-california-budget-goes-stop-aapi-hate-co-founded-sf-state-professor.

Bray, Mark. *Antifa: The Anti-Fascist Handbook.* New York: Melville, 2017.

Brickmann, Celia. *Race and Psychoanalysis: Aboriginal Populations in the Mind.* London: Routledge, 2017. Reprint, New York: Columbia University Press: 2003.

Britannica/ProCon. "Religion in the Original 13 Colonies." January 6, 2009. https://undergod.procon.org/religion-in-the-original-13-colonies/.

British Broadcast News Korea. "When Will I Get the Vaccine?" April 9, 2021. https://www.bbc.com/korean/news-56687547.

Brown, Wendy. *Regulating Aversions: Tolerance in the Age of Identity and Empire.* Princeton, NJ: Princeton University Press, 2006.

Bush, George W. "Address to the Joint Session of the 107th Congress, United States Capitol, Washington, DC." September 20, 2011. https://georgewbush-whitehouse.archives.gov/infocus/bushrecord/documents/Selected_Speeches_George_W_Bush.pdf.

———. *Selected Speeches of President George W. Bush: 2001–2008.* https://georgewbush-whitehouse.archives.gov/infocus/bushrecord/documents/Selected_Speeches_George_W_Bush.pdf.

Butler, Judith. "Violence, Mourning, Politics." *Studies in Gender and Sexuality* 4, no. 1 (2003) 9–37.

Callanan, Maggie, and Patricia Kelley. *Final Gifts: Understanding the Special Awareness, Needs, and Communications of the Dying.* New York: Simon and Schuster, 1992.

Carvalhaes, Cláudio, ed. *Liturgies from Below: Praying with People at the End of the World.* Nashville: Abingdon, 2020.

Center for Disease Control Newsroom, "CDC Confirms Possible Instance of Community Spread of COVID-19 in U.S." February 26, 2020. https://www.cdc. gov/media/releases/2020/s0226-Covid-19-spread.html.

Cesaire, Aimé. *Discourse On Colonialism*. 2nd ed. Translated by Joan Pinkham. New York: Monthly Review, 2000.

Chakrabarty, Dipesh. *Provincializing Europe: Postcolonial Thought and Historical Difference*. Princeton, NJ: Princeton University Press, 2007.

Chappell, Bill. "1st Known U.S. COVID-19 Death Was Weeks Earlier Than Previously Thought." April 22, 2020. https://www.npr.org/sections/coronavirus-live-updates /2020/04/22/840836618/1st-known-u-s-covid-19-death-was-on-feb-6-a-post-mortem-test-reveals.

Cheung, Tim. "Your Pick: World's 50 Best Foods." July 12, 2017. https://edition.cnn. com/travel/article/world-best-foods-readers-choice/index.html.

Chidester, David. *Empire of Religion: Imperialism & Comparative Religion*. Chicago: University of Chicago Press, 2014.

Cho, K. "Crossing Borderlines—An Ethnography on Korean Diplomats' Offsprings." Unpublished Master's Thesis, Yonsei University, Seoul, 1994.

Choi, Kyeong-Hee. "Impaired Body as Colonial Trope: Kang Kyong-ae's 'Underground Village.'" *Public Culture* 13, no. 3 (2001) 431–458.

Chow, Rey. *Entanglements, or Transmedial Thinking about Capture*. Durham: Duke University Press, 2012.

Civil Rights Heritage Trails. "The Bonnie Blue Flag." Civil War Lyrics & Civil War Music Index. https://www.civilwarheritagetrails.org/civil-war-music/bonnie-blue-flag.html.

Clebsch, William A., and Charles R. Jaekle. *Pastoral Care in Historical Perspective*. New York: Rowman & Littlefield, 1964.

Coakley, Sarah. *The New Asceticism: Sexuality, Gender, and the Quest for God*. London: Bloomsbury, 2015.

Coates, Ta-Nehisi. "The Cancellation of Colin Kaepernick." *The New York Times*, November 22, 2019. https://www.nytimes.com/2019/11/22/opinion/colin-kaepernick-nfl.html.

Coleman, Monica A. *Making a Way Out of No Way: A Womanist Theology*. Minneapolis: Fortress, 2008.

Cone, James H. *Black Theology & Black Power*. 3rd ed. Maryknoll, NY: Orbis, 1997.

Cooper-White, Pamela. *Cry of Tamar: Violence Against Women and the Church's Response*. 2nd ed. Minneapolis: Fortress, 2012.

———. "Is Forgiveness Necessary?" Paper presented at the International Association of Spiritual Care Plenary on Forgiveness in Jerusalem, Israel (unpublished), June 2017.

———. *Many Voices: Pastoral Psychotherapy in Relational and Theological Perspective*. Minneapolis: Fortress, 2007.

———. "The 'Other' Within: Multiple Selves Making a World of Difference." In *Braided Selves: Collected Essays on Multiplicity, God, and Persons*, edited by Pamela Cooper-White, 156–170. Eugene, OR: Cascade, 2011.

———. *The Psychology of Christian Nationalism: Why People Are Drawn in and How to Talk Across the Divide*. Minneapolis: Fortress, 2022.

Copeland, M. Shawn. "A Thinking Margin: The Womanist Movement as Critical Cognitive Praxis." In *Deeper Shades of Purple: Womanism in Religion and Society*, edited by Stacey M. Floyd-Thomas, 226–35. New York: New York University Press, 2006.

Couture, Pamela. "Reading Adam Hochschild's 'King Leopold's Ghost': A Story of Greed, Terror, and Heroism in Colonial Africa Side by Side with Luis Rivera-Pagán's *A Violent Evangelism: The Political and Religious Conquest of the Americas.*" *Journal of Pastoral Theology* 17, no. 2 (2007) 37–55.

Daily Gater. "A Non-White Struggle toward New Humanism, Consciousness." [San Francisco State College] May 22, 1969.

Das, Veena. *Life and Words: Violence and the Descent into the Ordinary.* Berkeley: University of California Press, 2006.

Davis, Fania E. *The Little Book of Race and Restorative Justice: Black Lives, Healing, and US Social Transformation.* New York: Good Books, 2019.

De Certeau, Michel de. *The Practice of Everyday Life.* Translated by Steven Rendall. Berkeley: University of California Press, 1984.

Derrida, Jacques. *On Cosmopolitanism and Forgiveness: Thinking in Action.* Translated by Mark Dooley and Michael Hughes. New York: Routledge, 2001.

———. "What Is a 'Relevant' Translation?" Translated by Lawrence Venuti. *Critical Inquiry,* 27, no. 2 (2001) 174–200.

Diamond, Anna. "Telling the History of the U.S. through Its Territories." *Smithsonian Magazine,* January/February 2019. https://www.smithsonianmag.com/history/telling-us-history-through-territories-180971004/.

Dinnerstein, Dorothy. *The Mermaid and the Minotaur.* New York: Harper & Row, 1976.

Doehring, Carrie. *The Practice of Pastoral Care: A Postmodern Approach.* Rev. ed. Louisville: Westminster John Knox, 2015.

Douglas, Kelly Brown. *Stand Your Ground: Black Bodies and the Justice of God.* Maryknoll, NY: Orbis, 2015.

Du Bois, W. E. B. "The Negro and the Warsaw Ghetto." *Jewish Life,* 1952. Reprinted in *The Social Theory of W. E. B. Du Bois,* edited by Phil Zuckerman, 45–46. Thousand Oaks, CA: Pine Forge, 2004.

———. *The Souls of Black Folk.* Reprint ed. Narragansett, RI: Millennium, 2014.

El-Hadi, Nehal. "Ensemble: An Interview with Dr. Fred Moten." *MICE Magazine,* 4 (2018) https://micemagazine.ca/issue-four/ensemble-interview-dr-fred-moten.

Fields, Rick. "Divided Dharma: White Buddhists, Ethnic Buddhists, and Racism." In *The Faces of Buddhism in America,* edited by Charles S. Prebish and Kenneth K. Tanaka, 196–206. Berkeley: University of California Press, 1998.

Fitzgerald, Timothy. *The Ideology of Religious Studies.* Oxford: Oxford University Press, 2000.

Foucault, Michel. *Discipline and Punish: The Birth of the Prison.* Translated by Alan Sheridan. 2nd ed. New York: Vintage Books, 1995.

———. *Security, Territory, Population: Lectures at the College de France, 1977–1978.* Edited by Michel Senellart. Translated by Graham Burchell. New York: Palgrave, 2007.

Freeman, Jo (Joreen). "Trashing: The Dark Side of Sisterhood." Originally published in *Ms. Magazine* (1976): 49–51, 92–98. https://www.jofreeman.com/joreen/trashing.htm.

Freire, Paulo. *Pedagogy of the Oppressed.* Translated by Myra Bergman Ramos. New York: Penguin, 1970.

Freud, Sigmund. *Civilization and Its Discontents*. In *The Standard Edition of the Complete Psychological Works of Sigmund Freud*, edited and translated by James Strachey, 21:59–146. London: Hogarth, 1961.

Friedman, Lawrence J. "Erik Erikson on Identity, Generativity, and Pseudospeciation: A Biographer's Perspective," *Psychoanalysis and History* 3, no. 2 (2001) 179–92.

Gampopa, *The Jewel Ornament of Liberation*. Translated by Herbert Guenther. Boston: Shambhala, 1986.

Garland-Thomson, Rosemarie. "Integrating Disability, Transforming Feminist Theory." *The Johns Hopkins University Press* 14, no. 3 (2002) 1–32.

Gates, Henry Louis, Jr. *Stony the Road: Reconstruction, White Supremacy, and the Rise of Jim Crow*. New York: Penguin, 2020.

Gebara, Ivona. *Longing for Running Water: Ecofeminism and Liberation*. Maryknoll, NY: Orbis, 1999.

Gibson-Graham, J. K. *Postcapitalist Politics*. Minnesota: University of Minnesota Press, 2006.

Goldberg, Susan B, and Cameron Levin. "Towards a Racial White Identity." November 4, 2009. https://www.awarela.org.

Gómez-Barris, Macarena. *The Extractive Zone: Social Ecologies and Decolonial Perspectives*. Durham: Duke University Press, 2017.

Griffin, Susan. *Pornography and Silence: Culture's Revenge against Nature*. New York: Harper & Row, 1981.

———. *Women and Nature: The Roaring Inside Her*. New York: Harper & Row, 1978

Griswold, Eliza. "A Pennsylvania Lawmaker and the Resurgence of Christian Nationalism." *The New Yorker*, May 9, 2021. https://www.newyorker.com/news/on-religion/a-pennsylvania-lawmaker-and-the-resurgence-of-christian-nationalism.

Grover, Angela, Shannon B. Harper, and Lynn Langton. "Anti-Asian Hate Crime During the COVID-19 Pandemic: Exploring the Reproduction of Inequality." *American Journal of Criminal Justice* 45 (2020) 647–67. https://doi.org/10.1007/s12103-020-09545-1.

Habersham, Raisa. "'Wuhan Plague' Plaques Found on Atlanta Businesses, Streets." *The Atlanta Journal-Constitution*, April 24, 2020. https://www.ajc.com/news/local/wuhan-plague-plaques-found-atlanta-businesses-streets/b9takSWmtKqfqai7wAk8iL/.

Haiku Society of America. "Official Definitions of Haiku and Related Terms." September 18, 2004. https://www.hsa-haiku.org/archives/HSA_Definitions_2004.html.

Halley, Janet. *Split Decisions: How and Why to Take a Break from Feminism*. Princeton: Princeton University Press, 2006.

Hallisey, Charles. "Roads Taken and Not Taken in the Study of Theravāda Buddhism." In *Defining Buddhism(s): A Reader*, edited by Karen Derris & Natalie Gummer, 92–116. 2nd ed. New York: Routledge, 2014.

Hamilton, Rebecca. "Pope Francis Grants Plenary Indulgence to those Affected by Coronavirus." March 23, 2020. https://www.patheos.com/blogs/public catholic/2020/03/pope-francis-grants-plenary-indulgence-to-those-affected-by-coronavirus/.

Ḥammād, Aḥmad Zakī Manṣūr. *The Gracious Quran: A Modern-Phrased Interpretation in English*. Arabic-English parallel ed. Lisle, IL: Lucent Interpretations, 2008.

Hamman, Jaco. "Reclaiming Caritas in a Hyper-Masculine World: A Response to Dr. Rivera-Pagán's Doing Pastoral Theology in a Post-Colonial Context." *Journal of Pastoral Theology* 17, no. 2 (2007) 29–36.

Hannah-Jones, Nikole. "The 1619 Project." *New York Times*, August 2019. https://www.nytimes.com/interactive/2019/08/14/magazine/1619-america-slavery.html.

Haraway, Donna. J. *Staying with the Trouble: Making Kin in the Chthulucene.* Durham, NC: Duke University Press, 2016.

———. *When Species Meet.* Minnesota: University of Minnesota Press, 2008.

Harney, Stefano, and Fred Moten. *The Undercommons: Fugitive Planning & Black Study.* Brooklyn, NY: Minor Compositions, 2013.

Harris, Melanie L. *Gifts of Virtue, Alice Walker, and Womanist Ethics.* New York: Palgrave MacMillan, 2013.

Harrison, Mark E., Lahiru S. Wijedasa, Lydia E. S. Cole, Susan M. Cheyne, Shofwan Al Banna Choiruzzad, Liana Chua, Greta Dargie, et al. "Tropical Peatlands and Their Conservation are Important in the Context of COVID-19 and Potential Future (zoonotic) Disease Pandemics." *PeerJ – Life & Environment* 8 (2020). https://doi.org/10.7717/peerj.10283.

Hegel, Georg W. F. *The Phenomenology of Spirit.* Translated and edited by Terry Pinkard. 1807. Cambridge: Cambridge University Press, 2018.

Herman, Judith. *Trauma and Recovery.* New York: Basic Books, 1997.

Herstein, Gary. "The Roycean Roots of the Beloved Community." *The Pluralist* 4, No. 2 (2009) 91–107.

Hiltner, "The Solicitous Shepherd." In *Images of Pastoral Care: Classic Readings*, edited by Robert C. Dykstra 47–53. St. Louis, MO: Chalice, 2005.

Holmes, Barbara Ann. *Joy Unspeakable: Contemplative Practices of the Black Church.* Minneapolis: Fortress, 2004.

———. *Joy Unspeakable: Contemplative Practices of the Black Church.* 2nd ed. Minneapolis: Augsburg Fortress, 2017.

———. *Race and the Cosmos: An Invitation to View the World Differently.* 2nd ed. Albuquerque: CAC, 2020.

Hudson, Michael. *. . . and Forgive Them Their Debts: Lending, Foreclosure and Redemption from Bronze Age Finance to the Jubilee Year.* Dresden, Germany: Islet, 2018.

Hurd, Hilary. "Butterflies Behaving Like Cuckoos," April 18, 2014. https://blogs.biomedcentral.com/bugbitten/2014/04/18/butterflies-behaving-like-cuckoos-2/.

Immerwahr, Daniel. *How to Hide an Empire: A History of the Greater United States.* New York: Farrar, Straus & Giroux, 2019.

International Labor Office. *Indigenous Peoples and Climate Change: From Victims to Change Agents Through Decent Work.* Geneva: International Labor Office, 2017. https://www.ilo.org/wcmsp5/groups/public/---dgreports/---gender/documents/publication/wcms_551189.pdf.

Isasi-Díaz, Ada-María. *Mujerista Theology.* Maryknoll, NY: Orbis, 1996.

Jabr, Ferris, and Brendan George Ko. "The Social Life of Forests." *The New York Times Magazine*, December 6, 2020.

Jain, S. Lochlann. "Living in Prognosis: Toward an Elegiac Politics." *Representations* 98, no. 1 (2007) 77–92.

James, Frank. "Slavery, Not States' Rights, Caused Civil War Whose Political Effects Linger." *National Public Radio*, April 12, 2011. https://www.npr.org/sections/

itsallpolitics/2011/04/12/135353655/slavery-not-states-rights-was-civil-wars-cause.

Jenny, Hans. *Cymatics: A Study of Wave Phenomena and Vibration*. New Market, NH: Jeff Volk, 2001. https://monoskop.org/images/7/78/Jenny_Hans_Cymatics_A_Study_of_Wave_Phenomena_and_Vibration.pdf.

Jeung, Russell, Aggie Yellow Horse, Tara Popovic, and Richard Lim. "Stop AAPI Hate National Report 2020-2021." March 16, 2021. https://stopaapihate.org/wp-content/uploads/2021/04/Stop-AAPI-Hate-National-Report-210316.pdf.

John of the Cross. *The Collected Works of St. John of the Cross*. Translated and edited by Kieran Kavanaugh and Otilio Rodriguez. Washington DC: ICS, 1991.

Johnson, Cedric C. *Race, Religion, and Resilience in the Neoliberal Age*. New York: Palgrave Macmillan, 2016.

Josephson-Storm, Jason A. *The Myth of Disenchantment: Magic, Modernity, and the Birth of the Human Sciences*. Chicago: University of Chicago Press, 2017.

Jung, Carl G. *Memories, Dreams, Reflections*. Edited by Aniela Jaffé. London: Fontana, 1995.

Kendi, Ibram X. *How to Be an Antiracist*. New York: One World/Penguin Random House, 2019.

Kilborn, Jason J. "The 5000-Year Circle of Debt Clemency: From Sumer and Babylon to America and Europe." October 22, 2012. https://www.iiiglobal.org/sites/default/files/19036430v1%20-%20The%205000-Year%20Circle%20of%20Debt%20Clemency-%20From%20Sumer%20and%20Babylon%20to%20America%20and%20Europe%20%28Jason%20Kilborn%29.PDF.

Kim, Eunjung. *Curative Violence: Rehabilitating Disability, Gender, and Sexuality in Modern Korea*. Durham, NC: Duke University Press, 2017.

King, Martin Luther, Jr. "Where Do We Go from Here?" Report delivered at the 11th Convention of the Southern Christian Leadership Conference on August 16, 1967.

Klein, Christopher. "Why Did the Pilgrims Come to America? They Were Less Religious Refugees Than Economic Migrants." History Channel, November 13, 2020. https://www.history.com/news/why-pilgrims-came-to-america-mayflower.

Klein, Melanie. "Notes on Some Schizoid Mechanisms." *International Journal of Psychoanalysis* 27 (1946) 99–110.

Kristeva, Julia. *Strangers to Ourselves*. Translated by Leon Roudiez. New York: Columbia University Press, 1991.

Kristof, Nicholas. "How Can You Hate Me When You Don't Even Know me?" June 26, 2021. https://www.nytimes.com/2021/06/26/opinion/racism-politics-daryl-davis.html?referringSource=articleShare.

Kwok, Pui Lan. *Postcolonial Imagination and Feminist Theology*. Louisville: Westminster John Knox, 2005.

Kwok, Pui Lan, and Stephen Burns, eds. *Postcolonial Practice of Ministry: Leadership, Liturgy, and Interfaith Engagement*. Lanham, MD: Lexington, 2016.

Kundera, Milan. *Laughable Loves*. New York: Harper Perennial, 1999.

Laird, Martin. *Into the Silent Land: A Guide to the Christian Practice of Contemplation*. New York: Oxford University Press, 2006.

Lartey, Emmanuel Y. "Be-ing In Relation: The Goal of African Spiritual Practice." In *Postcolonial Images of Spiritual Care: Challenges of Care in a Neoliberal Age*, edited by Emmanuel Y. Lartey and Hellena Moon, 17–28. Eugene, OR: Pickwick, 2020.

———. *In Living Color: An Intercultural Approach to Pastoral Care and Counseling.* London: Cassell; 2nd ed. London: Jessica Kingsley, 2003.

———. "Knowing Through Moving: African Embodied Epistemologies." In *Sensing Sacred: Exploring the Human Senses in Practical Theology and Pastoral Care*, edited by Jennifer Baldwin, 101–13. Lanham, MD: Lexington, 2016.

———. *Pastoral Counseling in Inter-Cultural Perspective: A study of Some African (Ghanaian) and Anglo-American Views on Human Existence and Counseling.* Frankfurt am Main: P. Lang, 1987.

———. *Pastoral Theology in an Intercultural World.* Cleveland, OH: Pilgrim Press, 2006.

———. *Postcolonializing God: An African Practical Theology.* London: SCM, 2013.

———, and Hellena Moon, eds. *Postcolonial Images of Spiritual Care: Challenges of Care in a Neoliberal Age.* Eugene, OR: Pickwick, 2020.

Latour, Bruno. *We Have Never Been Modern.* Translated by Catherine Porter. Cambridge, MA: Harvard University Press, 1993.

Lazaro, Fred de Sam. "How Colorism Haunts Dark-Skinned Immigrant Communities." *PBS Newshour*, May 19, 2021. https://www.pbs.org/newshour/show/how-colorism-haunts-dark-skinned-immigrant-communities.

Leezenberg, Michiel. "How Ethnocentric is the Concept of the Postsecular?" In *Exploring the Postsecular: The Religious, the Political and the Urban*, edited by Arie Molendijk, Justin Beaumont, and Christoph Jedan, 91–112. Leiden: Brill, 2010.

Lewis, Jeremy. "Intentional Rhythms and Organic Rituals: Urban Recipe as a Model of Care," In *Postcolonial Images of Spiritual Care*, edited by Emmanuel Y. Lartey and Hellena Moon, 134–142. Eugene, OR: Pickwick, 2020.

Long, Charles H. *Significations: Signs, Symbols, and Images in the Interpretation of Religion.* 2nd ed. Aurora, CO: Davis Group, 1995.

Longaker, Karisha. "We Shall Be Known." https://songsforthegreatturning.net/going-forth/we-shall-be-known-by-the-company-we-keep/.

Lorde, Audre. *Sister Outsider Essays and Speeches.* 2nd ed. Berkeley, CA: Crossing, 2007.

Louth, Andrew. *The Origins of the Christian Mystical Tradition: From Plato to Denys.* Oxford: Oxford University Press, 2007.

Makransky, John. *Awakening through Love.* Boston: Wisdom, 2007.

Malcolm X. *By Any Means Necessary.* New York: Pathfinder, 1992.

Mandela, Nelson. *No Easy Walk to Freedom.* Portsmouth, NH: Heinemann, 1990.

McGarrah-Sharp, Melinda. *Creating Resistances: Pastoral Care in a Postcolonial World.* Boston: Brill, 2020.

———. *Misunderstanding Stories: Toward a Postcolonial Pastoral Theology.* Eugene, OR: Pickwick, 2013.

Menakem, Resmaa. *My Grandmother's Hands: Racialized Trauma and the Pathway to Mending Our Hearts and Bodies.* Las Vegas: Central Recovery, 2017.

Merchant, Carolyn. *The Death of Nature: Women, Ecology, and the Scientific Revolution.* San Francisco: Harper & Row, 1980.

Meyer, Josh. "FBI, Homeland Security Warns of More 'Antifa' Attacks." September 1, 2017. https://www.politico.com/story/2017/09/01/antifa-charlottesville-violence-fbi-242235.

Migliore, Daniel L. *Faith Seeking Understanding: An Introduction to Christian Theology.* 3rd ed. Grand Rapids, Michigan: William B. Eerdmans, 2014.

Mignolo, Walter D. "Epistemic Disobedience, Independent Thought and De-Colonial Freedom." *Theory, Culture & Society* 26, nos. 7-8 (2009) 1–23.

———, and Catherine E. Walsh. *On Decoloniality: Concepts, Analytics, Praxis*. Durham: Duke University Press, 2018.

Miller-McLemore, "The Living Human Web." In *Images of Pastoral Care: Classic Readings*, edited by Robert C. Dykstra 40–46. St. Louis, MO: Chalice, 2005.

Mills, Charles. *The Racial Contract*. Ithaca: Cornell University Press, 1997.

Mingus, Mia. "Changing the Framework: Disability Justice." February 12, 2011. https://leavingevidence.wordpress.com/2011/02/12/changing-the-framework-disability-justice/.

Mishan, Ligaya. "The Long and Tortured History of Cancel Culture," December 3, 2020. https://www.nytimes.com/2020/12/03/t-magazine/cancel-culture-history.html.

Mollica, Richard. *Healing Invisible Wounds: Paths to Hope and Recovery in a Violent World*. New York: Harcourt, 2006.

Moon, Hellena. "Aporias of Freedom and the Immured Spirit." In *Postcolonial Images of Spiritual Care: Challenges of Care in a Neoliberal Age*, edited by Emmanuel Lartey & Hellena Moon, 169–89. Eugene, OR: Pickwick, 2020.

———. *Mask of Clement Violence Amid Pastoral Intimacies: Charting a Liberative Genealogy of Spiritual Care*. Eugene, OR: Pickwick, forthcoming.

Moten, Fred. *Black and Blur*. Durham, NC: Duke University Press, 2017.

———. *Stolen Life*. Durham, NC: Duke University Press, 2018.

———. *The Universal Machine*. Durham, NC: Duke University Press, 2018.

Muir, Donal E. & Eugene A. Weinstein, "The Social Debt: An Investigation of Lower-Class and Middle-Class Norms of Social Obligation." American Sociological Review 27, No. 4 (1962) 532–539.

Murakami, Tatsuo. "After Fetishism: The Study of Religion in the Age of Commodity." In *With this Root about My Person: Charles H. Long & New Directions in the Study of Religion*, edited by Jennifer Reid and David Carrasco, 51–62. Albuquerque, NM: University of New Mexico Press, 2020.

Neal, Mark Anthony. "Left of Black: S9:E7: A Conversation with Fred Moten. November 29, 2018. https://www.newblackmaninexile.net/2018/11/left-of-black-s9e7-conversation-with.html.

Nedelsky, Jennifer. "Communities of Judgment and Human Rights," *Theoretical Inquiries in Law* 1, no. 2 (2000) 245–82.

Nouwen, Henri J. M. "The Wounded Healer." In *Images of Pastoral Care: Classic Readings*, edited by Robert C. Dykstra 76–84. St. Louis, MO: Chalice, 2005.

O'Dell, Scott. *The Island of the Blue Dolphins*. Boston: Houghton Mifflin, 1960.

Oduyoye, Mercy Amba. *Hearing and Knowing: Theological Reflections on Christianity in Africa*. Maryknoll, NY: Orbis Books, 1986.

Oliver, Mary. *Thirst: Poems*. Boston, MA: Beacon Press, 2007.

Omi, Michael, & Howard Winant, *Racial Formation in the United States*. 3rd ed. New York: Routledge, 2015.

O'Reilly, Michelle, Diane Levine, and Effie Law. "Applying a 'Digital Ethics of Care' Philosophy to Understand Adolescents' Sense of Responsibility on Social Media." *Pastoral Care in Education* 39, no. 2 (April 3, 2021) 91–107. https://doi.org/10.1080/02643944.2020.1774635.

Ortner, Sherry. "Is Female to Male as Nature Is to Culture?" In *Woman, Culture and Society*, edited by Michelle Zibalist Rosaldo and Louise Lamphere, 67–88. Stanford, CA: Stanford University Press, 1974.

Our World in Data. "Share of People Paccinated Against COVID-19," July 23, 2021. https://bit.ly/2V2VHKx.

Pateman, Carole. *The Sexual Contract*. Stanford: Stanford University Press, 1988.

Patton, Laurie L. "Mircea Eliade, Patterns in Comparative Religion." *Public Culture* 32, no. 2 (2020) 385–96.

Pennsylvania Spotlight. "Doug Mastriano Threatened New Yorker Journalist Ahead of Damning Exposé." *Pennsylvania Spotlight*, May 9, 2021. http://www.paspotlight. org/2021/doug-mastriano-threatened-new-yorker-journalist-ahead-of-damning-expose/.

Piepzna-Samarasinha, Leah Lakshmi. *Care Work: Dreaming Disability Justice*. Vancouver: Arsenal Pulp, 2018.

Popper, Karl. *The Open Society and Its Enemies: The High Tide of Prophecy: Hegel, Marx and the Aftermath*. 5th ed. Princeton, NJ: Princeton University Press, 1996.

Puar, Jasbir. "Prognosis Time: Towards a Geopolitics of Affect, Debility and Capacity." *Women & Performance* 19 no. 2 (2009) 161–72.

Quijano, Aníbal. "Coloniality and Modernity/Rationality." In *Globalization and the Decolonial Option*, edited by Walter Mignolo and Arturo Escobar, 22–32. London: Routledge, 2010.

———, and Michael Ennis. "Coloniality of Power, Eurocentrism, and Latin America." Nepantla: *Views from South* 1, no. 3 (2000) 533–80.

Rawls, John. *A Theory of Justice*. Revised ed. Cambridge, MA: Harvard University Press, 1999.

Ray, Rashawn. "Five Things John Lewis Taught Us About Getting in 'Good Trouble.'" July 23, 2020. https://www.brookings.edu/blog/how-we-rise/2020/07/23/five-things-john-lewis-taught-us-about-getting-in-good-trouble/.

Rivera-Pagán, Luis N. "Doing Pastoral Theology in a Post-Colonial Context: Some Observations from the Caribbean." *Journal of Pastoral Theology* 17, no. 2 (2007) 1–27.

Robinson, Cedric J. *Black Marxism: The Making of the Black Radical Tradition*. 2nd ed. Chapel Hill, NC: University of North Carolina Press, 2000.

Rohr, Richard. "Liminal Space," July 7, 2016. https://cac.org/liminal-space-2016-07-07/.

Royce, Josiah. *The Problem of Christianity*. Reprint of 1913 ed. Chicago: University of Chicago Press, 1968.

Ryan, Thomas, ed. *Reclaiming the Body in Christian Spirituality*. New York: Paulist, 2004.

Said, Edward W. *Culture and Imperialism*. New York: Vintage Books, 1993.

Saldanha, Arun. *Psychedelic White: Goa Trance and the Viscosity of Race*. Minneapolis: University of Minnesota Press, 2007. Quoted in Jasbir Puar. "Prognosis Time: Towards a Geopolitics of Affect, Debility and Capacity." *Women & Performance* 19, no. 2 (2009) 161–72.

Scheiding, Oliver. "Native Letters and North-American Indian Wars." In *The Routledge Companion to Native American Literature*, edited by Deborah Madsen, 135–145. New York: Routledge, 2016.

Schüssler Fiorenza, Elisabeth. *Sharing Her Word: Feminist Biblical Interpretation in Context*. Boston: Beacon, 1999.

Shah, Khushbu, and Juweek Adolphe. "400 Years Since Slavery: A Timeline of American History." *The Guardian*, August 16, 2019. https://www.theguardian. com/news/2019/aug/15/400-years-since-slavery-timeline.

Shakespeare, William. *The Merchant of Venice*. Reprint ed. Mineola, NY: Dover Thrift Editions, 1995.

Sheppard, Phillis. "Hegemonic Imagination, Historical Ethos, and Colonized Minds in the Pedagogical Space: Pastoral Ethics and Teaching as if Our Lives Depended on It." *Journal of Pastoral Theology*, 27, no. 3 (2018) 181–94.

Shivaram, Deepa. "Illinois Has Become the First State to Require the Teaching of Asian American History." *NPR News*, July 13, 2021. https://news.sfsu.edu/news-story/10-million-california-budget-goes-stop-aapi-hate-co-founded-sf-state-professor.

Simard, Suzanne. *Finding the Mother Tree: Discovering the Wisdom of the Forest*. New York: Alfred P. Knopf, 2021.

Smith, Archie. *The Relational Self: Ethics and Therapy from a Black Church Perspective*. Nashville, TN: Abingdon Press, 1982.

Somé, Malidoma Patrice. *The Healing Wisdom of Africa: Finding Life Purpose Through Nature, Ritual, and Community*. New York: Jeremy P. Tarcher/Putnam, 1999.

———. *Ritual: Power, Healing and Community*. New York: Arkana, 1997.

Sontag, Susan. *Illness as Metaphor*. New York: St. Martin's, 1977.

Spivak, Gayatri Chakravorty. "Can the Subaltern Speak?" In *Marxism and the Interpretation of Culture*, edited by Cary Nelson and Lawrence Grossberg, 271–313. London: Macmillan, 1988.

Sprunt, Barbara. "Here's What the New Hate Crimes Law Aims to Do As Attacks On Asian Americans Rise." *NPR News*, May 20, 2021. https://www.npr.org/2021/05/20/998599775/biden-to-sign-the-covid-19-hate-crimes-bill-as-anti-asian-american-attacks-rise.

Swenson, Kyle. "Black-Clad Antifa Members Attack Peaceful Right-Wing Demonstrators in Berkley." August 28, 2017. https://www.washingtonpost.com/news/morning-mix/wp/2017/08/28/black-clad-antifa-attack-right-wing-demonstrators-in-berkeley/.

Tanaka, Stefan. *Japan's Orient: Rendering Pasts into History*. Berkeley & Los Angeles: University of California Press, 1993.

Taylor, Barbara Brown. *Learning to Walk in the Dark*. 1st ed. New York: HarperOne, 2014.

Teresa of Avila. *The Interior Castle*. Translated by Kieran Kavanaugh and Otilio Rodriguez. Mahwah, N.J.: Paulist, 1979.

Tetteh, Ishmael N.O. *The Fountain of Life: A Course in Metaphysics*. Accra, Ghana: Etherean Mission, 2017.

———. *Soul Processing: The Path to Freedom*. Accra, Ghana: Etherean Mission, 2002.

———. *Spirituality in Christianity: Awakening to Christ-Centered Christianity*. Accra, Ghana: Etherean Mission, 2018.

Thatamanil, John. *Circling the Elephant: A Comparative Theology of Religious Diversity*. New York: Fordham University Press, 2021.

Three Initiates. *The Kybalion: A Study of the Hermetic Philosophy of Ancient Egypt and Greece*. United States: publisher not identified, 2012.

Tucker, Emma. "States Tackling 'Qualified Immunity' for Police as Congress Squabbles Over the Issue." *CNN*, April 23, 2021. https://www.cnn.com/2021/04/23/politics/qualified-immunity-police-reform/index.html.

———. *A Violent Evangelism: The Political and Religious Conquest of the Americas*. Louisville: Westminster John Knox, 1992.

United Nations. *Mandates of the Special Rapporteur On Contemporary Forms of Racism, Racial Discrimination, Xenophobia and Related Intolerance; the Special Rapporteur on the Human Rights of Migrants; and the Working Group on Discrimination Against Women and Girls*. New York: NY: UN Headquarters, August 12, 2020. https://spcommreports.ohchr.org/TMResultsBase/DownLoadPublicCommunicationFile?gId=25476.

Van der Kolk, Bessel. *The Body Keeps the Score: Brain, Mind, and Body in the Healing of Trauma*. New York: Penguin Books, 2014.

Vesely-Flad, Rima. "Racism and *Anatta*: Black Buddhists, Embodiment, and Interpretations of Non-Self." In *Buddhism and Whiteness: Critical Reflections*, edited by George Yancy and Emily McRae, 79–98. London: Lexington Books, 2019.

Vuong, Ocean. *On Earth We're Briefly Gorgeous: A Novel*. New York: Penguin, 2019.

Walker-Barnes, Chanequa. "My Struggle with New Monasticism." *Sojourners*. September 18, 2008. https://sojo.net/articles/my-struggle-new-monasticism.

Wallace, David. "Fred Moten's Radical Critique of the Present," April 30, 2018. https://www.newyorker.com/culture/persons-of-interest/fred-motens-radical-critique-of-the-present.

Want, Frances Kai-Hwa. "Who Is Vincent Chin? The History and Relevance of a 1982 Killing." *NBC News*, June 15, 2017. https://www.nbcnews.com/news/asian-america/who-vincent-chin-history-relevance-1982-killing-n771291.

Watkins Ali, Carroll. *Survival and Liberation: Pastoral Theology in African American Context*. St. Louis, MO: Chalice, 1999.

Watson, Ivan, and Sophie Jeong. "South Korea Pioneers Coronavirus Drive-Through Testing Station." March 3, 2020. https://edition.cnn.com/2020/03/02/asia/coronavirus-drive-through-south-korea-hnk-intl/index.html.

Weber, Max. *The Protestant Ethic and the Spirit of Capitalism*. Edited by Richard Swedberg. Translated by Talcott Parsons. New York: W.W. Norton, 2009. Reprint. New York: Scribner: 1930.

Willow, Anna J. *Understanding ExtrACTIVISM: Culture and Power in Natural Resource Disputes*. New York: Routledge, 2019.

Wimberly, Edward P. *Pastoral Care in the Black Church*. Nashville, TN: Abingdon, 1979.

Wohlleben, Peter. *The Hidden Life of Trees: What They Feel, How They Communicate—Discoveries from a Secret World*. Translated by Jane Billinghurst. NewYork: Harper Collins, 2016.

Woodward, Aylin. "The Chinese CDC Now Says the Coronavirus Didn't Jump To People at the Wuhan Wet Market—Instead, It was the Site of a Super-spreader Event." *Business Insider*, May 28, 2020. https://www.businessinsider.com/coronavirus-did-not-jump-wuhan-market-chinese-cdc-says-2020-5.

Worldometer. "Reported Cases and Deaths by Country or Territory," July 23, 2021. https://www.worldometers.info/coronavirus/#countries.

Wynn, Natalie. "Takeaways from Natalie Wynn on Cancel Culture," September 19, 2020. https://ctliotta.medium.com/takeaways-from-natalie-wynn-on-cancel-culture-dofdoef3c7c9.

Yehuda, Rachel and Amy Lehrner. "Intergenerational Transmission of Trauma Effects: Putative Role of Epigenetic Mechanisms." *World Psychiatry*, 17, no. 3 (2018) 243–57.

Zahnd, Whitney E. "The COVID-19 Pandemic Illuminates Persistent and Emerging Disparities among Rural Black Populations." *The Journal of Rural Health* 37 (May 3, 2020) 215–16.